Management and Organization in Financial Services

Liz Croft, Maryam Herin, Ann Norton & Ian Whyte

institute of financial services

Financial World Publishing
c/o The Chartered Institute of Bankers
Emmanuel House
4-9 Burgate Lane
Canterbury
Kent
CT1 2XJ
United Kingdom

Telephone: 01227 762600
e-mail: editorial@cib.org.uk

Financial World Publishing publications are published by The Chartered Institute of Bankers, a non-profit making registered educational charity.

The Chartered Institute of Bankers believes that the sources of information upon which the book is based are reliable and has made every effort to ensure the complete accuracy of the text. However, neither CIB, the author nor any contributor can accept any legal responsibility whatsoever for consequences that may arise from errors or omissions or any opinion or advice given.

Typeset by Kevin O'Connor

Printed by Communications in Print, Basildon, Essex

© The Chartered Institute of Bankers 2000

ISBN 0-85297-572-4

CONTENTS

Contents

Contents

1

STUDY TECHNIQUES

Objectives

After studying this chapter you should be able to:

- State the considerations when studying the Management and Organization in Financial Services core subject

- Explain the examination structure

- Determine the importance of the set reading

- Identify an approach for case study analysis

- Identify the sources of advice on further reading

- Identify sources of advice on revision and preparation for the day of the examination itself

1   Studying for the Management and Organization in Financial Services Core Option

The purpose of the study text is to provide the framework for learning to help students to pass the Management and Organization in Financial Services module towards the achievement of a degree (BSc/ACIB) awarded jointly between The Chartered Institute of Bankers and UMIST. It must be recognized, however, that studying the study text alone is not a sufficient guarantee to pass this examination and its assessments. However, when used in conjunction with the recommended reading text, and other resources such as the worldwide web to access relevant current research, the student will gain an appreciation for the 'graduateness' now required to successfully pass this degree. For example it is a good idea to read the latest annual reports of the relevant Ombudsmen in the financial services area. The recommended texts have been selected because they have been written by people who are or have been examiners for this paper or by authors who have specialist knowledge of the industry through work experience, teaching and examining at undergraduate, postgraduate and professional level in the field of management and organization.

Additional support is provided for the examinations by The Chartered Institute of Bankers. For example, you are strongly recommended to obtain recent examiners' reports in this subject. These provide an important guide to what the examiner considers valid approaches as to how to answer the questions. It is important to remember that aspects of this subject area are constantly changing. Therefore you must keep up to date with developments in these key areas. *CIB News* is another important source for any articles and updates on the subject, especially those written by the Chief Examiner. Support is also provided by the Institute in the form of study texts and past examination papers.

The CIB recommends that you devote 200 hours study to each subject. If you are studying by distance learning you should agree a schedule of study with your tutor so that you know what you will be studying from week to week and also what progress you are making against the objectives. Remember that changes to the syllabus and to the examination format can occur since this book was produced, so it is important to keep in touch with your tutor and the Institute to keep abreast of the current situation.

2 Assessment

The assessment comprises:

- Assessed courses
- Examination.

Assessed Courses

There will be two assessed coursework assignments, each of which is worth 15% of the final mark.

The Examination Structure

The examination is worth 70% of the final mark awarded. At the time of writing, the format for this examination comprises two sections, section A and section B.

Section A consists of one question worth 40 marks.

Section B consists of five questions worth 20 marks each.

All candidates are required to answer a total of four questions, as follows:

Section A: Question 1

Section B: THREE questions

Section A

The question in Section A is worth 40 marks and is based on the set reading. Section A of the examination requires an analysis of the situation, and recommendations should be made to help to improve the situation.

The Set Reading

The set reading is designed to help to orientate the student specifically for a certain year's course of study. New set reading is distributed by the Institute at the start of your study.

It contains the details of the case study upon which the section A question will be based in your exam, and provides three possible scenarios within the case study organization. The section A scenario in your examination will be based upon one of these three situations, and students would be well advised to become familiar with these scenarios, analyse them, and consider the issues thoroughly in preparation for the examination.

As well as the details of the case study, the set reading also contains a collection of articles on different topic areas in the syllabus. This is designed to help students to read more widely. A question from section B will be based on one of the topic areas highlighted by the articles.

Section B

In section B there is currently a choice of five questions, each worth 20 marks, from which you will have to answer three. One of the questions in section B will be based on one of the articles provided in the set reading collection.

The questions are designed to allow you to evidence what you have gained from your course of study. All the questions can be answered in several different ways: in each case it is not necessary to search for the right answer. In some cases you may even find it sensible to challenge the question. What is important is you should support the approach that you choose with reasoned argument, make reference to relevant theory, and provide examples to support your points.

It will help markers to appreciate fully the points you are making if you define technical words or phrases that you use where there may be some ambiguity – even where these words and phrases are used in the questions. This helps to ensure that both the candidate and the examiner are starting from the same base point.

Choose your optional questions with care and read the section A question thoroughly. Remember that you should recognize most of the material from the set reading, so hopefully you will have had time to consider the key issues, the relevant theory and develop your points appropriately. This will help you to present the results of your studies in a way that justifies the investment you have already made in reading and learning theories and information.

3   Guidance for the Student

It is important to stress that a simple regurgitation of facts and knowledge is insufficient to pass this examination. In the past candidates have thought that management is a common sense subject and therefore a minimal amount of studying can be undertaken to achieve a pass in the examination. However it has been made perfectly clear from more recent examinations that this is not the case – if indeed it ever was.

If students do not have management experience this could hamper the way they analyse and interpret information, and inexperienced students may be better advised to take this examination at a later stage of their studies, when they have gained a little more experience. However it is also true to say that although candidates may lack management experience, they are all managed by other people and will still have a wealth of experience to draw on by observing the managerial activities of others. The trouble is that they may have difficulty tapping into this resource because they do not have sufficient knowledge of management to be able to formulate sensible approaches to learning from their observations.

Certainly by studying with this study text and the recommended reading texts the student should acquire the knowledge. For a candidate to succeed with this examination, what is required is a clear focus on the questions set and structured arguments developing the points by explaining the pros and cons and implications, and ending with a clear conclusion.

4 Case Study Analysis

The set reading has been highlighted as an important aspect of this course of study. A major part of it contains the possible scenarios for the section A case study. Because this section is worth 40 marks it may be helpful to highlight how students may choose to approach case study analysis. It is important to remember that this is only one suggested approach to analysis, and that the student must decide if it is appropriate for him or her.

Objectives of the Case Study

The BSc/ACIB approved by The Chartered Institute of Bankers and UMIST aims to provide a level of knowledge that is vital for success in the world of financial services. However knowledge on its own is not enough; managers have to be able to apply their knowledge in such a way that it benefits them, the people working with and around them and the organization. This means assessing situations and taking decisions, the implications of which have been properly thought through. Therefore a manager will be able to identify the main problem areas, and drawing on the knowledge he or she possesses, analyse the best course of action. This involves recognizing all the possible options, a consideration of the advantages and disadvantages of each, the risk factors and implications of each and selecting the most appropriate course of action given all the factors involved. The case study therefore provides a vehicle for candidates to demonstrate these skills and to apply the knowledge that they have gained throughout the course of their study.

The case study provides a realistic scenario set in the context of a financial services company. The students have ample time to familiarize themselves with this material because it is distributed by the Institute at the commencement of the study period. This means that there is the opportunity to discuss this with tutors and fellow students, ask questions, seek clarification if necessary, understand how different people view the same scenario and why. This type of discussion allows recognition of the fact that the same scenario is open to many alternative interpretations and hence there is no one 'correct' answer.

It allows students to assess, prioritize and justify the importance of the different problems suggested in the case study, and to defend their choices. This ability to defend their chosen course of action is a vital part of passing this examination. It may be through consideration of the implications of the decision by, for example, assessing the pros and cons of the arguments, and by making reference to the theoretical frameworks learnt throughout the course of study. Indeed to be successful in any degree, students must show that they have studied the existing theory on the subject in question. Students can use this knowledge as they choose, for example, use it to support a point being made. Students are rewarded for challenging the status quo and questioning the whys and wherefores of certain arguments, so again existing theory can be used as a means of debate and argument.

In summary, therefore, case studies are used to allow students to assess a given situation, analyse the extent of the problem and then apply the knowledge they have in a practical realistic way to achieve benefit for the organization and the people involved.

It is hoped that the use of case studies in this examination helps the student to acquire a key managerial skill, the ability to analyse a situation, identify the key issues and then decide on a way forward by making recommendations that will improve the situation.

One approach to case study analysis is provided below in the form of questions.

Case Study Analysis

Firstly, students should be completely familiar with the material and have read the case study as many times as is required to ensure that the key facts are clear and the major problems have been identified. Remember that although the scenarios are outlined in the set reading, aadditional material is also given in the examination, so before you begin your answer ensure that you understand the case study presented.

A useful structure for case study analysis is to ask the following questions

- What are the main problems? (It may be helpful to link them to the topic areas in the syllabus, e.g. leadership or motivation or culture etc.)

- Why do you think that this problem exists? (This is your chance to justify the problem, give evidence of why you think the problem exists from the case study.)

- What are the implications of this problem? Think about this is terms of the impact on the people, organization, budget etc.)

- Why are these issues important?

- What are the possible courses of action?

- What are the advantages and disadvantages of each?

- What are the key recommendations and why? What are their likely effects?

- What do you want to achieve from your recommendations?

- How will you know you have been successful? What are the critical success factors? How will you monitor and review progress?

- What resources do you need to consider? (Think about time, people budget etc.)

In writing any answer for a degree examination, it is important to establish a dialogue with the examiner through your script. This means explaining your rationale to the examiner about the things you write. Therefore explain to the examiner why you think there is a problem, what you think the implications will be and how and why you will take the actions you suggest.

This is only one suggestion for case study analysis, but it highlights the importance of planning your answer, so that you can make the key points and develop them. Hopefully these questions will assist you in analyzing a case study and then planning your answer in a coherent fashion, producing points that are well developed and well argued and supported by reference to relevant theory.

5 Further Reading

The set reading is very important aspect of this course of study. In the examination, section A is based on the case study material and is worth 40 marks. Therefore you will want to study it carefully before the examination. In addition one of the questions in section B which carries 20 marks will be based on one of the articles provided in the set reading collection.

All the time you are studying, look for relevant examples of what you have studied in the real world. If you work for a financial services organization, your company should provide a good source of material and knowledge. If you do not work for a financial services company, then think about your experiences as an individual customer of a building society or bank. Also keep an eye on the quality press for reports about banks and building societies and their activities.

6 Revision

Among the attributes of a good manager are the abilities to manage time and absorb and marshal new data. The management examination may appear challenging but for the well-prepared candidate there is ample time available to make the relevant points to achieve the marks required to succeed.

As with any examination, there is no substitute for preparation. You should therefore devise an approach that will enable you to complete this study text and still leave time for revision and further research of topics. Many candidates find that four weeks is about the right period of time to revise the material and update material relevant for the examination. You need to remember to allow time to work through the student activities and to practise writing up your answers to past examination questions. This is a critical part to obtaining success in this examination.

The period you have earmarked for revision is very important, and time is now ticking down to the actual examination date. It is important to plan your time between now and the examination so that you maximize the benefit for yourself.

- Make use of a timetable.

- Set clear objectives for each revision session.

- Use time sensibly. Remember that you need to be realistic. You will still need time to eat, sleep, perhaps do overtime, attend family events and for leisure!

- If you are studying for more than one subject, how will you split your time between the subjects? What are your weaker areas? You may decide to spend more time on one subject than another.

- Think about your learning style, and the time that is best for you, e.g. early morning, early evening or late evening.

- Take regular breaks. Most people find that that they can absorb more if they attempt to revise for long uninterrupted periods of time. However you also need a short five-minute break every 40 minutes or so, to give your brain a short rest, and when you recommence studying you should be able to retain information with increased efficiency.

- Believe in yourself. There is no reason why you should not pass the examination if you adopt the correct approach. Be confident. You have passed examinations before. You can pass this one – especially if you are well prepared.

- Book some time off leading up to the examination if you can. This will allow you to clear your mind of work and focus on passing the exam. Remember planning is important. Give your manager the opportunity to support you at this important time.

7 The Day of the Examination

Passing the examination is about having the knowledge and being able to present it in a way that will gain maximum marks in the exam. You must ensure that you satisfy the examiner's requirements:

- Familiarize yourself with the instructions on the front of the examination paper. Check that the exam format has not changed. Plan to answer the right number of questions.

- Read all the questions on the exam paper before you start writing and allocate time for planning your answers.

- Select questions carefully. Read through the paper once then quickly jot down any key points against each question in a second read through. Select those questions that you feel you can really focus on and develop relevant points in some depth. Also remember to check that you have got the right end of the stick before committing pen to paper for real.

- Plan your attack carefully. Consider the order in which you are going to answer the questions. It is usually a good idea to start with your best section B question. This will give you confidence and help you to relax knowing that you have made a good start and that marks are already starting to accumulate.

- Then attempt section A which is the case study and is worth 40 marks at the time of writing. Plan your time carefully in the exam room to ensure that you properly analyse the case study and make appropriate recommendations. Remember this material will be familiar to you because it is in the set reading.

- Present a tidy paper and plan your answers. You would be advised to submit your plans with your answer book. Again a good manager should be able to plan, and generally better answers can be seen after plans have been constructed because it helps you to structure your answer in a way that encourages a logical flow. When using your plan keep checking that you link your points back to the question. This will help to ensure that you maintain a good focus on the question asked.

- State the obvious. Sometimes candidates look for complexities which are not required and consequently overlook the obvious. Make basic statements first and build on these by developing the point. So, for example, say what you think of the point being made, explore the pros and cons and arrive at a conclusion, which is as a result of your argument. This captures the essence of graduateness in this paper.

- Use examples. This will help to demonstrate to the examiner that you keep up to date, and that you can apply your learning in the real environment. These anecdotes can be used to support your points and will help to explain your points appropriately. There are examples provided in this study text, but also in the quality press and academic books and articles that are available.

- Do not produce irrelevant answers. Do not see a topic area that you like or that you think you have revised. Look carefully at what the question is asking for. You must be able to cover the aspect requested. Make sure you answer the question set and not the question you would have liked to be set. Remember in the pressure of the examination room, your mind can play tricks, and you think you have answered the question but in fact you have answered a totally different question. Strange as it may seem this is a common occurrence and the reason why some candidates fail to achieve a pass mark. Therefore it is not because of a lack of knowledge necessarily, or that what the candidate has written is wrong. Rather the main problem can be a lack of focus on the question set.

- Produce an answer within a structure that promotes graduateness. For example to pass, it is vital that you construct arguments, which directly answer the question set. This means stating a point, and explaining why you think it is important, exploring the advantages and disadvantages of the argument and then drawing your work together in a conclusion, which needs to answer the question set. Your own views are important, as long as you justify them, explain why you believe in something (or not) and support your views by reference to theoretical frameworks. This is why the workbook and the text books are important to show the examiner that you have read around and are familiar with the main theories surrounding the topic area.

● Try not to leave the exam early. Remember if you have been given the time use it for your advantage. Plan to finish 15 minutes before the end of the examination so that you can read through all your answers, and check them to make sure you have said what you meant to say.

Finally...

Do not worry if you feel you have performed badly in the examination. It is likely that other candidates will have found the exam difficult too. Therefore forget about the exam. You cannot do anything now to change anything in your paper, so put it out of your mind until the day of results. Even if the worst comes to the worst you can always take the exam again, but if you have prepared well, you will have been preparing to pass.

Summary

Having studied this chapter you should now be aware of:

● The main considerations when studying the Management and Organization in Financial Services core subject

● The examination structure

● The importance of the set reading

● How to analyse case studies

● The main sources for further reading

● The key points to consider for revision and for preparation for the day of the examination itself.

2

THE CHANGING NATURE OF THE FINANCIAL SERVICES INDUSTRY

Objectives

After studying this chapter you should be able to:

- analyse the nature of an organization's external influences;

- identify the legal, ethical, political, economic, social, technological and competitive environments within which organizations and management operate;

- undertake an external appraisal of an organization;

- explain the consequences of economic deregulation, increased competition and advancements in technology on the operations of financial services organizations;

- explain the nature of ethical influences and discuss an organization's social responsibility;

- analyse and evaluate the external factors that exert an influence on business strategy.

1   The External Environment

Organizations do not operate in a vacuum nor is the context in which they operate static. It is important that organizations are able to analyse and respond to influences upon them.

The CIB Management and Organization in Financial Services Syllabus

The environment in which financial services organizations operate is constantly changing, with different factors exerting influences on the organization. It is vital that organizations constantly scan their environments and are aware of what is happening; only then can strategies be developed that fit both the internal capability of the organization and its environment. Environmental analysis helps the organization to develop a better understanding of how the external environment may affect it.

This chapter examines the general nature of the environment, distinguishing between turbulent as opposed to stable business conditions. It sets out a framework for assessing the different factors influencing the operation of organizations under the headings of legal, ethical, political, economic, social, technological and competitive.

2   Why Analyse the Environment

The end of the twentieth century saw a rapid pace and rate of change within the external environment of the financial services industry. The first decade of the new millennium will see even more transformation, with the world changing at an unprecedented speed. All organizations are vulnerable to environmental change because some features of change will provide new opportunities whereas others pose threats. The challenge for financial services organizations is to anticipate and be proactive to the changes in order to avoid launching inappropriate services and products with structures, costs and systems unable to meet customer demand and expectations.

Undertaking an environmental analysis can:

- enhance self-understanding, that is develop an awareness of the organization's own position vis-à-vis the environment both now and in the future;

- help the organization to avoid surprises by anticipating major changes in the business environment;

- help with swifter identification of opportunities and threats;

- improve planning and shorten reaction time – a good understanding of the environment should allow an organization to act more effectively once opportunities and threats have been identified.

The external environment can be defined as everything outside the organization that may affect performance either directly or indirectly. Environmental forces are often beyond the control of the organization. However, the contribution of environmental analysis is to help organizations to be proactive rather than reactive in managing in an uncertain environment. Environmental analysis must be an iterative process, not only analyzing the current situation but anticipating how the environment might change in the future. When analysing the environment it is important to evaluate and prioritize the different influences in order to understand the position of the organization and determine how it should respond.

3   The Nature of the Environment

The nature of the environment concerns the degree of turbulence and uncertainty and provides an understanding of the basic conditions surrounding the organization. Turbulence can be explained in terms of:

1. Changeability, that is the degree to which the environment is likely to change, and

2. predictability, which is concerned with the degree to which change can be predicted.

There are a number of factors that will determine the level of turbulence in the environment, for example:

● the changeability of the market environment;

● the speed of change;

● technological advancements;

● discrimination by customers;

● pressures from government and interest groups.

Uncertainty can be determined by examining the degree of complexity within the environment and the degree of dynamism. This involves assessing whether the environment is simple, or complex to understand and whether it is static or dynamic, facing rapid change? Johnson and Scholes (1997) propose that uncertainty increases when environmental conditions are more complex and dynamic. Where turbulence and uncertainty are high the organization will need to structure itself so that it is adaptable and flexible in order that it can cope with rapidly changing circumstances.

4   Environmental Influences

The external environment can be analysed at two levels:

1.   The macroenvironment, which includes developments in the wider business environment relating to political, economic, social and technological changes.

2.   The microenvironment, which is of more immediate concern and encompasses competitive pressures within the industry and demands from customers and suppliers.

It is important to note that the macro- and microenvironments are interrelated, so for example changes in legislation could alter the nature of the competition the organization faces.

A popular framework for analyzing the external forces driving change is the Le Pest & Co mnemonic which categorizes factors under the headings legal, ethical, political, economic, social, technological and competitive environments. Factors within each of these dimensions can affect, either directly or indirectly, the organization's business strategy and performance, and ultimately management policies.

Figure 1.1 provides an example of a Le Pest & Co analysis for the financial services sector. Once this analysis has been undertaken the headings can be used as a checklist to assess the relative importance of the different influences in order to identify the *key* drivers of change.

Figure 1.1: Factors in a Le Pest & Co analysis

Legal
- Employment law
- Monopolies legislation
- Industry regulatory framework
- Consumer legislation

Ethical
- Minority groups
- Social accountability & responsibility
- Green issues

Political
- Government stability
- Political parties at national, European or trading-block level
- Relations between government & organization
- Government attitudes towards competition

Economic
- Inflation levels
- Consumer income & expenditure
- Interest rate levels
- Investment
- Unemployment
- Exchange rate & currency fluctuations

Social
- Shifts in values
- Changes in lifestyles
- Attitudes to work
- Education & health
- Demographic changes
- Distribution of income

Technological
- Technological developments
- Speed of change
- Rate of adoption of new technologies
- Cost of technologies

Competition
- Market structure
- Intensity of competitive rivalry
- Market growth
- Stage in life cycle of products & services

The remaining part of this chapter uses the Le Pest & Co framework to examine some of the key factors that have influenced or might, in the future, influence the strategies of financial services organizations.

5 Legal Influences

It is helpful to try to categorize the legal influences that face a financial services organization. A possible approach is to divide the influences into three major categories:

- legislation governing the recruitment and employment of individuals;

- legislation governing customer relations and business operations;

● legislation regulating the activities of financial institutions.

UK organizations are controlled by both the European Community and UK Parliamentary legislation. There are also local regulations and custom and practice which set guidelines and which must be respected. Relevant legislation governing the employment of individuals will be explored in the later chapters on Human Resource (HR) policies and systems. However, it should be noted at this stage that statutes or codes of conduct govern all aspects of employment from:

● advertising jobs;

● recruitment;

● terms and conditions of employment to severance of employment;

● grievance and disciplinary procedure;

● equal opportunities.

An understanding of the implications of legislation is therefore an important aspect of a manager's role. This part of the chapter will, however, concentrate on legislation that governs customer relations and business operations, and regulates the activities of financial institutions, and as such has exerted an influence on their strategy over recent years.

Over the last 20 years legislation has been enacted that has both regulated and deregulated the financial services environment. Regulation refers to legislation that results in greater control and restriction of activities. Deregulation introduces new opportunities and less restrictive practices for some types of financial services organizations. Changes in the regulatory framework have encouraged alterations in the operations and strategy of financial institutions. Some examples of official deregulation are:

● Building Society Act 1986;

● EU Second Banking Co-ordination Directive 1993.

Examples of official reregulation are:

● Financial Services Act 1986;

● Financial Services and Markets Bill (proposed legislation for 2000)

There are also examples of unofficial regulation and deregulation, applied by professional bodies, trade associations and cartels. Most of these have tended to be deregulatory in nature, e.g. abandoning building society interest rate cartel (1992) and changes in the membership rules and allowable activities of London Stock Exchange (1986).

Until the 1970s there were clear divisions between the operations of different types of financial institutions because of the regulative restrictions on the scope of their activities. With the deregulation of the industry, since the beginning of the 1980s the competitive pressures within the UK financial system have ensured that organizations provide a broader range of financial services. This has increased competition between banks, building societies and insurance companies and has led to new entrants (e.g. Marks and Spencer, and Virgin) and to alliances and mergers between organizations (Lloyds-TSB, and Cheltenham and Gloucester Building Society, and Halifax and Leeds Permanent Building Society, and Clerical and Medical Insurance Group). The clear divisions between the different types of organizations, the products offered and their activities no longer exist.

The next section examines in more detail the acts mentioned above and considers their effects. These acts have been selected because of their influence in altering the nature of the financial services sector, but of course many more have been enacted which are outside the scope of this book.

Deregulation

Building Society Act 1986

Building societies are mutual institutions owned by members. The late 1960s to the early 1980s saw rapid growth in terms of the size and activities of building societies. Since the Building Societies Act 1986 there has been some consolidation occurring with the end result being a smaller number of larger organizations. This rapid growth could be explained in terms of:

- the high demand for mortgages (encouraged by the tax relief scheme introduced by the government),

- the ability of the banks to compete with the building societies because of changing monetary controls,

- the lower cost/income ratio of building societies due to the simplicity of their operations and smaller branch networks and new delivery channels.

In January 1987 the Building Society Act came into force, and was designed to update the legislative framework for building societies. It gave the societies, especially the larger ones, more flexibility to manage their affairs and more opportunities to provide a better quality of service for customers in terms of the wider product range they could offer. It was not intended that the societies should fundamentally change their role but be able to offer complementary services to the customer.

Specifically the Act:

- allowed societies to extend their unsecured lending;

- allowed societies to offer a range of financial and banking services hitherto forbidden;

- formalized the position on societies raising wholesale funds;

- provided a mechanism for societies to relinquish their mutual status and become plcs (convert to banks);

- established the Building Society Commission to supervise their activities.

In February 1988 it was decided that the powers of the building societies would be widened further. Building Societies could now take equity stakes in life and general insurance companies, undertake fund management, and establish and manage personal equity plans and unit trusts through associated bodies and stockbroking firms offering a wider range of bank and related services. As a result many organizations offered a wider range of products.

Now very few of the large Building Societies have retained their mutual status.

EU Second Banking Co-ordination Directive 1993

Another example of major deregulation affecting the Financial Services Sector is the EU Second Banking directive. Prior to the late 1980s the EU had little impact on bank activities in the UK. However, the single European Market Initiative (1992) gave a major boost to the relevance of EU legislation.

The Second Banking Directive was adopted in January 1988. It introduced the concept of a single European bank licence whereby any bank authorized in any European state could operate freely in any other state without further authorization. This authorization gave the home country the responsibility for the overall supervision of the EU-wide operations of banks based in the respective countries. The Directive came into force on 1 January 1993, so encouraging increased competition between financial services organizations within Europe.

Reregulation

In contrast to the legislation above which indicates deregulation of the industry has occurred, other acts have been introduced which provide for reregulation.

Financial Services Act 1986

This Act was designed to protect consumers from the adverse effects of deregulation and was designed to cover all types of investments and the giving of advice related to investments. It made the Department of Trade and Industry (DTI) responsible for the regulation of investment business in the UK. In turn the Secretary of State for Trade and Industry delegated operating powers to the Securities and Investment Board (SIB). In 1992 the DTI's responsibility in respect of the Financial Services Act was transferred to the Treasury to consolidate a wide range of financial regulations under one ministry.

The Financial Services Act explicitly made the Bank of England responsible for the regulation of the gilts bullion market, wholesale money markets and foreign exchange. The DTI also has considerable power over the operations of insurance companies and unit trusts although marketing activities rest with the Treasury.

The SIB (from October 1997 renamed the Financial Services Authority) formulated the rulebook with codes of conduct and regulations for those involved in the investment business. It delegated to the Self Regulatory Organizations (SROs) their responsibility. Each SRO produced its own rulebook. Although initially there were five new boards there are now only three:

- Securities and Futures Authority;

- Investment Management Regulatory Organization;

- Personal Investment Authority.

Originally the boards were very legalistic and detailed and were criticized because of their increasing costs, but now they have been rationalized and follow certain core rules. The SIB structure also includes recognized professional bodies (such as chartered accountants) and recognized investment exchanges.

Financial Services and Markets Bill

In July 1998 the Government published the draft Financial Services and Markets Bill, (likely to become law during 2000) which proposed giving wide-ranging powers to the Financial Services Authority (FSA). Included in this bill was confirmation of the Labour Government's desire to bring under a single authority the regulation and supervision of virtually all banking and financial services activities and products in the UK. The main exceptions were mortgage loans, banking and building society deposits and general insurance. Even with these products the bill proposes reserve powers to allow the government to bring the products under FSA control without further recourse to Parliament in the future.

The FSA will receive all of the powers currently available to the existing regulatory bodies, plus additional powers to deal more effectively with market abuse.

The main objectives of the proposal are:

- To maintain confidence in the UK financial system – this will be achieved by both prudential regulation (emphasizing the solvency and the soundness of the financial institutions) and the conduct of business regulation (the ways financial institutions conduct business with customers, the disclosure of information, integrity etc.).

- To promote public understanding so that consumers become better purchasers, enhancing financial literacy and providing generic advice (helplines, publications etc.).

- To protect customers and provide mechanisms to handle customer complaints.

- To prevent financial crime by ensuring financial service organizations have systems in place to protect them against money laundering situations.

The Act also brings together the rules governing financial advertising and promotion, for example making explicit the cost of borrowing by quoting the equivalent annual percentage rate (APR).

Financial Services Ombudsman

In 1999 the Financial Services Ombudsman scheme was established, bringing together the existing schemes (e.g. Banking Ombudsman, Building Society Ombudsman, Insurance Ombudsman) under one umbrella. This established a single financial services ombudsman and a unified compensation scheme within which there is a differentiation between markets and different types of customers (for instance the knowledge that could be reasonably expected of a corporate client is far higher than for a personal customer). Although it is impossible for any scheme to fully protect customers, the Ombudsman's primary purpose is to act as an independent arbitrator. The aim is to provide customers, where disagreements between the organization and the customer cannot be resolved, with the opportunity to have their case investigated without the costs involved when this is done through litigation

In summary, recent legislation has to some extent restructured the financial services sector in the UK. Many building societies have sought conversion to plcs (e.g. Abbey National in July 1989 and Halifax in 1997). The industry has seen the entry of non-financial institutions and consequent increased competition, so it is difficult to distinguish between different types of financial service providers. However there has also been increased regulation with the Financial Services Act, and the proposed Financial Services and Markets Act will shape the behaviour of financial suppliers and increase the protection offered to consumers. The Financial Services Authority, now the single regulator for the industry, will have stronger powers as a result.

6 Ethical Influences

Ethics

Ethics is the 'study of principles of human duty' (*Oxford Dictionary*). As such it impacts upon considerations of organizational activity both in respect of the ways in which organizations treat the personnel who work for them and in the ways in which organizations manage the relationships with their external stakeholders.

Unfortunately the practical application of ethics to business activity is far from simple. This is because in the context of the global marketplace there is little agreement on what constitutes the 'principles of human duty' both in the practical and the philosophical sense.

To appreciate the difficulty, consider some of the current 'problem areas' of business activity:

- genetic modification
- cloning
- moving production centres to areas where wage rates are low
- deforestation
- nuclear reprocessing
- disposal of waste materials
- withdrawal of subsidies to farmers – without provision of assistance to restructure the industry
- overfishing, etc.

There is often no simple answer to problems posed by activities in these 'ethically grey areas'. For example – should a manufacturer of sports equipment exploit child labour by siting its production in areas where child labour is both the norm and a significant source of family income?

Philosophers arguing from a Utilitarian basis (the 'greatest happiness of the greatest number' ethic) would suggest that the answer to this question should be 'Yes' because the greatest good is produced by the provision of resources to underdeveloped areas. Economists may well argue in the same way from a practical point of view.

On the other hand, philosophers following Kant's ideas on the 'categorical imperative' (the concept that there are duties by which human actions can be determined without any consideration of the consequences of the action) could argue that exploitation of child labour is morally obnoxious and consequently ethically unjustifiable. Many potential consumers within the producer's developed markets would share this view.

This very confusion itself suggests that that which is ethical is contextual. Thus what I regard as ethical is determined by my genes, my upbringing, education and development, by the influences to which I have been exposed and by the decisions which I have had to make. In a more general sense ethical thought depends on the body of tradition that supports it and the problems with which it is asked to grapple – not many of the world's great philosophers have addressed the question of whether genetic modification is morally defensible.

More advanced considerations on ethics

On a practical level – when grappling with potential ethical problems in the business environment – there are helpful frameworks against which to make judgements.

Johns and Connock (1995) outline three broad approaches to ethics.

(a) Social ethics: which describe the basic rules for existence within a given society. A 'society' could be a group as large as a nation or one as small as a family unit: it includes a commercial organization in which social ethics will probably manifest themselves as underpinning the organization's vision statement, its codes of conduct and its corporate values. Social ethics – as a foundation for business ethics – suffer from inherent insularity and tend to break down in situations that involve competition between differing groups (such as employees as a group – or 'society' and customers as a group).

(b) Transcendental ethics: which are founded on the concept that there is a set of absolute standards of right and wrong behaviour which have universal applicability. While this is an appealing concept it is of little practical benefit because it ignores the essentially contextual nature of ethics and the idea that different cultures will operate from different ethical bases.

(c) Tactical ethics: whereby what may be regarded as ethical standards are observed not because such observation is 'right' but primarily because such observation is in the best interests of the individual – or group of individuals – concerned.

Carroll (1990) suggests that there are eleven different ethical criteria which managers may use as a basis of judgement in relation to business issues.

1. The **categorical imperative** whereby principles of action will be adopted only if they can be adopted, without inconsistency, by everyone else – i.e. the principles are transcendental in nature.

2. The **conventionalist ethic** whereby acting in your own self-interest is permissible provided that the laws imposed by society are not thereby infringed.

3. The **golden rule** – do unto others as you would have them do unto you.

4. The **hedonistic ethic** – if it feels O.K. then it probably is O.K.

5. The **disclosure rule** whereby the rectitude of any particular action is judged by reference to one's projected feelings should it happen to be reported on the front page of a tabloid newspaper.

6. The **intuition ethic** – do whatever your emotional as opposed to rational decision-making machinery tells you to do.

7. The **means to an end ethic** whereby it is permissible to act if the end result is defensible.

8. The **might equals right ethic** whereby acting in accordance with the strength of your power base, even though this runs contrary to social convention, is permissible.

9. The **organization ethic** in accordance with which loyalty to the organization takes precedence over all other considerations.

10. The **professional ethic** under which adherence to the code of your profession transcends other considerations.

11. The **utilitarian principle** under which the guiding principle is attaining the 'greatest good of the greatest number'.

It is becoming increasingly important for commercial organizations to grapple with this problem. More and more they are judged by those with whom they come into contact on the basis of their capacity to behave in an ethically correct manner. Within the business world the ethical agenda includes not topics of the order of those mentioned above but also the relationship between business and its stakeholders; issues of remuneration policy; questions of excess profits; the impact on the community at large of inadequate business systems – such as led to pensions mis-selling etc. For many of these topics there is no long tradition of philosophical thought with the result that organizations are having to determine on the hoof approaches to unexplored issues. So, having an ethical framework in place makes it easier for business to choose the 'right' behaviour – even if that ethical framework is contextual.

7 Developing an Ethical Organization

There are two basic approaches to developing an ethical organization:

a) compliance-based, and

b) integrity-based.

A compliance approach seeks not so much to promote ethical behaviour but to eradicate that which is unethical. It is designed fundamentally to eliminate competitive disadvantage. Compliance approaches have the virtue of being readily manageable. They can also be actively promoted by forces external to the organization either by punishing non-compliant behaviour (as is happening in the U.K. in respect of the rectification of pension miss-selling) or by encouraging compliant behaviour through tax breaks and sentencing policy as is happening in the USA.

Compliance can be in accordance with the requirements of the organization itself – through the medium of an ethical policy, or its mission, aims, goals, objectives and strategy, or in accordance with the requirements of external elements – governments, regulators, markets, consumers etc. – provided that these elements have sufficient power to impose a competitive disadvantage on non-compliant businesses.

For example the rectification of the pensions mis-selling was aided by the naming and shaming policy of the government – designed to produce a competitive disadvantage. On the other hand governments are relatively powerless against businesses manufacturing tobacco products who – in relation to the defence of those products – act collectively and are thus not susceptible to competitive advantage/disadvantage.

Integrity-based approaches aim to integrate into day-to-day activities the organization's guiding values, hopes and patterns of behaviour. Elaborate programmes exist to achieve such ends involving, among other things, orientation; consultation on the articulation of values and standards; integrated systems and feedback channels for employees.

Such programmes are important but likely to fail unless the organization's leadership is prepared to 'walk the talk'. Thus, for example, remuneration systems must be designed to give credit to – or at least not to discourage – ethical behaviour. Similarly the organization should strive to establish such a climate of trust that mistakes can be openly discussed and worries regarding the ethical credentials of a product or service shared internally.

8 Political Influences

Political influences are closely linked with legal ones because the government of the day determines in part the legislation which reflects its own areas of interest and policy. The major changes to the regulatory and supervisory framework were explored in an earlier section. There has been over recent years widespread dissatisfaction with the quality of supervision and investor protection in the UK. A number of high-profile cases (Maxwell pension scandal, personal pension mis-selling, etc.), combined with confusion about the split responsibilities of the SIB/SRO structure made an attractive case for a single regulator with statutory powers.

The increasingly complex nature of financial services business at domestic and international levels, together with the trend towards diversified financial institutions, makes the inclusion of all financial service organizations into a single regulatory framework logical. The draft Financial Services and Markets Bill referred to in the earlier section will address the issue of a single regulatory authority.

Another area is international relations between powers. This can have a profound effect on investment and trade. For example, unrest in the Middle East and Africa can alter the investment strategy of foreign powers and inhibit growth by multinationals. The issue of lending to less developed countries and country risk will continue to be strategic issues. The policies of governments and local authorities can also influence banking activities, e.g. policies of regeneration in areas of high unemployment.

Other political influences on financial service organizations include government policies on interest rate control, European alignment of rules such as the employee's rights, rationalization of the European Stock exchange and the continued policy of privatization.

An example of government activity in the scrutiny of financial services organizations was the Cruickshank report commissioned in November 1998 by the Labour government to examine:

● the UK banking sector except investment banking;

● levels of innovation, competition and efficiency in different banking markets;

● how these levels compare with international standards;

● the options for change.

The findings of the report made four main recommendations:

● the creation of a stronger policy framework, so the relationships between banks, the treasury and the Financial Services Authority (FSA) should be strengthened;

● the supervision of money transmission which should be subject to a payment system licensing regime supervized by a payment systems commission (paycom);

● fairer banking services for personal banking customers so consumers can compare products and have more information about complaints procedures;

● fairer banking services for small businesses.

As a result of the report the government is considering the actions needed.

9   Economic Influences

It is sometimes difficult to distinguish between economic and political influences because again governments follow particular economic polices. Diverse factors influencing the economy are:

- changing levels of disposable income,
- rates of inflation,
- fiscal policy,
- income/wealth distribution,
- unemployment
- the availability of raw materials

The recessions of the early 1990s in the UK resulted in many defaults on loans and a move from borrowing towards saving. Over the last 10 years the population of the UK generally is better off. Between 1987 and 1997 the total household income increased by 30.5% in real terms to reach £769 billion in 1997 and disposable income increased by 36% over the same period (due mainly to the decrease in income tax). Despite the general increase in household income one quarter of all full-time employees had gross weekly wages of under £250 and a national minimum wage came into effect in April 1999.

Over recent years the economic changes in the UK have resulted in:

- the decline of manufacturing industries
- the growth of service industries,
- differences in the distribution of wealth
- economic recession with high unemployment.

These factors have led to the emergence of giant multinational firms which have a political influence because of the transfer of tax and funds between countries. There is far greater competition for the UK financial services institutions from overseas companies and other organizations extending or moving into financial service activities. Also playing a part are quasi-legal entities, e.g. rating agencies, which ascribe a credit rating to banks. This can have serious implications for their stock market rating.

By relinquishing control of interest rates to the Bank of England in May 1997, the Labour government tried to introduce distance between the government and the body charged with fixing interest rates. The Bank of England has operational freedom in respect of the implementation of the government's monetary policy. The Bank's monetary policy committee now determines whether or not changes should be made in the short-term interest rates in pursuit of the goal of maintaining a target rate of inflation (+/-1%) as specified by the government.

10   Social Influences

It is predicted that changes in the social environment will increase in importance over the next decade. Social influences will affect both the demand for financial services and the supply of what could arguably be an organization's most important resource, its staff. The trends that can be discerned which will impact on the financial services industry include:

Changing customer needs and attitudes

- More educated customers with more sophisticated financial services needs;

- Customers with an increased real disposable income, although the gap between high and low incomes has widened;

- More discerning customers demanding higher quality yet at the same time competitively priced products;

- Society is expecting greater social responsibility from organizations with regard to ethical conduct towards employees, customers and ethical protection.

Demographic

Demography is the study of population trends and is one of the most important social changes that will affect the demand for financial services products. In the UK the following trends can be identified:

- The number of young peopled entering the marketplace will continue to decline;

- There will be an increase in the proportion of people over retirement age;

- The ageing population will continue to dominate government welfare spending, along with greater self-reliance for individuals and financial well being in the future in terms of provision of health care and retirement.

Household and family structure

- Increasing divorce rates have led to the decline of the traditional family unit (i.e. working husband, wife and dependent children) and a growth in single-parent households;

- Later marriage and delayed child bearing with an increase in the economic activity of women;

- Greater financial independence for women and an increase in single-person households;

- Increase in the number of household with joint incomes.

Nature of the workforce

- Decline in the manufacturing base and a massive growth in the services sector;

- Decline in blue collar work, while at the same time there has been an increase in white collar, supervisory and management jobs;

- Increase in women working and a growth in part-time and temporary work.

All these developments and trends will have implications for the strategies of financial services organizations in terms of the customer base they serve, the product range they offer, delivery channels and the quality of service. They will also impact on the available labour market for recruitment and the drive for more flexible working arrangements.

1 1   *Technological Influences*

Developments in technology over the last twenty years have dominated the revolution in the financial services sector, transforming financial services organizations in terms of the nature of their work, the structure of the organization and the way they design and deliver their products and services to customers.

Developments have included:

- The miniaturization of technological solutions, the falling cost of computer power, and the growth of computer literacy and software applications;

- Worldwide explosion in telecommunications increasing the globalization of capital flows of funds;

- Advancements in processing and money transmission activities with systems developed to speed up the transfer of money from one place to another. Examples of such systems include, CHAPS (Clearing House Automated Payment System); BACS (Bankers Automated Clearing Systems); SWIFT (Society for World Wide InterBank Financial Telecommunications);

- Consumer payment systems have changed with an increased reliance on credit and debit card payments, and, more recently, the introduction of alternative methods such as smart cards;

- The changing nature of work as technology reduces the amount of basic administrative and routine tasks, particularly in the area of processing activities. It is predicted that the introduction of image scanning technology will result in a paper-less environment. Automation has seen a shift from the traditional back-office branch activities towards centralized processing and service centres, often 'greenfield' sites, employing 'factory' type workers who do not necessarily have or need any knowledge of the financial services sector;

- Technological changes which have also encouraged the de-layering of the organizational hierarchy with the reduction in management layers, the skills required and working methods. Developments in credit scoring and risk analysis technology systems have led to a de-skilling of the traditional lending role. Unskilled staff supported by expert systems are now able to sanction loans to the personal and small business markets;

- Advancements in technology have also impacted on the way financial services organizations interface with their customers, with the proliferation of new products and emergence of new delivery channels. 'Self-service banking' means that there is no need to go to the traditional outlet, with remote sites available at more convenient locations such as in supermarkets, shopping malls and train stations. Telephone banking, PC banking and smart card technology have all contributed to the change in the way financial services transactions are enacted. The advent of digital TV will further revolutionize the delivery of financial services. Nellis (1998) suggests that technology will make it possible for customer demand to be satisfied 'anytime, and place, anywhere'!;

- Advances in database marketing techniques have led to the development of sophisticated database systems which provide organizations with tools to analyze customer information and to provide a better understanding of the marketplace. This enables them to more accurately predict consumer needs and to identify cross-selling opportunities;

- There has been a revolution in communication methods as a result of technological advancements which have implications for work practices. E-mail, Intranet and the Internet are all examples of modern communication methods, speeding up and making information more accessible.

Technological advancements have enabled organizations to seek greater operating efficiencies, productivity and service quality in their quest to sustain profitability and provide more reliable security to cut down on fraud and improve risk assessment utilizing expert modelling techniques. However, there are risks associated with this heavy reliance on technological support, for example there is the risk of systems going down, along with the dangers of computer viruses and possible sabotage by disgruntled staff or customers.

12 Competitive Influences

One of the key forces for change in the way financial services operate has been the increase in competition. As mentioned earlier deregulation has changed the nature of competition with organizations competing not just on a national arena, but increasingly at an international and global level. It is suggested that financial services markets are oversupplied and margins are being depressed in a highly competitive marketplace. Profitability will be determined by the extent to which organizations develop appropriate strategies to 'combat' the growing competitive forces.

The nature of competition in the financial services industry can be characterized by:

- existing players who all provide similar services. The boundaries between different types of institutions have become blurred with banks, building societies and insurance companies now all offering very similar product ranges and competing in the same markets;

- niche players offering a more restricted range of products, but which are strong competitors in their specialist field;

- new entrants, including non-financial services organizations who have diversified into the financial services arena. Supermarkets such as Tesco and Sainsbury's, and other well established names such as Marks and Spencer, Virgin, General Motors, the AA and SAGA all now have a portfolio of financial services on offer;

- new entrants, particularly foreign competition attacking the UK marketplace, some launching new brands, such as Goldfish.

The factors driving change at the micro level can be analyzed using Porter's five forces model (Porter 1980). This framework identifies five basic competitive forces that influence the state and structure of competition in an industry, and which will collectively determine the long-run return on capital and the profit potential of the industry as a whole. These five competitive forces are:

1. The threat of new entrants to the industry;

2. The threat of substitute products or services;

3. The bargaining power of customers;

4. The bargaining power of suppliers;

5. The rivalry among current competitors in the industry.

The threat of new entrants

A new entrant into the industry will bring new capacity, so posing a threat to established players. The strength of this threat depends on how easy or difficult it is for other organizations to enter the industry. Barriers to entry could include scale economies, product differentiation, capital requirements (e.g. major investment in technology), switching cost (i.e. the cost and inconvenience which customers would experience by changing supplier), access to distribution channels (e.g. branch networks), government policy and legislation, and other factors such as access to key skills/experience and competencies.

The threat of new entrants is real within the financial services sector where deregulation and consumer acceptance of technology-based delivery channel developments have significantly reduced barriers to entry. Non-bank retailers, such as Virgin, Marks and Spencer, Tesco and Sainsbury's, view the financial services sector as an attractive business to enter, allowing them to capitalize on their strong brand image and exploit their large customer databases. These new players bring different marketing skills and are playing by different rules. Traditional providers of financial services must be proactive and willing to adapt their strategies if they are going to survive the new competition.

It is suggested that in the future it will be the telecommunication companies who pose a new threat in the financial services market place.

The threat from substitute products and services

Substitutes are different goods or services that satisfy the same customer need. Given the nature of financial services products, which do not attract patents and can be easily copied, this presents a major threat. Most financial services products essentially satisfy the same customer needs, for example the need to deposit funds, the need to borrow funds, the need to insure. The costs of switching to alternative providers are low and customers can easily move to alternatives that offer better rates of interest for loans and savings products, or which have cheaper premiums in the case of some general insurance products.

The availability of close substitutes means that financial service organizations may find it difficult to charge higher prices for what might be termed 'commodity' products.

The bargaining power of customers

Where customers are in a strong position they have the power to force organizations to reduce prices or improve/change products and thus force down the profitability of the industry.

Legislation in the financial services sector has increased customer rights while at the same time greater access to information of what is on offer and competition has increased customer choice of both products and suppliers. The result has been a rise in consumerism with customers expecting better quality products at lower prices. Traditionally financial services organizations relied on customer inertia not to move but this is no longer the case as new entrants actively pursue new customers. A key strategy of most financial services organizations is one of customer retention with a focus on how to better meet customer needs. Organizations are already implementing strategies designed to develop closer relationships with high net worth customers.

The bargaining power of suppliers

Suppliers can influence an industry's profitability by exerting pressure for higher prices.

For financial services organizations the supply chain is complex. It involves getting the right staff, skills and technology. A further complexity is that along with the money markets, customers could also be classed as suppliers of raw material, in the sense that they provide the deposits which can be then manufactured into loans.

The intensity of competitive rivalry

This is concerned with assessing the intensity of competitive rivalry because this will affect the profitability of the industry as a whole. Rivalry is intensified where organizations are competing for a greater market share in a total market where growth is slow or stagnant and where exit barriers make it difficult to leave the industry.

Within the financial services sector competitive rivalry is intense, and is likely to increase as organizations fight for their share of the marketplace and as more new entrants from the telecommunications and computer technology industries join the marketplace. This is likely to result in a continued squeeze on profit margins and a continued search for cost reductions and sources of new revenue. Brand strength, efficient delivery systems, quality of products and service and an increased emphasis on identifying the customer using database management and predictive marketing techniques will be key elements of strategies to maintain market position. However, it is likely that there will be more merger activity as existing organizations seek to minimize risks through cost reductions and increased market share.

Summary

Now you have studied this chapter you should be able to:

- Explain why it is vital for an organization to understand its external environment;

- Analyse the nature of the financial services operating environment;

- Use the Le Pest & Co framework to examine the external environment in order to identify some of the key environment forces impacting on financial services organizations' operations;

- Assess the influence of ethics and social responsibility on business strategy;

- Evaluate some of the changes in terms of the structure of the financial services industry and its development;

- Discuss how the competitive environment can be analysed using the five forces model.

References

Johns T and Cannock S (1995) *Ethical Leadership*, Institute of Personnel and Development

Johnson J & Scholes K (1997) *Exploring Corporate Strategy*, 4th ed. Prentice Hall

Nellis (1998) *The Chartered Banker*, The Chartered Institute of Bankers

Porter M E (1980) *Competitive Strategy, Techniques for Analysing Industries and Competitors*, Free Press

3

MANAGING THE STRATEGY PROCESS IN FINANCIAL SERVICES ORGANIZATIONS

Chapter 2 explored the influences that the external environment can exert on financial services organizations. This chapter examines the process of how organizations can develop strategies to respond to those pressures. It sets out the frameworks and activities involved in the strategic management process and shows how an understanding of the process can help financial services organizations in the development and implementation of appropriate strategies for business growth and survival.

Objectives

After studying this chapter you should be able to:

- describe the concept and role of strategic management;

- explain why organizations need strategic management and planning;

- contrast the different levels of strategy and planning;

- identify the different stages of the strategic management process;

- apply the various analytical models;

- discuss the alternative approaches to strategic management;

- explain stakeholder influences on strategy development.

1   The Concept of Strategic Management

The viability of an organization in both the long and short term is fundamentally dependent upon its capacity to establish and achieve objectives.

> The CIB Management and Organization in Financial Services Syllabus

The dynamic, unpredictable and complex environment in which financial service organizations operate, already discussed in Chapter 2, makes it essential that financial services organizations plan for the future. The strategic management process is concerned with determining the organization's future direction and the formulation and implementation of strategies that will enhance the overall competitiveness of the organization. For most financial services organizations the overall aim is to develop strategies that will deliver long-term added value.

There are many different approaches to strategic management but they all have the aim of establishing a business purpose and guiding managers on how to implement strategies to achieve organizational goals. The strategies adopted will determine the internal character of the organization and how it relates to the outside world, the range of its products, the markets in which it operates and its intentions for the future.

2 Defining Strategy

There is no universally agreed and accepted definition of the term strategy. Some examples of different definitions include:

- "strategy is the direction and scope of an organization over the long term: ideally, which matches its resources to its changing environment, and in particular its markets, customers or clients so as to meet shareholder expectations". Johnson and Scholes (1997)

- "the pattern of major objectives, purposes or goals and essential plans for achieving those goals, stated in such a way as to define which business the company is in or is to be in and the kind of company it is or is to be". Andrews (1971)

Strategy therefore could be said to be concerned with the **scope** of the organization's activities and the **actions** required to achieve its **objectives**.

There is a whole vocabulary associated with the subject of strategic planning, which it is helpful to be familiar with prior to discussing the strategic management process. For example, Johnson and Scholes (1997) offer the following definitions of some key terms:

- **Vision/Strategic intent**   Desired future state or aspiration of the organization.

- **Mission**   The overriding purpose of the organization in line with the values or expectations of shareholders. An organization's rationale for existing.

- **Mission statement**   Document in which the mission is formally stated.

- **Goal**   General statement of aim or purpose, while not quantifiable this interprets the mission.

- **Objective**   Quantification (if possible) or more precise statement of goal, used to plan the achievement of mission and monitor performance.

- **Competitive advantage**   Factors that enable the organization to compete successfully with competitors on a sustained basis.

- **Core competencies**   Resources, processes or skills that provide competitive advantage

3   The Need for Strategic Management and Strategic Planning

The terms 'strategic management' and 'strategic planning' are often used interchangeably. They are both concerned with an analytical approach to making decisions within an organization and determination of what an organization needs to do in order to achieve its goals and objectives. The activities involved include:

- analysing the external environment;
- analysing the internal resources;
- determining and evaluating strategic options;
- managing the implementation of the strategies chosen.

So strategic management and planning are important activities because they impact on the future direction and survival of the organization, and as such are long-term in nature. Without planning an organization may find itself becoming out of touch with its environment, leaving itself vulnerable to competition.

A formal system of strategic management will help the organization to cope with uncertainty and managing risk by:

- anticipating the opportunities and threats presented by the external environment;
- providing a sense of purpose for the employees of the organization and an understanding of their own roles and responsibilities;
- provide guidelines for management actions in terms of identifying the resources needed and ensure the efficient allocation of these resources to achieve organizational goals and objectives;
- drawing attention to the need to keep changing and adapting;
- encouraging cooperation and coordination of efforts at all levels;
- evaluating the implications of future decisions;
- helping to improve the quality of decision-making;
- improving the consistency of actions across the organization.

An analogy often used to explain the strategic planning process is that of planning a journey. Before embarking on a journey you need to know first of all where you are now and where you want to get to (i.e. current position and goals and objectives). This will allow you to consider the alternative routes you could take and to decide how are you going to get there (i.e. alternative strategies and actions). Finally, having set out on the journey you need to check progress in order to ensure you are not deviating from your route in arriving at the final destination:

- where are we now?
- where do we want to be?
- how are we going get there?
- have we arrived?

Although the above would perhaps suggest the process of strategic management is a set of clear steps and activities, it is, in reality, a far more complex process because of the constant changing nature of the environment

4 The Different Levels of Strategy and Planning

It is important to note that planning and decision-making occur at different levels. A categorization put forward by a number of researchers distinguishes between strategic level, business level and operational/functional level plans and decision-making. However, the different levels are interdependent, i.e. one level should be consistent with the strategies at the next level and all levels should be directed towards contributing to the overall corporate strategy. The hierarchy and interrelationship of strategic decision-making is illustrated in the diagram below:

Figure 3.1: The hierarchy and interrelationship of strategic decision-making

Strategic level

Strategic decisions are of a higher order than other management decisions and tend to be complex and non-routine in nature because they often involve a high degree of uncertainty based on what *might* happen in the future.

Strategic level planning addresses issues such as:

- What type of business or businesses should the organization be in? This is concerned with decisions of scope. For example, should the organization diversify or limit its business activities? An example of an organization that has constantly stretched the scope of its business is Virgin, moving into new business areas such as financial services, rail transport and retailing.

- Should the organization invest in existing businesses or buy new business? This is a key question facing the building societies who have demutualized and have capital to invest.

Business level

This level is concerned with how an operating unit or strategic business unit (SBU) approaches a particular market and how it should compete in order to be superior to its rivals. It is therefore concerned with how to secure and sustain competitive advantage. For example:

- which products/services should be developed?

- how should it segment the markets; should it specialize in particular profitable segments?

Generally, financial services organizations are not single businesses but a range of different businesses serving different customer markets. The division into the retail sector, corporate sector, capital markets, etc. could illustrate examples of how a financial services organization may divide its activities into distinct strategic business units.

Operational/functional level

This level of planning and decision-making is concerned with determining the operational strategies of the various functional areas and would include, for example, marketing strategies, production strategies, finance strategies, information systems strategies, and human resource management (HRM) strategies. These are of strategic significance in that they will all contribute to the overall success of the corporate strategy.

While the corporate strategy formulation tends to be the concern of top managers, other levels of management will be responsible for ensuring the successful implementation of strategy. Therefore, strategic management involves the entire organization, and management from all levels will be involved in some aspect of the planning activity.

5   The Process of Strategic Management

The traditional approach to strategic management is often termed the formal or rational approach. This approach is based on four interrelated building blocks:

● strategic analysis;

● strategic choice;

● strategy implementation;

● review, evaluation and control.

Within each of these elements are a number of different activities, as illustrated in Figure 3.2.

Figure 3.2: The process of strategic management

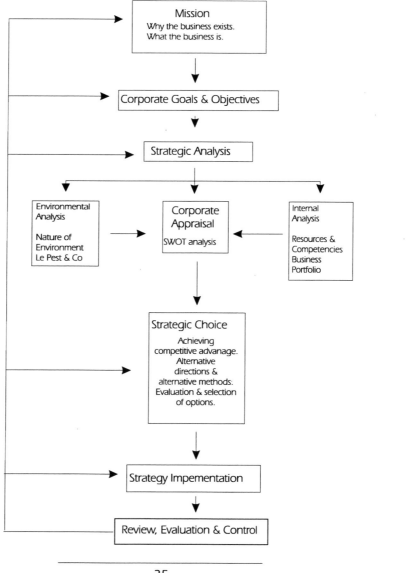

Figure 3.2 does tend to show the process as a set of orderly steps, which in practice it is not. Nevertheless, the framework is helpful as a starting point to understanding the different elements and activities of the process. Each of the different activities will now be explored.

Strategic analysis

Strategic analysis is basically concerned with gaining a better understanding of the strategic position of the organization relative to the competition. The process will start with an analysis of the organization's **present situation**. The first step is to determine the purpose of the organization – i.e. why the organization exists and what business it is in. Any business must have a clear *raison d'être*; without a clear knowledge of its purpose the business will drift, falter and may eventually fail.

Traditionally the banks would probably have identified 'banking' as their business domain. However this is now perhaps too restrictive a definition given the merging of boundaries of financial services suppliers and the emergence of new entrants. The parameters of 'what business are we in' are often summarized in a mission statement which should encapsulate the long-term vision of what the organization wants to be and what it wants to achieve.

Examples of mission statements for financial service organizations include:

- 'To be the UK's leading provider of personal financial services'
- 'To be the first choice of financial services for customers, shareholders and staff'

The sentiments of the mission must then be translated into goals and objectives. Goals and objectives are concerned with the outcomes that the organization seeks to achieve. Whereas goals are more general in nature, objectives are often more specific statements which can be quantified and measured. Examples include profit targets, return on investment (ROI), return on capital employed (ROCE), growth rate targets, size of market share, sales volume, etc. However, some objectives may not lend themselves to quantifiable measures and are more qualitative in nature, for example, creating a favorable image in order to attract funds. Goals and objectives are important because they provide:

- a basis for strategy formulation;
- a standard of performance;
- guidelines for decision-making and providing justification for action taken;
- some indications as to the priorities for the organization.

Referring back to the analogy of planning as a journey, the present situation determines where the organization is now, the next step is to determine where it wants to go in the future. This will be influenced by the nature of the external environment and the organization's own internal distinctive competencies Therefore, it is important for the organization to have a solid understanding of its external and internal environment.

(i)   Analysis of the external environment

The main purpose of analysing the external environment is to gain an understanding of the factors which will impact on the organization's current and future activities, since the strategy of an organization should fit its environment by taking advantage of opportunities and countering threats. An analysis of environmental factors should explore the legal, ethical, political, social, technological and competitive influences, perhaps using the Le Pest & Co and Porter's five forces frameworks described in Chapter 2.

(ii)   Internal analysis

An organization's ability to compete will also depend upon the resources that it has at its disposal. Internal analysis focuses on determining the strategic capability of the organization by appraising its internal resources and identifying its core and distinctive competencies. This involves the identification of those things which the organization is particularly good at in comparison to its competitors, and which are relatively difficult to imitate.

The analysis starts by undertaking a resource audit to evaluate the resources the organization has available and how it utilizes those resources, for example an appraisal of financial resources, human skills, physical assets, technologies, etc. The internal analysis should also consider cultural issues and the structure of the organization. Additionally it may involve benchmarking exercises in terms of financial measures of performance, ranking against the competition, and market shares for different product/ service areas.

The outcome of the analysis should assist in providing an understanding of the organization's core competencies and strategic capability relative to the competition.

It is also important to examine the strategic capability in terms of the balance of different business units and product areas of the organization, often referred to as portfolio analysis. One method which can be used for this type of analysis is the Boston Consulting Group (BCG) growth share matrix which is identified in Figure 3.3. According to this matrix two factors define a business's or product's strategic stance in the marketplace:

● the relative market share compared to the competitors;

● market growth, which is concerned with the rate of growth of the product category in the market as a whole.

This leads to four categories:

The **question mark**, sometimes referred to as problem child, which has a small market share but is in a high-growth market. A question mark business requires high investment and resource allocation in the hope that the business or product is viable and will become a star in the future.

A **star** is a business unit with a high market share in a high-growth market and by implication has the potential for generating significant earnings both now and in the future.

The **cash cow** has a high market share but is in comparatively mature and slower-growing markets. There is less need for heavy investment and therefore the cash cow should make a substantial contribution to overall profitability.

A **dog** can be characterized by low market shares and low growth rates in a static market and may be a drain on resources, leading to cost disadvantages.

Figure 3.3: The Boston Consulting Group growth/share matrix

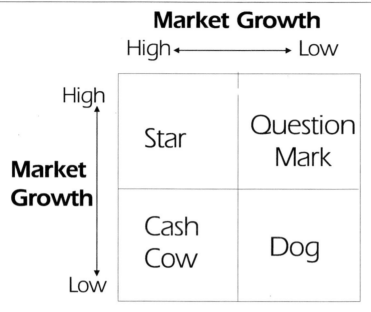

Portfolio analysis provides a picture of the balance of an organization's strategic capability. It can be used within the strategic planning process to determine the relative position of business units and inform decisions relating to resource allocation. An organization should be seeking to maintain a balanced and strong portfolio, ensuring that there are enough cash generating products/business to match those requiring investment.

(iii)   Corporate appraisal

Having undertaken an analysis of the trends and possible external and internal environmental developments that may be of strategic significance now or in the future, the next step is to bring together the results. This step of the process is often referred to as corporate appraisal. A useful framework to assess the various factors is SWOT analysis, which is essentially an inventory of key external environmental opportunities and threats and strategically important internal strengths and weaknesses. The analysis should not simply be a list of the factors but should involve some evaluation of the relative importance of the factors. This is often presented as a matrix of strengths, weaknesses, opportunities and threats:

Strengths
- a strength is a particular skill or distinctive competence which the organization possesses and which gives it an advantage over competitors;

Weaknesses
- a weakness is something which may hinder the organization in achieving its strategic aims, such as a lack of resources, expertise or skills;

Opportunities
- an opportunity is something happening in the environment which is favourable to the organization and which may be exploited to obtain benefits;

Threats
- a threat is something happening in the organization's environment which is unfavourable to the organization and which must be overcome or circumvented.

Adapting to the environment means responding to environmental opportunities while coping with threats. A strength is potentially of strategic importance because it can be used either to take advantage of an opportunity or as protection against a threat.

Having determined the organization's present situation in conjunction with its objectives (i.e. where are we now and where would we like to be), specific strategies must be developed to close the 'gap'. This is often referred to as 'the planning gap' and represents making choices on what needs to be done to achieve the goals and objectives of the organization.

Strategic choice

This stage involves the generation and evaluation of strategic options in order to bridge the planning gap and involves making decisions on:

- on what basis should the organization compete and on what basis can it achieve competitive advantage?

- what are the alternative directions available and which products/markets should the organization enter or leave?

- what alternative methods are available to achieve the chosen direction?

(i)   Achieving competitive advantage

When developing a corporate strategy the organization must decide upon which basis it is going to compete in its markets. This involves decisions on whether to compete across the entire market or only in certain market segments. This can be referred to as the competitive scope. A further consideration concerns how to gain competitive advantage. Competitive advantage is anything that gives one organization the edge over its rivals and which can be sustained over time.

Sources of competitive advantage can be found in every aspect of the way an organization competes, for example, prices, products, service levels, low-cost production, delivery channels etc. However, for the competitive advantage to be sustainable, organizations must seek to identify the activities that competitors cannot easily copy and imitate. In the financial services sector many products and services are easily copied, so organizations must seek other ways to achieve competitive advantage and add value.

Value has to be defined by the customer because ultimately value is judged by customers in terms of the amount that they are willing to pay for the product/service. Therefore, organizations must assess why customers choose to purchase from one organization rather than another and what constitutes value in their terms. The answer to this question can be broadly categorized into two areas:

1. The price of the product/service is lower.

2. The product service is perceived to provide better added value.

These general terms represent the generic strategy options for achieving competitive advantage, An organization can, for example, compete on price-based strategies by focusing on price-sensitive market segments and portraying a cheap and cheerful image. Alternatively, it can choose to pursue a differentiation strategy which seeks to be unique on dimensions valued by buyers and which is also different from competitors, for example in terms of product design, performance, or quality of service.

(ii) Alternative strategic directions

Having looked at the basis for achieving competitive advantage, the second element is to consider the alternative directions for strategic development. Ansoff (1988) provides a useful framework for setting out the alternative directions. This matrix is illustrated in Figure 3.4 and suggests that the strategy decisions are based on the fact that an organization can choose to develop by utilizing existing products or developing new products, and by operating in existing or new markets. This produces a number of possible strategy options:

Figure 3.4: Growth vector matrix

Product

	Present	New
Present	Strategies based on existing markets and products (e.g. market penetration for growth; or consolidation to maintain position; or withdrawal)	Strategies based on launching new/or improved products into existing markets (e.g. product development)
New	Strategies based on finding new markets for existing products (e.g. market development)	Strategies based on launching new products in new markets (e.g. related or unrelated diversification)

Market

Market penetration is where the organization seeks to maintain or increase its share of existing markets with existing products and as such is the least risky option. Specific strategies could involve attracting customers away from the competition through, for example, competitive pricing and promotional activities.

Alternatively, the organization may try to increase the usage of products by existing customers. This could be achieved through the introduction of incentive schemes such as loyalty bonuses. This strategy has been pursued by a number of credit card issuers, such as Barclaycard Profile points and HSBC Choice points for their Visa and MasterCard cardholders. However, the benefits of operating such schemes must be greater than the costs.

Product development requires the organization to develop new products or to make enhancements to its existing products. In financial services this often takes the form of modifications to existing products. It can also be in response to government initiatives, as for example with the launch of ISAs and stakeholder pensions.

Market development is a strategy of moving into new markets with existing products. At a local level market development may involve the creation of new distribution channels to attract new customer segments. This strategy is being pursued by a number of the major banks and building societies through direct channels such as telephone, PC, and Internet and Digital TV banking. The increasingly global marketplace will also provide opportunities for geographical market development for financial services product areas. However, globalization may also present a threat as foreign competition enters the UK marketplace.

Diversification is the most risky of the growth strategies because it involves the organization moving into areas where it has no experience, with new products and new markets. There are two broad classifications of diversification: *related diversification* and *unrelated diversification*.

Related diversification involves development beyond the present product market but still within the main confines of the industry, building on the assets and capabilities which the organization has already developed. This strategy has been a feature of many financial service organizations, which have diversified beyond their traditional product and market areas. For example, the clearing banks moving into mortgage and insurance products and markets and the building societies introducing money transmission services and unsecured lending products.

Unrelated diversification is where the organization moves into products/markets which are beyond the present industry and which may not have any close relation to the current activities of the organization. This method is one pursued by the conglomerates such as Hanson but can also be seen in the financial services arena with non-traditional suppliers, such as Virgin, entering the marketplace. It could be argued that the supermarkets, Marks and Spencer, Boots and some car manufacturers such as General Motors are also pursuing this strategy as they move into the financial services sector.

In addition to the above strategies an organization may decide to do nothing, or consolidate or withdraw from a product market completely. To do nothing means that the organization continues to follow, in broad terms, existing strategies while events around it change. Consolidation is different from doing nothing in that while the range of products and markets remain constant, a positive approach which adapts to the changing circumstances is being taken in order to maintain market position. Withdrawal implies that the organization withdraws from a product/market combination and this may be appropriate if, by selling out from one activity, funds are released to develop another area. This may be the only viable option if the market is declining rapidly, or losing money – for example it is a strategy adopted by a number of the major banks who withdrew from the estate agency business.

(iii)   Alternative methods

Not only must the organization consider on what basis to compete and the direction of strategic development, it must also decide how it is going to pursue its strategic direction (i.e. what method is most appropriate). In simple terms the organization could decide to develop by:

- internal development;
- takeovers/acquisition or merger;
- strategic alliances/joint ventures.

Internal development

Internal development, sometimes referred to as organic growth, is where the organization uses its own internal resources to pursue the chosen strategy. This may involve building up a new business from scratch and developing it. The launch of First Direct by Midland Bank in 1989 and more recently Egg launched by Prudential are examples of a strategy achieved through internal development.

Takeovers/Acquisitions and mergers

An alternative would be to acquire resources by taking over or merging with another organization in order to acquire knowledge of a particular product area, obtain a new product range, or market presence, or as a means of eliminating competition.

A takeover or acquisition involves the purchase of a controlling interest in another company. On the other hand, a merger involves the joining of two separate organizations to form a single organization. Both acquisitions and mergers have been prevalent in the financial services sector. This can be illustrated by the activities of Halifax plc which merged with Leeds Permanent Building Society and which more recently acquired interests in Clerical and Medical and Birmingham Midshires.

Strategic alliances

The aim of joint ventures and strategic alliances is usually to gain exposure to new markets or to gain access to technology. There are a variety of arrangements for strategic alliances, some of which are very formalized and some are much looser arrangements. Joint ventures involve the formation of a company whose shares are owned jointly by the parent companies. Alliances are weaker than contractual agreements between different organizations who work together.

Joint ventures and strategic alliances have become increasingly popular in the financial services sector as organizations struggle to cope with environmental pressures from their internal resources alone. The move by supermarkets into the financial services industry has been facilitated by strategic alliances with the banks. For example, Tesco Personal Finance is a joint venture between Tesco and the Royal Bank of Scotland, while Abbey National has opened branches in Safeway stores.

Evaluation and selection of strategic options

Once the alternative strategic options have been identified they must then be evaluated and a selection made. Johnson & Scholes (1997) categorize the criteria that can be used to evaluate alternative strategies into three broad categories: *suitability*, *acceptability* and *feasibility*.

Suitability is concerned with an assessment of whether the strategy fits the situation of the firm in terms of its resources and environment. This can be done against a number of criteria, for example:

● does it increase the organization's strengths?

● does it rectify existing weaknesses?

● is it suitable for the organization's existing position, and is it consistent with other activities? In other words, does it have strategic fit?

The *suitability* of a strategy must also be evaluated in the context of the political and cultural factors operating in the organization.

Acceptability of a strategy relates to people's expectations of it. Therefore, it is concerned with assessing whether the strategy is acceptable to the organization's most powerful stakeholders. Evaluating *acceptability* involves assessing the financial considerations in terms of how far the strategy will meet the objectives for return on investment, profits and growth, and the level of risk involved in pursuing the strategy. The key issue here is that different stakeholders will have different expectations from any particular strategy.

Feasibility refers to the extent to which the strategy can be implemented and is achievable in practice. It is concerned with the resourcing implications and capabilities of the organization. For example, are the financial, technical and other resources available and are there no obvious barriers to its implementation?

Strategic implementation

Having determined the strategic route the next step is to plan the implementation of the strategy. In other words, the strategy that determines what must be done in broad terms must be translated into more specific actions and tactics. This includes:

- the detailed specification on how the activities will be carried out and by whom;
- the targets that need to be achieved;
- resource planning (finance, human resources, physical resource) involving the allocation of resources to the key tasks.

The implementation of the strategy may require strategic change in terms of organization redesign and restructuring and day-to-day routine. This theme will be explored in Chapter 4.

Review, monitor and control

Returning to the analogy of the journey the final stage is to determine whether you have succeeded in completing your journey, arriving at the desired destination. With strategy formulation and implementation it is important to establish the extent to which the strategies are fulfilling the intended mission of the organization and bridging the 'planning gap'. Monitoring is concerned with watching what is happening in order to detect things that are going wrong. The control process should be oriented to measuring performance against the standards, and taking action where there are deviations to close gaps. The strategic control process should ensure that there is a clear agreement on the strategic targets that the organization is pursuing and that there is a means of monitoring achievement against them. Control systems will be explored in greater depth in Chapter 5.

An effective strategic management process that follows the various stages outlined above should result in the organization having a clear view of its purpose, its goals and objectives and its strategic approach.

6   Different Approaches to the Strategic Management Process

So far this chapter has used the formal or rational approach to explain strategic management. This suggests a well-ordered logical process; however in reality it is not. There are alternative views on how strategies develop and are formulated and that successful strategies can emerge without prior planning. An organization may take different approaches depending on factors such as the nature of the organization, its culture, its management style and the environment in which it operates. Some organizations may adopt a more informal or unplanned approach. This perspective suggests that strategy 'emerges' and develops over time in an incremental and continuous way developed from a pattern of behaviour not consciously imposed by senior management. The stance here is that managers cannot and do not operate in a rational and logical manner, and that the development of corporate strategy is far more complex than the rational approach suggests. People, politics and culture all need to be taken into account in the process. However, emergent strategies should be evaluated and any inappropriate strategies stopped.

Essentially, the formulation of intended/planned strategies tend to result in a top-down approach, whereas the formulation of emergent strategies can be viewed as a bottom-up process.

The above does not do justice to the research on the complexities associated with the different approaches to strategic management. What is important for the purposes of this workbook is to appreciate that there are different approaches and that the whole process of strategic management is more complex than is perhaps suggested by the step-by-step approach described.

7   Strategy and Stakeholder Influences

There are a number of different individuals and interest groups, both inside and outside the organization, who will have views about the strategy of the organization, and who will have a vested interest in the behaviour of the organization. These groups or individuals are referred to as stakeholders. The stakeholders of a financial service organization could include:

- Shareholders and Owners
- Competitors
- Employees
- Senior Management
- Customers/Clients
- Government – National
- Regulatory Bodies
- Government – European
- Trade Unions
- Pressure Groups
- Media
- Interest Groups
- Local Community
- Suppliers

Stakeholders are not just those individuals and groups 'inside' the organization but include individuals and groups 'outside' the organization. So for example, internal stakeholders might include employees and management; connected stakeholders: shareholders, customers, and suppliers; external stakeholders which could included the community, government, and pressure groups.

Each of the different stakeholder groups will have invested something in the organization and will expect a return. They will also wish to influence how this is determined. Conflict may arise when the expectations of stakeholder groups differ. The organization must identify which stakeholders have priority by analysing stakeholder power because the level of power and influence will vary between different stakeholder groups.

In making a strategic choice management must consider its responsibilities to the different groups. For example, it has a responsibility to:

- shareholders to provide a good return on the risk of investment;
- customers in terms of the quality of products/services, security, pricing levels, etc.;
- employees in the form of reward systems, working conditions, training and career

development, job satisfaction, equal opportunities; and the community in terms of creation and maintenance of employment, and providing financial assistance to charities and community activities.

In determining and formulating its corporate strategy the organization will have to balance the demands of the different stakeholder groups. For example, the demands of customers for longer opening hours versus the needs of employees, the needs of the community to have branches in rural areas versus the banks' delivery strategy, and more generally the short-term pressure to deliver shareholder value versus management's desire to invest in longer-term developments.

Ultimately, according to Johnson & Scholes (1997), objectives and strategies will be influenced by:

- who are the stakeholders concerned?

- what is their relative power?

- how important to them is a particular strategy, which they will then support or oppose?

- where and how will they exert their influence and power?

Summary

Having studied this chapter you should be able to:

- Define the key terms associated with the strategic management process;

- Explain the role of strategic management;

- Discuss the different levels of strategy and their interrelationship;

- Describe the framework and activities involved in the strategic planning process;

- Apply the various analytical models;

- Discuss the alternative approaches to strategic management;

- Identify the key stakeholder groups;

- Explain how the different stakeholders might influence the strategic direction and decisions of an organization.

References

Andrews K (1971) *The Concept of Corporate Strategy*, Irwin

Ansoff H (1988) *Corporate Strategy*, Penguin

Hofer C W & Schendel D (1978) *Strategy Formulation: Analytical Concepts*, West

Johnson G & Scholes K (1997) *Exploring Corporate Strategy*, 4th ed. Prentice Hall

Lynch R (1997) *Corporate Strategy*, Prentice Hall

4

MANAGING CHANGE – THE
INTERNAL DIMENSION

Objectives

After studying this chapter you should be able to:

● determine the nature of change;

● identify the different forces for change in the financial services sector;

● describe different models of change;

● analyze change situations in order to determine the appropriate method for managing and implementing change in terms of a hard or soft approach;

● explain the reasons for resistance to change and discuss strategies for dealing with resistance;

● discuss the role of change agents;

● demonstrate how project management techniques can be used in the context of managing change.

1   The Context for Change

Much of the difficulty which is inherent in the implementation of change can be ameliorated by an understanding of the process and the application of appropriate models.

The CIB Management and Organization in Financial Services Syllabus

Change is a certainty for those operating in the financial services sector where organizations are under pressure to adapt and respond to fast-changing business conditions. External and internal forces are challenging the traditional ways of working. If organizations are not prepared to change they may well not survive in today's uncertain and unpredictable business environment. Financial services organizations must shed traditional structures and ways of working and move to more dynamic and flexible structures and processes that are responsive to change

There are, however, no simple recipes for successful change and all too often change fails. Different change situations require different approaches. Where change is managed skillfully the results can be enormous with a revitalized organization and improved performance.

Everyone in the organization is concerned with and involved in change, with change affecting all areas of the operations and functions of the organization. Change could therefore relate to changes in the environmental conditions, to working methods, to working relationships, to organization structure or size, to the products and services the organization offers, to the markets it serves. This chapter will consider the nature of change and the forces for change on the financial services industry. The different approaches to managing change will be discussed and the reasons for resistance to change examined. The final part of the chapter will consider the role of the change agent in the change process and the contribution of project management as a tool for effecting change.

2   The Nature of Change

All organizations are subject to change as a result of the natural ageing process of organizational resources and systems. Physical assets such as buildings and equipment will have a finite life span, as will human resources in terms of skill and abilities. However, organizational change more often takes place because of the need to respond to changes in the external environmental conditions.

There are a number of different ways of categorizing organizational change. Strebel (1996) suggests that although change may be a constant it is not always the same, and it can be characterized as falling along a continuum ranging from incremental change to discontinuous or fundamental change.

Incremental change

This type of change occurs slowly in a systematic and predictable way and is often associated with change as it emerges within the organization. It involves fine-tuning and making adjustments to procedures that will improve the efficiency of organizational performance, but which will not fundamentally alter the organization. Most organizational changes tend to be of this type.

Discontinuous change

This type of change is sometimes referred to as transformational or fundamental change . It can be defined as large-scale change that is marked by rapid shifts in either strategy, structure or culture (Grundy 1993). The forces of external pressures which could threaten the continued existence of a firm often bring about discontinuous change and the result is often a major strategic shift, such as a merger with another organization. Discontinuous change has been a feature of the financial services industry in recent years as organizations have embarked on major structural change. For example, there have been a number of mergers and acquisitions such as Lloyds/TSB and RBS and NatWest. The outcomes have been changes to individual employment contracts, job roles, delivery channels and products and services.

Other writers have come up with alternative categorizations but they all tend to follow the pattern of small-scale incremental versus large-scale transformational change. The classification of different types of change is helpful in identifying the way in which the change process should be managed.

3 The Forces for Change

Organizations operating in the financial services sector face an uncertain future, with the forces bringing about change being complex and interrelated. It is important that managers and decision-makers analyse the factors that trigger organizational change. Forces/pressures for change have largely been brought about as a result of changes in legislation. Primary drivers of change are the demands of the evolving marketplace, the emergence of new technologies, swings in the economic climate, the increase in the number and quality of competitors, and shifts in the behaviour of existing competitors. One way of grouping the different environmental factors is to use the Le Pest & Co framework described in Chapter 2.

The Le Pest & Co analysis will reveal forces for change brought about by the external environment, but there are also internal factors which may result in change, such as the appointment of a new chief executive.

As with the nature of change, Strebel suggests that the forces for change can be distinguished in terms of:

- Weak change forces whose nature and direction can be difficult to discern and imply proactive changes;

- Moderately strong forces whose direction can be seen but will have only a minor impact on performance;

- Strong change forces which will have a substantial impact on performance and demand rapid change.

Changes will inevitably affect both the individual and the organization, for example:

- changing the individuals who work in the organizations in terms of, for example, skills, values, attitudes, behaviours;

- changing organizational structures and systems;

- changing the organizational culture or style.

However, while strategic change is necessary in all organizations if they are to survive, managing change is not an easy task. The next section explores the different approaches to managing change but it is important to note that the approach adopted will be contingent on the nature of change facing the organization.

4   Approaches to Managing Change

It is perhaps helpful to distinguish between two types of change, that which just happens and that which is planned and deliberately executed by management. The focus of this chapter is planned change. Planned change aims to increase an organization's effectiveness and improves the ability of the organization to cope with alterations in its operating environment. It is usually triggered by the need to respond to new challenges, opportunities and threats presented by the external environment.

Planned change

Lewin (1951) proposed one of the first fundamental models of planned change, which encapsulates a number of steps, including:

- recognizing the need for change;
- identifying a solution;
- selecting a solution;
- implementing a solution.

He also developed a programme of planned change to explain how the change process could work more effectively. It involves three phases in changing behaviour:

Unfreezing

For change to take place old behaviours must be altered. This stage involves reducing those factors that maintain current behaviours and by so doing provide recognition of the need for change. This means getting rid of existing practices, which stand in the way of change.

In order to achieve this, people need to be made aware of the benefits of the changed behaviour. Unfreezing may occur through dramatic events, such as redundancy programmes, or softer approaches, e.g. persuasion. Both may lead to doubts and fears of the future. Effective communication is critical at this stage.

Movement/change

This involves the development of new attitudes or behaviours and the implementation of change through communication and the work of project teams.

Refreezing

This stage is where the change is stabilized and reinforced, through supporting mechanisms such as reward policies and structures, which help to establish the new norms.

A comment which could be made is that change follows change, in the current environment of the financial services industry, and instability and uncertainty are the norm, therefore refreezing may not always occur before further change.

Implementation of change – hard and soft approaches

It is possible to categorize the approaches to implementing change into two broad groups: the hard and soft approaches. The hard approach views change as needing a systematic and rigorous approach. It is typified in methodologies like business process reengineering, which involves restructuring the way business activities, departments and entire companies operate. Many financial services organizations have instigated BPR projects as a means of identifying how to improve organizational efficiency through systems and procedures.

The soft approach to implementing change is much less rigid and can be described as the organizational development approach. This method considers issues not always acknowledged in the hard approach such as organizational culture, power bases and leadership styles. If there is a lot of complexity and the change required is far-reaching then consideration of the soft approach, sometimes termed organizational development, may be more appropriate.

The organizational development approach relies on teamwork and participative leadership styles. If a participative style is used then the changes tend to be more widely accepted and are long lasting because commitment is present. The disadvantages of the organizational development include the fact that this approach tends to lead to slow and evolutionary change.

The hard approach to change tends to be quicker in terms of implementing change but can occur only if the leader holds a position of power. Any changes occurring within the organization are likely to have an effect on its culture and structure.

5 Implications of Change for Structure and Culture

The topics of organizational structure and culture will be dealt with in separate chapters, however organizational change will impact to some degree on both.

A relationship exists between the development of the organization and the structural forms it may adopt. In the early stages of development the structure of an organization tends to be simple and focused around one individual. When this early entrepreneurial phase gives way to a more settled phase of sustained growth, the structure is likely to be formed into specialized departments or functions. As a company expands geographically and becomes global in nature its structure will reflect this geographical expansion.

It is argued by some researchers, for example Morgan (1989), that most bureaucratic organizations are being reshaped in response to the changing demands of the world. Some changes are marginal but others are more radical and result in network structures such as the matrix organization. Bartol and Martin (1994) suggest that organizations using a matrix structure have passed through four identifiable stages. These are:

1. Traditional structure normally functional in nature.

2. Temporary overlay in which posts are allocated to managers to integrate the various projects. These have cross-functional or departmental boundaries.

3. Permanent overlay in which the integrators are permanent posts with often permanent interdepartmental teams.

4. Mature matrix structures is the final stage where the matrix managers have equal power with functional managers.

Although it is possible to discern the different structures an organization can adopt as it changes and develops, one issue that must be addressed is the feasibility of frequently changing structures. There are difficulties associated with organizations changing their formal structure at frequent intervals, therefore there has to be a considerable change in environmental factors before an organization will respond by changing its structure. There are also time lags between the factors creating the pressure to change and the change occurring.

Changes impacting on the financial services sector in the last decade resulted in many organizations moving towards flatter organizational structures that are more flexible and responsive to different markets and less functional. Customer responsiveness places a greater emphasis on horizontal processes and incorporates the concept that everyone is someone else's customer.

A change in organizational structure is one of the overt signs that change has occurred. Less obvious are the cultural changes that are required. Since one of the key aspects of the change process is that it will alter 'the way things are done around here' so that some change in culture will be inevitable.

Changing the culture of the organization is often the most difficult change to manage because it means a change in the beliefs and values that the staff working for the organization have adopted. Developing a new corporate culture management may involve:

●   Making changes to a dysfunctional culture

●   Reinforcing or embedding an existing culture to adapt to its changing environment.

Researchers and academics continue to debate the extent to which culture can be managed and changed with some taking the view that the culture of an organization develops over years and is therefore such a deep-seated phenomenon that it is impossible to change. Silverwieg and Allen (1976) identify a number of steps that can be used when implementing a programme of cultural change.

Step One

Analyse the existing culture and establish the gap between the actual and desired culture in terms of:

●   leadership;

●   team culture;

- communication systems;

- organizational policies and structures;

- reward systems;

- training.

Step Two

Experience the desired culture by involving the employees affected in workshop sessions.

Step Three

Modify the culture through a discussion of issues and problems at work group level.

Step Four

Sustain the culture with continued measurement and evaluation.

Human Resource Management (HRM) policies and procedures play a key part in managing cultural change in terms of recruitment, selection, induction, training and development and reward systems. These can be used to both shape and reinforce the desired organizational cultural values.

Leadership is also vital to the success of any cultural change programme because the leader will play a crucial role in setting the vision that the organization wishes to move towards. As an organization moves through different stages it may be appropriate for a leader to utilize different styles. For example, in the soft approach or organizational development approach to managing change a participative style would be most appropriate. In other situations where there is a need to drive change quickly it may be more appropriate to use an authoritative style.

6   The 7 S Framework

Although both structure and culture are critical aspects to managing the change process, there are other important aspects. The 7 S approach, developed by the McKinsey Consultants, suggests that managing successful change is complex and should focus on the whole organization. This can be considered as consisting of seven sub-systems, all of which are important in achieving success. They all interact with one another, and if any one is changed then any or all of the others may need to be changed to achieve organizational effectiveness. The seven Ss are:

1. *Strategy* – the actions are planned in response to environmental changes in order that the organization achieves its objectives.

2. *Structure* – the issue of structure should not only be concerned with whether the organization should be of a functional/divisional or matrix form but should also consider

the coordination between different areas operating in a changing environment.

3. ***Systems*** – are concerned with how the organization gets things done. This includes the formal and informal procedures that ensure the organization operates, for example accounting systems, budgeting systems, information technology systems, training, etc.

4. ***Style*** – relates to the management and leadership style which will be critical, because this will convey what is important in the organization.

5. ***Skills*** – concern the key capabilities of the organization. A change in strategic focus may mean that new skills need to be acquired as other skills become redundant.

6. ***Staff*** – this is concerned with the way people in the organization are managed, developed and allocated.

7. ***Superordinate goals*** (Shared values) – refers to the guiding concepts, values and aspirations of the organization that go beyond the formal statement of corporate objectives. In managing change it may be necessary to alter or introduce new guiding concepts.

The contribution of the 7 S framework is that it clearly reveals that the relationships between the different areas are important in managing change. When implementing change all aspects of the framework need attention.

7 Resistance to Change

It is widely acknowledged that effective change in organizations is difficult to achieve. One factor, which can inhibit successful change, is resistance to change. When management plans change, there will be forces that encourage change and forces that resist change at work. Lewin's force field analysis framework can be helpful in predicting the likely consequences of introducing change and the ways of understanding resistance to change. Lewin proposes that organizations exist in a state of equilibrium, which is not conducive to change and is the result of opposing forces constantly acting upon the organization and individuals. The framework identifies forces that push change forward, and forces that work against change. To promote the appropriate conditions for change individuals must identify the driving and restraining forces and blockages. The driving forces **for** change can be categorized in terms of external forces and internal forces.

Driving forces for change

1. External forces

    ● Role of the state;

    ● Social pressures;

    ● Changing technology;

    ● Constraints from suppliers;

- Stakeholder demands;
- Competitor behavior;
- Customer needs.

2. Internal forces

- Organizational growth;
- Pressures for increased performance;
- Managerial aspirations;
- Political coalitions;
- Redesign of jobs;
- Restructuring.

Driving forces against change

Resistance to change, in other words the driving forces **against** change, can happen at several different levels, including the individual and organizational level.

At an individual level Lewin identifies security and comfort arising from familiarity and habit as a source of resistance to change. Also security associated with economic factors and status can be another cause of resistance.

At organizational level well-defined structures, rules and procedures can lead to resistance to change. The lack of resources to commit to new projects can also hinder change. Consideration of stakeholder interests also leads to resistance.

McCalman and Paton (1992) suggest that individuals and organizations go through certain stages when resisting change, these include.

- *denial and confusion*, where new ideas are rejected because they do not fit in;
- *defence*, when there is depression and frustration with ritual behavior and so performance sags;
- *optimism* can start to emerge which can question the commitment to the new trial behavior;
- *adopting learning*, whereby performance starts to recover and change is assimilated;
- *internalize and accept change* with self esteem rebuilt and new ways of doing things arise.

Kotter and Schlesinger (1979) detail a range of different approaches for dealing with resistance to change. These are:

- Education and communication
- Participation and involvement

- Facilitation and support
- Negotiation and agreement
- Manipulation and cooptation
- Explicit and implicit coercion

It is widely recognized that consideration of resistance and resulting action is vital if change is to be successful. Within this change process several other major factors require consideration:

- the degree of change required, whether it is minor (layout of forms) or major (strategy), the greater the change the more difficult it will be to implement and the more time and resources will need to be invested in its design and implementation;

- the time frame, whether the change is happening over several months or years, because the longer the time frame the greater the degree of success;

- the impact on culture, whereby the greater the impact the greater the resistance and the greater the difficulty in implementing it;

- the evaluation of standards or levels of performance (critical success factors) used to measure the degree of change and its impact on organizational effectiveness;

- the consultant: whether he or she should be internal or external to spearhead the process.

8   Who Should Manage Change?

There can be a number of people involved in the implementation of change. These can be categorized according to the time of their involvement in the project or according to whether they are internal or external agents.

At the beginning of the change project there may be involvement by:

- *a catalyst*, often the chief executive or managing director, who has reduced involvement in the change processes but is a key player at the beginning of the process. A catalyst will select a change agent to carry through the process of change.

- *a change agent* who can be an internal or external player and who is responsible for starting up the change process.

Later, as the project progresses there may be involvement by :

- *the steering agent* who works with the change agent to channel change and ensures the initiative is not diverted and does not lose momentum (acting as a project manager).

- *the maintenance agent* who maintains the change achieved and the progress made.

A further categorization in terms of involvement by different parties is the use of external or internal consultants. Some organizations feel there are considerable advantages in using external consultants to manage the change process.

External consultants

External consultants have some advantages because:

- they are independent and objective;

- they are invited into the firm and so have increased leverage and freedom of operations;

- they are not influenced by internal power and political issues and not dependent upon their clients for promotions, pay increases, etc.;

- they have a more independent attitude to risk-taking and confrontation with clients.

However not all organizations favour using external consultants. The problems, which can arise, are:

- the external consultant may not possess a thorough understanding and knowledge of corporate culture and there can be a reluctance by some organizations to hand over culture-specific problems;

- doubts are often expressed about the effectiveness of standard solutions and packages frequently provided by consultants;

- consultants often appear reluctant to get to grips with the unique situations and circumstances of each company but rather offer standardization. They can have an inadequate understanding of the internal context of the client firm and 'push' their own solutions rather than work with clients to produce new ones;

- it is difficult to recruit quality practitioners who can move between corporate cultures. Consultants are technical specialists but often it is managerial problems that are at the root of the issue;

- there is a perception that much of what is provided by consultants is over-elaborate;

- the tendency for consultants to focus on the short-term rather than try to develop longer-term relationships.

Some organizations would therefore favour the use of internal consultants.

Companies making progress with change find internal agents are more aware of the corporate's unique nature and the requirements of their own companies. Internal consultants have familiarity with organizational cultures and norms and behave in accordance with these. They also know the power structure of the organization and how to get leverage. Therefore no time is wasted. Finally there is a personal interest in the organization succeeding.

The disadvantages include:

- the internal consultant can often lack the specialist skills that may be needed;

- he or she can lack objectivity;

- colleagues can be influenced by the consultant's previous role;

- the internal consultant can lack power and authority.

Organizations have tried to achieve the best of both worlds by either developing a long-term relationship with an outside consultant or providing their own internal consultancy department. But even with these there are drawbacks. The long-term external consultant may provide benefits in terms of familiarity with the organization but a high degree of specialization means the multi-disciplinary team approach will not exist. Billing tends to be on time spent rather than tangible outcomes. Many consultants are reluctant to stray outside their own area of expertise and can resist the formation of network links. Similarly internal consultants are not able to draw on the experience of working with other companies.

Another solution is to use a team containing both internal and external consultants so the advantages of one offset the weaknesses of the other. This solution can offer less chance of compromise and promote greater continuity.

9 Project Management

An area of management that is particularly relevant to the successful implementation of change is project management. A project can be defined as an undertaking which has a beginning, an end and is carried out to meet established goals within cost, schedule and quality objectives. Some of the characteristics of a project is that at the start it has clear aims and objectives to follow so that tasks and deadlines can be allocated to the team involved. The scope of the project should be determined; this often involves the development of a project definition with the identification of milestones. This approach should:

- Ensure the project's purpose is achieved;
- Specify the work that must be done;
- Specifically exclude work that is superfluous or unnecessary.

Also necessary is a clear timetable of events so, where possible, activities can be scheduled concurrently. Network analysis or critical path analysis are useful techniques in the planning of a project. This type of analysis involves the mapping of the sequential relationships between the different tasks in a project in order to assist planning and to find the shortest possible time for doing them.

All projects need a sponsor. This is essential to change management projects where full support and commitment from senior management is likely to be critical to the successful implementation. Someone with power and influence is needed to make sure that the project happens and resources are made available.

The project team should be carefully selected to ensure that the required expertise is available and that the members of the project team can work well together. It is important to have a clear structure so that people are aware of their responsibilities and accountabilities. In many cases managers are expected to deal with project work in addition to their existing jobs and few managers have been trained in project management. The key skills required by a project manager are:

- Leadership skills in order to harness resources and guide the process;

- Energy and initiative to make sure the project is driven forward;

- Problem-solving skills and results orientation to overcome any barriers and remain focused;

- Good communication skills;

- Good negotiation skills to set clear contracts.

Although project management has been discussed in the context of introducing change, the use of project teams is increasing in financial services organizations dealing with tasks from strategic level, for example the implementation of a new delivery system, to lower-level activities.

10   Managing for Successful Change

The whole subject of change is a complex and difficult area with failure to implement change often being reported rather than success stories. Change effort often fails according to Kotter (1995) through:

- Not establishing a great enough sense of urgency

- Not creating a powerful enough coalition

- Lacking a vision

- Under-communicating

- Not moving obstacles to the new vision

- Not systematically planning for and creating short-term wins

- Declaring victory too soon

- Not anchoring changes in the organization's culture

It is, however, often difficult to measure how effective strategies to achieve change have been, and what the measures used to assess the 'success' of change should be. Schein (1988) suggests that effectiveness of organizational change can be assessed as the capacity to survive, adapt, maintain and grow. Other features of successful change, which can be identified, include:

- appropriate organizational structure and design;

- appropriate cultures and values;

- suitable leadership and managerial style;

- supportive HR policies;

- identification and removal of blockages to change;

- effective communication systems;

- attainment of employee commitment and involvement;

- sufficient resources for implementation of change.

What is apparent is that there is no single recipe for implementing successful change. However, in today's fast-changing environment, organizations need to constantly consider the appropriateness of their structures, cultures and systems, and how best to plan and implement the change process. To ignore change could be fatal to their future survival .

Summary

Now you have studied this chapter you should be able to:

- Identify the nature of change, contrasting incremental and discontinuous change;

- Discuss the forces for change impacting on financial services organizations;

- Explain the different approaches to managing change, distinguishing between planned change and hard and soft approaches to change;

- Analyse some of the reasons why there is resistance to change and how this can be minimized;

- Assess how change agents can be used to facilitate change;

- Describe the features of project management in the context of implementing change;

- Explain the criteria for 'successful' change.

References

Bartol K M & Martin D C (1994) *Management*, 2nd ed. McGraw Hill

Grundy T (1993) *Managing Strategic Change*, Kohan Page

Lewin K (1951) *Field Theory in Social Science*, Harper & Row

McCalman J & Paton R (1992) *Change Management*, PCP

Morgan G (1989) *Creative Organization Theory*, Sage

Schein E H (1988) 'Coming to a New Awareness of Organizational Culture', *Sloan Management Review*, Vol. 25, No. 1

Silverwieg S & Allen R F (1976) 'Changing the Corporate Culture', *Sloan Management Review*, Vol 17 No 3, 33-49

Strebel (1996) 'Choosing the Right Path', *Mastering Management*, Part 14, Financial Times

5

ORGANIZATIONAL SYSTEMS

Objectives

After studying this chapter you should be able to:

- Describe the key elements of organizational information systems;
- Explain how organizations use budgets to manage finances;
- Explain the basis of approaches to the management of risk;
- Describe organizational approaches to the management of quality.

1 Organizations and Information Technology

In July 2000 the world's richer nations pledged to make available to the world's poorer nations significant funding for the development of the use of information technology ('IT') in the poorer nations. Although the merits of this offer can be debated, it illustrates the importance attached to IT within the 'developed' world. This in turn emphasizes how the business world has been revolutionized by IT in the relatively short time since computers first appeared, in a business context, in the late 1960s. It does however disguise the idea that the business world has undergone not one but three IT revolutions.

Initially business was hesitant about engagement with IT largely because of the arcane nature of the work involved. However the benefits of running mechanically key operations that had hitherto to be paper-based and labour intensive – for example payroll and payment systems – were an appealing introduction of IT to many larger businesses. From there such organizations began to explore what other operations could be moved away from human resources towards mainframe computers. Gradually the relationship between business and IT began to be built.

In its early stages this relationship was characterized by the insistence, by business, that IT should seek to replicate the tried and tested systems of the organization. This was not necessarily the best approach because the constraints under which the paper and human resource based system was originally devised and subsequently developed were not necessarily the constraints under which a mechanical system could best be built.

As business became more comfortable with IT the merits of developing new systems based on what IT could produce rather than on replication became apparent and, as a result, IT became a key strategic feature of many larger businesses.

This change of organizational mindset coincided, more or less, with a fundamental change within the IT industry which led to the second of the three revolutions. This was the shift from 'mainframe to micro', the outcome of which was that the power of IT was no longer reserved to specialist departments but rather was delivered to the desktops of an increasingly computer-literate workforce.

The workforce itself was, collectively, making greater and greater demands of IT in terms of speed, capacity and functionality, which in turn led to the development of networks firstly within organizations and then between organizations and other organizations where there was some element of mutual benefit in establishing a link.

An essential feature of these networks – be they intra-company (Local Area Network or LAN) or inter-company (Wider Area Network or WAN) was their exclusive nature. They were designed to be secure and accessible only by people within the organization or consortium, as the case may be.

By contrast the Internet grew up as an inclusive system – open to all those who could access the appropriate software. The development of the Internet as a means of communication firstly between academic institutions and then later between interest groups and individuals meant that it grew into a key communication tool within the world's more developed countries.

The Internet became the foundation of the third IT revolution experienced by organizations for any product that can be commoditized – i.e. produced in such a way that dialogue between buyer and seller is unnecessary. The Internet is now becoming the electronic equivalent of the High Street. Organizations are now turning more and more to electronic media as delivery channels and prime among these will be the Internet, if only because it can present multi-media images to the potential customer.

The implications for organizations, particularly within the financial services industry, are profound – though as yet no doubt not fully recognized. The demise of the High Street as an interface between the organization and its customers was already in train before the advent of e-commerce – but hitherto the replacement delivery mechanism was still a presence within key shopping areas (e.g. cash points) coupled with a more remote but nonetheless accessible regional office. Once the number of transactions using electronic communication builds to a critical mass the need for a local albeit remote presence diminishes. Transactions in commoditized products can be agreed in one place, processed in another, despatched from a third and followed up from a fourth. None of these locations needs to be in the locality of the customer – they need not necessarily be in the same country (e.g. the concentration of securities and insurance centres in Glasgow and Edinburgh serving the whole of the UK and beyond). They need not even be in the same continent as the customer (e.g. the fragmentation of the automotive products industry) with the implication that – as with car assembly – organizations will site their operations where they can achieve significant cost advantages.

2   Management Information Systems

A sensible working definition of 'information' is 'that which is known': in opening up the subject of Management Information Systems ('MIS') it is necessary to embellish this definition and to point to the difference between 'data' and 'information'.

'Data' comprise statistics, facts, opinions, figures, estimates which are as yet unmarshalled and therefore of little interest or direct relevance.

When data are presented to the right person, at the right time, in the right context, and in the right combinations to allow for inferences to be drawn they become 'information' in the sense in which that word is used in connection with MIS.

The term 'Management Information System' thus refers to the gathering, processing and re-presentation of data derived both from internal and external sources.

Typical internal sources for data are the functional departments, such as marketing; sales; production; personnel; finance etc.

Typical external sources would be the supply of data about market conditions and competitors.

In the context of this definition, 'processing' involves the analysis of data; comparisons with similar data from other areas; comparisons with past data to identify trends; integration of data from diverse sources and the marshalling of that data into strategically relevant information.

Although this is not dependent upon the use of computers, where an organization has the desire and capacity to make full use of an MIS the premium which will be placed on speed, accuracy and the ability to manipulate the information implies that the use of IT is inevitable.

What does MIS do?

Essentially MIS is an aid to corporate decision-making.

An essential element in decision-making – particularly in relation to the solving of problems – is to attempt to base the decision on the best information available.

This is even more important when decisions are being taken at the strategic level where more often than not problems concern the future rather than the present or past. In this context an MIS is a vital tool.

The quality of the strategic decisions made by an organization both in an absolute sense and in comparison with the decisions made by that organization's actual and potential competitors will to a large extent determine whether that organization has, or fails to have, a competitive advantage.

In turn the quality of those decisions will be based upon two fundamental aspects:

    a) the quality of the information loading into the decision, and

    b) the ability of the senior management to use that information.

The use of an MIS should help in both of these aspects and is likely to do so if it contains the key elements outlined below.

Additionally the use of an MIS enables management more readily to record the information on which decisions were based, thus allowing a more rigorous evaluation of that decision. This can itself be useful information when loaded into future decisions after the extent to which the original decision was appropriate has been determined.

3 Key Features of an MIS

Because the information provided by an MIS must be strategically relevant to the organization, each MIS should be individually designed. Nevertheless there are a number of features which all MISs are likely to contain. The MIS will be:

- adaptable to meet the changing needs of the organization;
- capable of meeting the needs of all potential users whatever their level in the organization;
- geared to the future rather than to the past or the present;
- able to encompass all areas of the organization's activities i.e. all products/services and all functions;
- interlinked with all the other information systems within the organization e.g. the budgetary system;
- user friendly;
- easily accessible;
- capable of presenting information in an easily digestible form.

A sensible organizational approach to the management of its internal data is that of 'warehousing'. Under a warehousing scheme all items of both data and information generated within an organization are required to be dumped in or copied to a data warehouse. From the warehouse this data can be accessed and marshalled to provide useful information for the organization as a whole.

The key advantage of data warehousing is that it allows functions and departments within an organization to marshal relevant information in ways that are useful to their operations without either having to conform to organizational templates for presenting information or subsequently having to rewrite the information in a format required by the organization. With data warehousing it is the responsibility of those wishing to access the information to structure the information output in ways that they find useful.

4 Financial and Budgetary Systems

Within large and complex organizations 'budgets' are often equated with 'returns' which have been made at monthly, quarterly, half-yearly or yearly intervals. Unfortunately, viewed in this way there is little emphasis placed on the more useful and fundamental aspects of budgeting, namely forecasting future financial performance and monitoring and analysing the actual financial performance in comparison with the forecast – i.e. basic management but with money added!

Budgets are forecasts that specify the financial resources which have been allocated to an organization's activities or to the achievement of its objectives for a given period of time. If properly prepared they form the basis of a plan against which the performance of the budgetary unit can be monitored and any variance analysed so that appropriate action can be taken.

Within a large and complex organization they are important because:

- they concentrate upon an area which it is important to control – namely costs;

- variances between forecast and performance can usefully be analysed;

- they set very clear, and relevant, standards of performance;

- they are directly comparable with the statistics produced by the organization at the end of the period;

- they simplify the production of end-of-period accounts;

- they are useful for cross-organization comparison (and negotiation in the competition for resources) because they are stated in terms that are common throughout the organization;

- they give senior management the opportunity to compare, coordinate, control and prioritize a wide variety of organizational activities.

There are two prime difficulties with budgets; firstly, they often take a long time to compile and agree, and secondly, possibly because of this investment of managerial time, they tend to take on the aura of rigidity – which could mean that business opportunities are lost.

5 Budget Problems: Time Investment

The budget setting process is often tortuous, particularly in a large and complex organization. This is because budgets are ideally built 'bottom up'. This means that each individual manager is asked to forecast his requirements for the forthcoming year and on the basis of these forecasts bid for a proportion of his boss's budget.

The senior management amalgamates the bids of all subordinate managers and passes the combined bid up to the next layer of management, and so on until the total of the bids for the corporate budget is established. Generally at this point it is clear that the organization cannot afford to do all that its managers want to do and so in some way the bids have to be pared to match what the organization reckons it can afford.

This can be done either on a pro rata basis; or on some system which allows prioritization or on a combination of both approaches. Naturally it is preferable that a prioritization mechanism is used because this allows the organization to decide the order of priority in accordance with its strategic goals and its long-term plan.

Whatever method is used the resulting figures are then passed down through the layers of the budgetary hierarchy with at each stage managers trimming their original budgets in accordance with the amount of the resources which are to be made available to them.

This processes of building up and trimming down may go through more cycles before the budget is finally set. Set out in this way the budgetary system does not appear to be too onerous or difficult to operate – and neither should it be – provided that all management are available to go through the budget setting exercise at more or less the same time each year.

Unfortunately life does not work like that and so the length of time during which the budget is set tends to extend over a far longer period than is ideal. Typically the managers in a large organization which accounts to 31 December will start setting budgets in September or August. This means that managers are being asked to forecast requirements for up to 16 or 17 months ahead!

6   Budget Problems: Rigidity

Budgeting works well for stable organizations operating within a stable environment. Where, however, either the organization or the environment (or both!) is not stable it is often not feasible to expect management to be tied down to budgets to which they agreed up to a year before and which were based on assumptions made months before the agreement.

This is not to say that managers in such circumstances should not be required to budget, but it does suggest that the budgetary system itself should be susceptible to controlled flexibility. If it is not then there will tend to be a move among managers to abuse the system and provide flexibility within their own budgets.

Where the system does allow for controlled flexibility care should be taken to ensure that the process of gaining sanction to deviate from the budget is not fraught with delays – otherwise the benefits of that flexibility will be lost.

7   Risk

All entrepreneurial activity involves the taking of risk. The more successful businesses, particularly where they operate in a competitive environment, are likely to be those that are better at relating risks to the rewards that are likely to flow from the acceptance of those risks.

At an organizational level there is a need to balance the relationship of risk to reward in order to ensure that, as a business, unacceptable risks are not taken and acceptable risks are appropriately managed and profitable. In simple terms risk at the organizational level can be categorized according to two criteria:

1. Those that we DO accept – as opposed to those that we DON'T, and

2. Those that we SHOULD accept – as opposed to those that we SHOULD NOT.

Using these criteria we can draw up a matrix:

Figure 5.1: Risk matrix

	Should Accept	Should Not Accept
Do Accept	O.K.	Management Problem
Do Not Accept	Lost Opportunity	O.K.

From the diagram we can see that organizationally we have made decisions which are 'correct':

a)   where we DO accept a risk which SHOULD have been accepted; and

b)   where we DO NOT accept it and SHOULD NOT have done so.

Conversely a decision is 'incorrect' if:

c)   we DO NOT accept the risk but SHOULD have done so – in which case the opportunity has probably gone to a competitor; and

d)   where we DO accept a risk but SHOULD NOT have accepted it – in which case our organization is saddled with a problem which it would rather not have.

On this analysis, for the organization, the key to the acceptability of risk decisions lies in the management of those decisions which are so marginal that it is not clear into which box they should properly fall. This is difficult because at the individual level the decision will, in the final analysis, be reached subjectively by the decision taker.

Nevertheless, to enable the organization to evaluate its decision takers' abilities as risk assessors, and to manage the marginal risk decisions, the more objective data that is available the better. This implies that the better a company's risk management systems are the better able it is to undertake appropriate entrepreneurial activity.

Risk management involves:

●   analysis of the risk;

●   quantification of the risk;

●   recording of the objective data that has loaded into the decision;

●   determining the reward level expected from the acceptance of the risk;

●   monitoring the effects of the decision – particularly against the recorded data;

- feedback and adjustment of the risk analysis methods.

Naturally for complex decisions the use of IT will facilitate risk management.

8 Risk Analysis

Basically risk analysis is concerned with two types of measurement:

a) the probability that a given event will occur

b) the impact should it occur

Consider the following table:

Figure 5.2: Managing risk

IMPACT		LOW	MEDIUM	HIGH
	HIGH	Manage closely	Reject	Reject
	MEDIUM	Accept	Accept	Reject
	LOW	Accept	Accept	Manage closely
		LOW	MEDIUM	HIGH
		PROBABILITY		

This is a very simple matrix which could be used to manage risks that can be categorized into one of the nine boxes indicated. (Naturally a more sophisticated model would contain more boxes). At an organizational level there will of course be arguments over the boundaries between boxes and the merits of the categorization of boxes in terms of the acceptance or rejection of the risk, but the essential point is that using a model such as this imposes some level of objectivity on the process that generates the profits of an entrepreneurial operation. If after using such an analysis it becomes clear that profits are not in line with strategic requirements, the approach to risk analysis can be adjusted by redefining the levels of acceptability within risk-laden activities.

9 Quantification, Recording and Monitoring

Decisions at organizational level are rarely as simple as implied by the model on managing risk sugggests. This is because of the great number of factors that load into the decision and hence into the risk analysis. It is because of this that IT is being used more and more in the realms of risk analysis – because IT enables complicated and sophisticated models to be built which are capable of producing the quantifiable data that is so necessary for decision-making at this level.

Basically the process involves the input of data into a financial model. As a result of this, output is obtained which quantifies the chances of particular outcomes and indicates the likely returns should those outcomes occur.

The risk manager must assume that the unthinkable will happen. This should be done at either or both of the level of the individual risk and, centrally, at the portfolio level. Facts, opinions and assumptions which have loaded into the lending decision – for example, interest rate levels, security values, bouyancy of the local economy, management ability etc. – should be documented and where possible quantified so that 'What if' questions can be asked that will show the effects of changes in any one (or a combination of any number) of these factors.

Concurrently thought (at least) should be given as to the extent to which hedging should be undertaken as a means of damage limitation.

It matters not that it is difficult, if not impossible, to measure risk accurately; risk measurement is such a fundamental entrepreneurial activity that organizations should install risk measurement systems even though they must acknowledge that they will be less than perfect.

Two things will then happen:-

a) as the systems are used, many of the acknowledged imperfections will gradually be eradicated, and

b) those that remain will be recognized and managed by human intervention.

As the use of MIS becomes more prevalent within the financial services industry it is clear that they are likely to be developed to allow their use in the assessment of risk. Already sophisticated systems have been installed by many companies to enable senior management to assess investment risks at the strategic level; familiarity with the capacity of MISs will enable operational management to use them as an aid to the quantification of risk at their own level.

10 Balancing Risk and Reward

Financial services organizations are in the business of buying risk and thus of demanding a reward for their acceptance of risk. It is not unnatural that they expect that the greater the risk that is assumed the higher the reward will be. This can be represented diagrammatically (see page 71).

Again it is sensible that decisions as to the level of reward demanded from the acceptance of a risk are well documented and monitored because it is only then that the level of profitability from that area of activity can be properly assessed.

Figure 5.3: Return on risk

Even after adapting the model to take account of the risk/reward relationship, the model is not complete – it requires a further dimension – that of Time.

One of the problems faced by large organizations, particularly where decisions are supported by a centralized bureaucracy, is the difficulty of accepting that decisions, once made, should be susceptible to adjustment. A risk that was acceptable when first assumed may subsequently become unacceptable, or move into a category requiring more careful management. This consideration applied for example to many of the 'good' lendings of the mid- to late-1980s (made when the UK economy was buoyant) that subsequently became the non-performing debt during the recession of the early 1990s.

For financial services organizations this highlights an organizational dilemma: in general, lending organizations are geared to manage relationships rather than transactions – their cultures are such that having created or continued a relationship with a customer by lending to him or her it seems to be incumbent upon the organization not to sever that relationship except in the most extreme circumstances.

At the level of the actual risk decision it is important that the culture of the organization – and the values of the individuals involved – does not prevent a decision being revisited. The 'correctness' of a decision is liable to change over time. From the risk management point of view such decisions should be reassessed as fresh data, assumptions, opinions etc. materialize. Culturally – if the reassessment leads to a re-adjustment of the original decision – it is important that this is seen as related to the PRESENT and the FUTURE rather than to the PAST so that the original decision is not categorized as a 'mistake' rather than as a decision which, while correct at that time, is no longer appropriate.

11   The Management of Quality

The influx of other commercial organizations into the already over saturated financial services industry has meant that FSOs have had to become sharper as regards their competitive instincts. This, coupled with the mauling which the industry in general has received at the hands of the media, has limited the scope for price competition and at the same time provided the impetus for differentiation on the basis of the quality of service provided to existing and potential clients.

The senior management of many of the UK's financial institutions have since the onset of the recession of the early 1990s publicly restated their organization's commitment to quality. However it is one thing to exhort a workforce to ensure that the work which it produces is consistently of a high quality; it is quite another thing to ensure that such standards of consistency are achieved and, more importantly, sustained.

The Systemic/Mechanistic Approach

The difficulty of managing quality has led many Western organizations to pay close attention to the techniques used in Japan – an economy that since the end of the Second World War has built an enviable reputation as a consistent provider of high-quality goods. It is ironic that the Japanese learnt about quality management from American gurus who were ignored in their own country where – in the postwar years – the drive for efficiency of production was of paramount importance.

W. Edwards Deming and Joseph Juran encouraged the Japanese to install appropriate systems for managing quality that allowed their organizations to reverse completely – within the space of a few years – a reputation for producing sub-standard goods.

Although Deming recognized that quality – as an organizational issue – could only be effectively implemented through people, he was primarily concerned to ensure that organizations adopted a systematic approach to quality. Thus, for example, he advocated the abolition of quality control (or inspection) departments because these underpinned a dependence on the rejection of sub-standard product rather than on the production of goods of high standard. This philosophy is now enshrined in the approach of 'Right First Time' which is designed to ensure that output – of whatever sort – has 'zero defects'.

Deming identified that the route to good quality production lay through the elimination of variances from a predetermined norm. This was achieved by checking product at each stage of a process to ensure that it conformed to expectations; if it did not then the reason for variation was to be identified and eliminated.

Juran, a disciple of Deming, was concerned to ensure that organizations saw quality as a company-wide issue, responsibility for which could not be assigned or delegated because the whole of the workforce – from the chief executive officer down – should be personally responsible for quality within their sphere of operation.

This implied that company-wide quality management (in Juran's phrase) could only be achieved through the empowerment of the workforce (because they had to accept responsibility for quality) but that such empowerment had to be supported throughout the organization by the 'quality trilogy' of quality planning: quality management and quality improvement.

The combination of the approaches of Deming and Juran led the Japanese towards the development of the 'quality circle' which more recently has come into vogue in the West. Basically, the idea behind the quality circle is that small teams of workers, the ones who best understand the processes by which they contribute to their organization's output, meet regularly to discuss, recommend and plan the implementation of ways in which the quality of those processes and outputs can be improved.

In practice, the systemic approach can be incorporated into a service environment by thinking in terms of products. In this way mortgages, savings accounts, debit cards, insurance policies etc. are regarded as products rather than as services. By 'getting close to its customers' the organization designs a range of standardized 'products' to meet the needs of the customer. There are, for instance, many more types of mortgage now available (floating rate; fixed rate; term fixed rate; capped etc.) than was the case some years ago. These products in a general sense meet the needs of the customer base; the consumer has the choice of which product to select. Quality is imported into this approach through the medium of the back- and front-end systems which support the products so that at the point where the consumer has to exercise choice the features of each product are readily available; staff are trained to help the consumer to buy the right product for his or her needs and access to the product – form filling – is easy. Subsequently the paperwork is rapidly processed; commitment and support is readily offered; statements and interest payments are accurate and timely – in short the aim is to have zero defects.

BS ISO 9002

Currently there is a vogue among service organizations to apply for a recognized standard whereby the organization is accredited with having installed and maintained sufficiently robust systems designed to ensure that output is consistent – and can therefore be managed to high quality standards. BS ISO 9002 was developed to apply within the service industry.

The TQM approach

Whereas it is easy to imagine the gradual development of a product from one which meets a very high standard specification to one which is perfect – i.e. one which has zero defects consistently – it is more difficult to envisage this with services that have not been commoditized.

Services depend upon humans for their delivery and this implies that however standardized the service can be made, and however high a standard the deliverer can reach, there is still considerable scope for imperfection because ultimately the quality of the service will depend upon the interpersonal skills of the human charged with its delivery.

Accordingly, quality management in the service industries tends to rely less on a systemic or mechanistic approach and more on a 'values driven' approach leading to Total Quality

Management ('TQM'). This in itself is a development from Juran's CWQM but takes the concept further by aiming to imbue the values of the organization – and hence the entire workforce – with a commitment to quality as a way of life rather than as a means to products which approach perfection.

One of the more interesting contributors to the TQM approach was Chester Barnard whose book *The Functions of the Executive*, published in 1938, has been influential in a number of spheres but principally in its identification of the role of the chief executive in relation to the values – and hence the culture – of the organization.

Barnard argued that it was the function of the CEO to ensure that there was coherence, and a degree of stability, within the values, the informal social networks, the formal systems and the purposes of an organization and that the presence of such stability and coherence enabled organizations to withstand, and benefit from, operating in a changing environment.

He pointed to the importance of communication and expounded three principles:

- everyone should know what are the channels of communication,

- everyone should have access to a formal channel of communication, and

- lines of communication should be as short and direct as possible.

Because the concept of TQM requires that all members of the organization espouse the cause of quality, it is necessary for the commitment to quality to be exhibited throughout the organization in order that those staff who interface with customers will feel that they are part of a 'quality' organization and thus act appropriately with customers.

This presents obvious difficulties with multi-function/multi-site organizations, and brings to the fore Chester Barnard's emphasis on the importance of communication within the quality organization. Accordingly, much of the message of quality has to be delivered by the most senior executives in three ways:

- by use of the 'Corporate' video – generally tied to key corporate events such as the annual conference or results announcements;

- by raising profiles within and without the organization in ways that are connected with – in this instance – quality; so, for example, when Brian Pearse became CEO at Midland he asked the bank's customers to write to him with suggestions for improvements;

- by consistently delivering personal 'quality' messages to those staff with whom the CEO does have contact – and requiring those personnel to do the same with their subordinates.

Thus in each division, area, branch, department, cluster, section and work unit the senior manager needs to take on personal responsibility for the quality of the output across the sphere of his operation; remember Juran's ideas that responsibility for quality cannot be delegated!

One of the interesting elements of BS ISO 9002 is that it requires those seeking accreditation to pay attention not only their own quality systems but also to those of their suppliers. In this way there can be a greater level of consistency in the eventual output from the organization.

Within financial services institutions the chief elements of the supply chain lie within the organization itself. Thus, for example, a bank is likely to control not only the development of a new product but also the design and printing of the stationery, the design and development of the computer software, the computer hardware on which the support systems will run, the networks across which they will run, the training of the staff who will deliver the product and a myriad of other things connected with that product.

In terms of quality management this implies that each department has to manage quality in three areas:

- firstly, as regards the input to its own processes (which will generally be the output of another department)

- secondly, as regards the processes by which it adds value to those inputs, and

- thirdly, as regards its own output – which must reach the quality standard of the next department in the supply chain or of the organization as a whole if the output is effectively the finished product.

On the above analysis the approach to quality management looks very much like a mechanistic one but because the essence of adding value to the products of a service institution is essentially an intellectual process rather than a physical one, added value derives from people rather than machines. This in turn implies that of paramount importance to the quality process is the approach to quality adopted by employees and this to a large extent is determined by three crucial factors:

- the message they receive about quality from their bosses and colleagues, and

- the quality they perceive in the way their internal suppliers treat them or their branch, department etc. as internal customers, and

- the quality which they perceive in the way in which the organization treats them as individuals.

Summary

Now that you have studied this chapter you should be able to

- Critically assess an organization's information, budgetary, risk management, and quality management systems.

References

Deming, W. E. (1982) *Quality, Productivity and Competitive Position* Massachusetts: MIT, Center for Advanced Engineering Study

Juran, J. M. (1988) *Juran on Planning for Quality* New York: Free Press; London: Collier Macmillan

Barnard, C. (1938) *The Functions of the Executive*, Cambridge, Mass.: Harvard University Press

6

APPROACHES TO MANAGEMENT

Objectives

After studying this chapter you should be able to:

- describe the various functions of management;

- explain the historical development of management as a discrete activity;

- appreciate the different systems of organizing, such as bureaucracy and scientific management;

- examine the developments in management approaches and ways of working, e.g. the classical, human relations, systems and contingency schools.

- evaluate the different theoretical approaches to management

1   Definition of Management

Organizations facilitate the achievement of things that could not be done by an individual alone. The role of an effective manager is to encourage and enable the transformation of the efforts of many individuals into corporate achievement.

A good starting point for exploring the approaches to management theory is to define what is meant by the term 'manager'. Some definitions of the term appear to be closer to leadership than management, interpreting management as getting others to follow, rather than considering the role in relation to the organization of work. Most definitions of management do seem to have a common thread. For example: managers are those with the responsibility for getting things done through other people instead of doing the job themselves. In order to achieve organizational objectives and goals, managers direct the use of human and other resources. This provides the link between leadership and management. Managers do not only have to get things done but they also have to ensure efficiency and effectiveness in operations.

The study of management as an activity began in the late 19th century and today there is still considerable interest in examining management as a specialist area in its own right. Research in the 1980s and 1990s by Charles Handy and others has led to increasing emphasis being placed on the education and development of effective managers.

Because of the complexity of processes and services today all managers appear to face certain key problems, including:

● the efficiency and effectiveness of operations,

● the clarification of aims and objectives,

● the design of a suitable structure,

● the performance of administrative functions.

Mullins (1997) emphasizes the importance of studying management thinking and its development. He believes this study is worthwhile because:

● examining the development of management theory is helpful in understanding organizations;

● knowledge of the writings of management theory assists in a wider understanding of the role of managers;

● understanding the development of the theory also helps to determine how management has progressed. Many of the findings and recommendations made in the earlier writings are still used and practised today.

2   The Development of Management Theory

The writers on the management of organizations can be divided into four major groups, classical, human relations, systems and contingency. The groups are distinguished by differences in their approach. Within this framework, there are also a number of different strands, for example the classical school can be subdivided into scientific management, administrative management and bureaucracy. This illustrates the complex nature of the theories and writings on management. Figure 6.1 opposite illustrates the four broad groupings or approaches in chronological order, although the boundaries between each are not always clearly visible.

Figure 6.1: Approaches to management theory

Contingency: 1960s-present
Systems: 1950s-present
Human Relations: 1920s-1950s
Classical: 1880s-1920s

The oldest of these four groups or 'schools' is the classical approach. As mentioned earlier this could be said to comprise three different strands:

● scientific management;

● administrative management;

● bureaucracy.

Across all these strands there are some common threads. So, for example, while the classical approach examines the technical and economic aspects of organizations, it tends to neglect the behavioural, social and sociological aspects of management and organizations.

The second school or group is the human relations school, and this emphasizes the study of behaviour and the behavioural aspects of organization, examining specifically individual and group productivity, individual development and job satisfaction.

The classical and human relations schools have now been replaced by more comprehensive approaches to the study of management and organizations in the systems and contingency approaches. The systems school, which has its roots in the biological theories of organisms (cybernetics), views organizations as systems, i.e. as an interrelated set of activities that converts inputs to outputs within an operating environment.

The most recent development has been termed contingency, and is regarded by most writers as forming a separate approach in its own right . This approach emphasizes the need to look at specific circumstances or contingencies when designing organizations or management systems.

3   The Classical Approach

Certain common themes or features exist within each approach even though the areas of interest and outcomes may differ. The classical writers tend to focus on:

- the purpose and structure of organizations;

- the technical requirements of each job;

- the principles of management;

- all behaviour as rational.

There are also significant differences in approach. These different approaches can be identified as scientific management, administrative management and bureaucracy.

Scientific Management

One of the best known writers within the scientific management school is Frederick Taylor (1856-1917).

Taylor stated that the major objective of management should be to obtain maximum prosperity for the employer, and maximum prosperity for each employee. This could be achieved by:

1. The constant cooperation of management and workers. There is a division of work and responsibility between management and workers. Management takes over all the work for which it is best fitted, i.e. the specification and verification of methods of working and the continuous supervision and control of the employee doing it. The worker executes the task to the best of his or her ability.

2. The development of a true science of work. This involved establishing a 'large daily task', and was determined after a scientific investigation into the amount to be done by a suitable, selected and trained person under optimum conditions. This later formed the basis for work study and piece rate systems.

3. The scientific selection and development of the worker. In order to ensure the best person to perform the job was obtained, careful and scientific selection would occur. This would also ensure the worker receives a high rate of pay for performing a job to which he or she is suited.

4. The bringing together of this science of work and the scientifically selected and trained workers so that employees could be specifically matched through recruitment and training for a job.

The insistence on maximum specialization of work was fundamental to Taylor's thinking. There are two aspects to this:

- the detailed division of labour so that complex tasks are split up into sub-tasks;

- the role of management in gathering this information and reducing it to rules, laws and formulae.

Taylor also believed that the four management functions (production, finance, personnel and marketing) should be separated out and performed by different specialists. He called this system 'functional management', a term still used today. Taylor also formulated the 'exception principle' whereby all management reports were condensed, giving details only of exceptions to established standards or averages, and so providing an immediate picture of progress. This is now termed 'Management by Exception'.

The advantages to employers of adopting his methods are considerable, for example:

- reducing the skill component can cheapen labour costs;

- streamlining the tasks can increase flexibility of labour;

- streamlining production systems means that unnecessary tasks are eliminated, physical layouts are improved and the work is speeded up.

The basic principles contained in Taylor's techniques have been adopted by many industries, including the financial services sector. The high degree of specialization and the maximum use of technology are principles widely adopted in processing centres, telephone call centres and similar business units. However Taylor's ideas were widely criticized. He was viewed as trying to increase the employer's profitability at the expense of the employee, by establishing highly efficient work methods that required lower labour levels.

Many writers would claim that Taylor's views had severe limitations. Bravermann (1974), for example, has argued that Taylor's thinking characterizes a progressive degradation of work. With Taylor establishing a system of control by managers and maintaining discipline through labour method development, the workers are effectively left without any opportunity to make decisions about the way their work is to be carried out. This can lead to the deskilling of work.

Taylor was focusing on efficiencies in the workplace and although his principles may be effective it is important to consider how they are implemented; account needs to be taken of employees' needs and reactions. A more sophisticated philosophy was that of the human relations movement, which recognized the emotional and human needs of employees.

Administrative management

The second grouping within the classical approach is that of administrative management. It is reflected in the writings of Henri Fayol (1841-1925). Fayol acknowledged, like Taylor, the importance of specialist functional activities and a manger's role.

The features of a manager's role were identified by Fayol as:

- forecasting and examining the future;

- planning and following a path of action;

- organizing and building up the structure and resources of an organization;

- commanding and maintaining activity;

- coordinating, bringing together, and harmonizing activity and effort;

● controlling and ensuring that everything conforms.

Fayol also defined fourteen principles of management, which he believed should be applied in organizations if maximum efficiency is to be achieved:

1. Division of work. The work is to be divided among all within the organization so that the burden does not fall too heavily on any one person.

2. Authority. The right to give orders should be commensurate with responsibility.

3. Discipline. Employees should obey orders but only if management provides good leadership.

4. Unity of command. Employees should have to report to only one head.

5. Unity of direction. Everyone should be working towards the same end in the organization.

6. Subordination of individual interests to general ones.

7. Remuneration. Pay should be fair to both employees and the firm, although the goals of the firm are the most important ones.

8. Centralization. Control should be retained centrally for maximum efficiency.

9. Scalar chain. There should be a clear line of authority from the top to bottom of the organization, but lateral communication is also important. It is crucial leaders know what is happening.

10. Order. The organization should be ordered with a place for all employees and activities.

11. Equity. Employees should be treated fairly and equitably.

12. Stability of position. Employees should experience stability of position and long-term appointments, and no unnecessary change should be introduced even in management.

13. Initiative. All levels within the organization should be encouraged to show initiative.

14. Esprit de corps. A spirit of harmony and cooperation should exist within the organization.

Many of Fayol's principles of management continue to be respected because they encourage sensible structures and practices for managers to follow. However it is acknowledged today that there is no one best way to manage; other factors have to be considered and greater flexibility is demanded.

The third aspect of the classical approach focuses on structure and administration. It is termed 'bureaucracy'.

Bureaucracy

Max Weber (1864-1920) explored the concept of rationalization and bureaucracy. Originally Weber was interested in why people in organizations obey orders. He distinguished between power (the ability to force people to obey regardless of resistance) and authority (the right to expect obedience). He categorized the various types of authority shown in organizations as:

- charismatic authority, derived from the influence of one man on the organization (i.e. personality);

- traditional authority, based on precedent;

- rational-legal authority, based on the use of rules and procedures which are applicable to any office.

Weber also developed the concept of bureaucracy as the ideal organization. However, the term 'bureaucracy' has negative connotations today, with images of red tape and unbending rules, but in management theory the term is used merely to describe the structural features of a particular type of organization.

Weber identified the following as the main features of bureaucracy:

1. A hierarchy of authority exists within the organization and is assigned to various positions, not people.

2. Work is allocated to this hierarchy of positions. Each position has a defined area of competence.

3. There is a high degree of task specialization, with supervisors controlling the work of subordinates.

4. A formally established structure of rules and regulations ensures uniformity of decisions.

5. Officials are expected to administer these rules impartially.

6. Employment and promotion are based on objective criteria and promotion is usually on the basis of seniority and merit.

7. Reward for effort is regular payment on a fixed scale.

Weber maintained that the growth of bureaucracy had come about because of the increasing size and complexity of organizations. This dictated the need for specialization, which in turn led to a need for procedural rules.

Criticisms of bureaucracy as a form of organizational structure are related to this. It is governed by rules, a lack of responsiveness, a lack of flexibility and an inability to change. As with the other classical writers, Weber takes no account of individual or group feeling in organizations.

Many financial service organizations have been said to possess bureaucratic structures, especially those in existence at head or regional offices where there are long lines of command, rules and procedures to be followed. Many would maintain, however, that organizations are now moving away from a bureaucratic structure and towards a matrix or project structure, because bureaucratic structures are not appropriate in a dynamic and fast-changing environment.

Some criticisms of bureaucratic structures have been made (Gouldner, 1955). For example, bureaucracy can lead to:

- increased supervision to ensure that rules are carried out;

- an increased emphasis on authority, creating greater interpersonal tension and resistance to change.

It is also suggested that an inherent contradiction exists within bureaucracies between a system of authority based on the appointment of experts, and authority based on hierarchy and discipline. The second authority arises from the office held by the individual, the first from superior knowledge. This represents an incompatibility in many professional organizations, where large numbers of employees may have more technical knowledge than their hierarchical superiors do.

4   The Human Relations Approach

The classical approach to management lacked any consideration of human behaviour in organizations. The human relations approach develops into a study of human behaviour, explaining how and why people behave and act as they do.

The major areas of study within this approach can be grouped into:

- individual needs and motivation;

- behaviour of work groups;

- behaviour of supervisors/leaders;

- inter-group behaviour.

All of these areas will be discussed in more detail in the chapters on groups and leadership and motivation.

The start of the human relations approach is generally assumed to be the Hawthorne Experiments at the Western Electric Co. in Ohio, USA (1924-1932). The experiment was originally designed to examine the effects of the environment on productivity. Elton Mayo, as research supervisor, showed that productivity in the experimental groups increased even when lighting conditions deteriorated. Something, other than environmental conditions, had affected productivity. Other experiments then followed.

The researchers revealed that the extra attention given to the employees, and the increased interest in them shown by management, was the main reason for higher productivity.

The Hawthorne Experiments are viewed as a significant milestone in management thinking because they emphasized the importance of people in an organization, and focused upon work groups, leadership and motivation, communications and job design, i.e. the social system. The research concluded that role of management should be concerned with providing a work environment that fulfils the social needs of employees, by providing interesting work and encouraging team-building and cooperation. The writers within this school assume that management can manipulate social factors and use social needs to achieve managerial aims and objectives. The influence of their work can be seen in many management practices, for instance the importance accorded to the development of teams and teamworking in financial service organizations.

The major criticism that has been levelled at the human relations writers is that they have been concerned with 'people without organizations' i.e. they do not address issues such as structure, administration and the external influences an organization can face (Bendix, 1956). It was assumed that employees were solely motivated by social needs. Bendix also questioned the extent to which the human relations philosophy and models have been accepted. Many examples of managerial control still tend to be founded upon classical rather than human relations models. Resources are constrained in all organizations and a balance has to be struck between the costs and benefits of different practices.

The third argument is that the human relations theorists still represent a strategy of organizational control and not a new humane approach, although control is based on manipulation and is more covert than the earlier classical approach. However, it must be acknowledged that the human relations movement has affected many areas of managerial activity, leadership style, new job design, etc.

The systems approach tries to some extent to remedy the criticisms of the human relations school, being concerned with the 'formal organization' of the classical school as well as the 'people' of the human relations school.

5   Systems Approach

In recent years attention has focused on an approach that views organizations as systems, replacing the earlier classical and human relations models. This approach sees organizations as an interrelated set of activities, which converts inputs to outputs (as system).

This view of organizations is set out in diagrammatic form in Figure 6.2.

Figure 6.2: The systems view of organizations

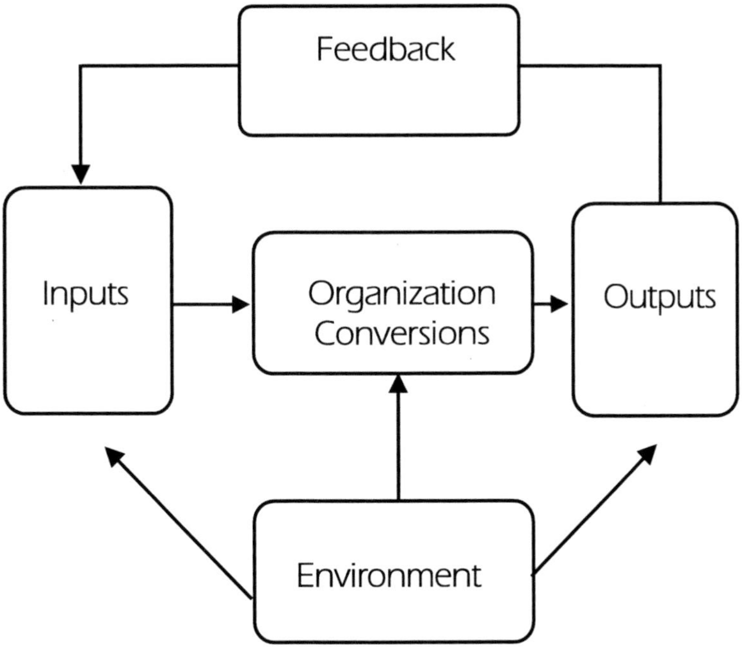

This approach studies the key elements in an organization, how they interact with one another, and the influence of the environment. It therefore examines people, structures, technology, the environment, and their effect on each other.

Organizations, by definition, are open systems because they interact and respond to their environment. Each system is composed of subsystems. For example, the organization has financial, production and marketing subsystems and where each of the subsystems meet are interfaces. The larger companies within the UK financial system could all be regarded as 'complex' systems. They are a conglomeration of a number of subsystems, as indicated above and, as identified in Chapters 2 and 3, need to respond to external environmental influences.

There are a number of advantages associated with the systems approach to management:

● helps identify problem areas quickly within a system by revealing blockages at particular points;

● provides a means of systematizing factors and influences in the organization;

● aids the understanding of the contribution of each part of the system to the whole;

● indicates the importance of communication and information systems;

● indicates the interaction of the environment with the organization.

However, a number of disadvantages can also be discerned, such as:

- it is difficult to understand and apply directly to organizations;

- it is difficult to understand how a large complex organization works, and this needs a highly sophisticated approach;

- it is difficult to see how the subsystems interact and define the boundaries of each;

- when examining systems the people tend to be overlooked.

6   Contingency Approach

The study of management and organizations has expanded further into what is known as the contingency approach. Once again the focus is on structure and administration, but unlike the classical view, the contingency school believe that there are no universal principles. Managers must face situations and then choose whatever seems appropriate in the circumstances. This approach therefore provides an insight into how to formulate responses in complex situations. Structure is one feature, which must change to suit circumstances, as must technology and it tries to identify links between causes and results.

Like other schools there are a number of key writers associated with the contingency approach, for example Burns and Stalker, who distinguished between two systems of organization: mechanistic and organic.

According to Burns and Stalker, the mechanistic system is characterized by a high degree of specialization, a rigid hierarchy of authority, and responsibility with clearly defined boundaries of rights and privileges. Communication is vertical (between superior and subordinate), rather than lateral. This system was perceived by Burns and Stalker to be most appropriate to those firms operating in stable conditions. It would be fair to say this type of structure has some similarities with bureaucracy.

The organic structure is more appropriate, according to Burns and Stalker, to conditions of change, because an individual's responsibility and job definition are never clearly described. Responsibilities are given to those best qualified in the sense of knowledge and skill rather than position. Control, authority and communication operate in a network. A consequence of the flexibility of the organic structure is the sense of insecurity expressed by members, who can never be sure where their job and responsibilities end.

An organization has a need to develop the right structure for its particular circumstances.

Joan Woodward, another researcher within the contingency school, examined the relationship between organizational structure, technology and performance in manufacturing firms. She identified three major types of production systems that seemed to show some relationship to structure:

- unit and small batch;

- large batch and mass production;

- process production (continuous production as for chemicals).

The organizations using process production tended to use decentralization and delegation more than the large batch systems. It was also observed that the span of control of middle management (the number of subordinates reporting to one superior) tended to decrease with technical complexity. The more complex the technological process, then, the greater the chain of command. This is perhaps evidenced within the financial services industry in processing centres, where production is frequently organized in small teams.

All the researchers and writers who could be said to belong to the contingency school tried to establish links between causal factors and efficiency and effectiveness. They therefore developed the concept of the appropriateness of certain types of structures to technology. The attempts to try to establish the factors, which lead to success throughout all businesses, are part of this approach. In the next chapter the different types of organizational structure and the factors that influence their development will be explored.

Evaluation of the contingency approach

A number of problems could be said to exist with the contingency approach. Child (1984) cites them as being:

- Causality – it cannot be certain that organizational performance does not have an effect on structure rather than vice versa;

- Measurement – the measurement of performance used in the contingency studies has not always been precise;

- Environmental influence – some organizations may be able to ignore environmental contingencies and still function effectively, e.g. those in a monopolistic position;

- Importance of different contingencies – although firms may be affected by a number of contingencies, it has not yet been established which are of importance to whom.

In defence of contingency theory, Robey (1982) maintains that it has provided a wealth of empirical research and that it draws the attention of managers to factors that should be considered in organizational design. He concedes that one difficulty with the contingency approach is that it emphasizes differences between organizations to the exclusion of similarities. The contingency approach draws attention to the situational variables, which account for differences in the structure of organizations. It is more concerned with variances than similarities, and rejects the idea that there is one best structure. The success of the organization is more dependent upon the ability to assess situations and to respond accordingly.

It could be concluded, as Mullins (1997) states:

> *That although there are limitations to the contingency approach ... it does direct the attention of the manager to the situational factors to be considered in the design of organization structure.*

Summary

Now that you have studied this chapter you should be able to:

- Evaluate the contribution of various theorists from the classical, the human relations, the systems and the contingency schools.

- Explain the influence of the different approaches on management processes and practices today.

- Compare the theories and writings of the different schools.

References

Bendix R (1956) *Work and Authority in Industry,* Wiley

Bravermann H (1974) *Labour and Monopoly Capital: The Degradation of Work in the 20th Century,* New York Monthly Press

Burns T & Stalker G M (1961) *The Management of Innovation,* Tavistock

Child J (1984) *Organization,* Harper and Row

Fayol H (1949) *General and Industrial Management,* Pitman

Gouldner A (1955) *Patterns of Industrial Bureaucracy,* Routledge and Kegan Paul

Mullins L J (1997) *Management and Organizational Behaviour,* Pitman

Robey D (1977) 'Computers and Management Structure', *Human Relations* Vol. 30, pp 963-976

Taylor F W (1903) *Shop Management,* Harper Row

Taylor F W (1911) *Principles of Scientific Management,* Harper Row

Weber M (1947) *The Theory of Social and Economic Organization,* Free Press

7

ORGANIZATIONAL DESIGN – STRUCTURE

Objectives

After studying this chapter you should be able to:

● explain the meaning of the term organizational structure;

● describe the different types of organizational structure;

● critically evaluate the approaches to the structural design of organizations;

● analyse and evaluate options relating to the organization of work.

1 The Formal Arrangement of Organizational Structures and Systems

In order to successfully implement an organization's strategy, not only do organizations need a clear understanding of external influences but they also need some appreciation of the internal environment. The internal environment involves the strategic capabilities and resources of the organization.

In this chapter some aspects of the internal environment of the organization will be explored. This will involve examining the possible structures an organization can adopt and the consequences of each. The formal organizational arrangement of structures and how this can aid or hinder the ultimate performance of the organization will be examined.

Firstly it is important to distinguish between the terms organizing and organization. The former is a process of management, whereas the latter is the social grouping or formation of positions and relationships. The organization is commonly depicted through the structure of the firm. The relationship described above is usefully summarized by Mullins (1997):

> *Structure makes possible the application of the process of management and creates a framework of order and command through which the activities of the organization can be planned, organized, directed and controlled.*

The process is therefore determined by both the structure and ordering of the organization. Mintzberg (1979) refers to these two aspects as:

1. The building blocks of the organization.

2. The coordinating mechanisms.

Both aspects are needed to support an organization's strategies and can be viewed as fitting with the strategic situation. The building blocks of organizations proposed by Mintzberg comprise:

● the operating or production core, where basic work is produced, for example a factory floor or branch outlet;

● the strategic apex, where general management occurs, for example the head office of a financial services organization;

● the middle line, that is the managers positioned between the strategic apex and the operating core;

● the techno-structure, the analysts who design the systems for work processes;

● the support staff, who facilitate the work of the operating core, for example, secretarial, catering, human resource management;

● the ideology or culture of the organization.

These building blocks of the organization are coordinated through supervision, informal contact, and standardization of processes and outputs. The choice of building blocks and coordinating mechanisms led Mintzberg to conclude that there were six major organizational configurations or structures:

1. The simple structure, which is characterized by the entrepreneurial style and which has few of the activities formalized.

2. The machine bureaucracy, following centrally established rules and principles, which is often found in mature organizations.

3. The professional bureaucracy, where power is based on expertise not formal position in the hierarchy.

4. Divisionalized structures, in which the business is divided up into autonomous regions or product businesses. Each division is configured as a machine bureaucracy.

5. The adhocracy, with few formal structures or procedures.

6. The missionary organization, which is dominated by the culture of the organization, and relies little on structures and systems.

In practice the match to the organization's strategic situation should determine the choice of configuration.

When organizations have grown past a size where owners can exercise direct control, a degree of differentiation is inevitable and issues such as the amount of specialization, the degree of standardization, the levels of authority to be established and the centralization of decision making must be decided.

As mentioned in the previous chapter, the study of structuring work was of major interest to early writers on organizations such as Fayol and Weber and it still features in contemporary theories of complex organizations.

In the following section the different ways of organizing and structuring activities will be explored. There are a number of alternative designs. The major ones used by financial service organizations are:

- functional;
- product specialization;
- geographic;
- divisionalized;
- matrix structures.

2   Types of Structure

It is now proposed to look at these structures in more detail.

Functional specialization

This structure can be achieved by grouping activities together on the basis of their function, e.g. personnel, marketing, finance and information systems. The advantages are that this structure groups together those with similar technical expertise, thus providing better co-ordination and promotion opportunities. However, this type of structure can create sectional conflicts and a strong sense of territorial power. It is also more difficult to judge the performance of different services and products and it can slow down the response time for innovations. It is typified in the central head office departments adopted by many financial service organizations.

Product specialization

In this structure the organization is grouped on the basis of the products developed, e.g. mortgage, lending or pensions products. This type of structure can encourage diversification, allowing individuals to cope better with technological change because expertise and specialized equipment are grouped together. The structure also allows units to be run as profit centres and can lead to better targets and control systems. However it can lead to the promotion of one product at the expense of others because the profitability of each product line and its use of resources are clearly indicated. There is also no encouragement of functional competence because each product division will employ its own marketing, human resource staff, etc. and therefore no significant grouping of functional expertise.

Geographical

The structure is grouped geographically, allowing for decisions and control to be exercised at national or regional level. This structure enables the organization to incorporate a sound knowledge of local markets and conditions into its strategy. However, it can create difficulties associated with a loss or lack of centralized control. An example of this type of structure within the financial services sector would be the organization of the branch network into regional groupings or indeed global companies who group their structure around countries e.g. National Australia Bank and its subsidiary Yorkshire Bank.

Divisionalized structure

This structure is divided on the basis of products or geography, and each division is in a functional form. However it differs from both the geographic and product structures mentioned above because some control is retained at head office, especially if cooperation across countries is required and the business is diversified. A balance is needed between corporate control and independence at local and functional level. It is a common structure in multinational organizations or even major national ones when separate divisions are established for credit cards, retail and corporate banking.

The key benefits of this are that it allows clear accountability for the different business units. However, problems can occur in coordinating the activities across several different units, e.g. providing IT support for several different business areas.

Figure 7.1: Divisionalized structure

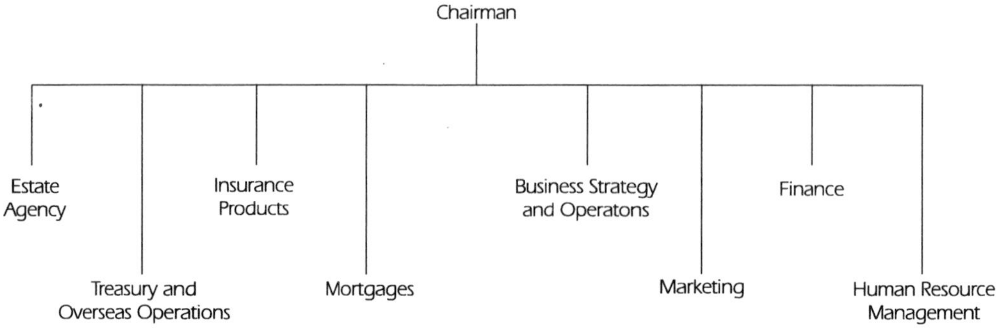

Matrix structure

New types of structure have resulted from the difficulties of coordinating activities across products or functional areas, especially where the development of new products or designs is involved. The matrix structure is sometimes referred to as a project structure, which has a functional base but allows a project structure to occur within it.

Figure 7.2: Matrix structure

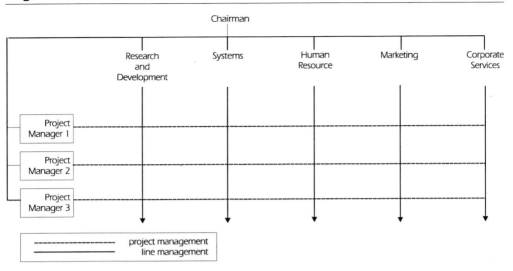

The advantages of this type of structure are that it combines lateral and vertical communication and authority so there is the efficiency of the hierarchical structure, with reporting lines to project managers and project sponsors, but the informality of the organic structure in working across product lines and functional areas. It allows the focus to fall on the requirements of the client and it clarifies who is responsible for success. It encourages managers to understand their contribution and role.

The disadvantages of this type of structure are the potential conflicts that can arise about the allocation of resources, the division of authority, the dilution of the responsibility of functional managers and the divided loyalties that can result for employees concerning their own project managers and their functional managers. It can be unclear who is responsible, which may lead to delays in decision-making.

Many financial service companies now have a mixed structure, which combines the benefits of two or more of these organizational forms e.g. functional and product structures at head office and a regional structure in the network. Few organizations adopt only one of the structural types mentioned earlier. The skill of management lies in balancing the structures to suit the circumstances as the company develops and evolves.

3 Virtual Organization

The virtual organization is similar in concept to a networked organization where companies are linked together. The virtual organization is a group of companies joined together to exploit fast-changing opportunities. The emphasis is on partnership and alliances rather than one organization being in control. The key features of virtual organizations appear to be:

- Technology – this is the key to helping companies and entrepreneurs link up and work together;

- Opportunism – partnerships are less formal and permanent and more opportunistic;

- Borders – the borders are redefined with greater cooperation between companies;

- Trust – greater trust is required and companies are more reliant on each other than ever before;

- Excellence – because each partner brings core competencies to the organization the best of everything is available.

This definition of a virtual organization includes within its scope the structure where employees are not physically present in the office but networked to other firms and locations.

However these new structures are not without their problems because effective team working relies on individuals being trained and developed in these methods of working and HR policies supporting the system through payment policies, training, development and employee relations.

4 Centralization and Decentralization

There are other issues concerned with organizational structure that firms need to address. These are based around the degree of centralization (bringing under central control) versus decentralization (reorganizing into more autonomous units), and the power to delegate both responsibility and authority.

The major advantages of decentralizing a structure are that:

- top management is not overloaded;

- top management can concentrate on strategic issues, as operational decisions are made elsewhere;

- operational decisions are speeded up;

- local management remains flexible;

- attention is centred on cost and profit centres;

- the contribution of different groups of employees is clearer;

- responsibility is passed down.

The main disadvantages of decentralization are:

- the potential loss of control. This means there is the need for adequate control systems to avoid errors;

- greater coordination with senior management is needed;

- it can lead to inconsistent treatment of customers;

●   it can encourage a parochial attitude in the subsidiary units.

However, it can provide a plentiful supply of managers to assume the increased levels of responsibility.

As organizations increase in size there is a pressure to decentralize. Studies at the University of Aston have shown that large size leads to less centralization but a greater amount of rules, procedures and specialization. Indeed multinational companies are an increasing feature of the financial services sector and decisions need to be taken about the degree of local independence and responsiveness versus global coordination.

5   The Importance of Structures

Researchers (Urwick 1952, Child 1984) are convinced of the importance of appropriate organizational structures. Poor structures can lead to:

●   low morale;

●   late and inappropriate decisions;

●   conflict and lack of coordination;

●   poor response to new opportunities and external changes;

●   rising costs.

These hinder the implementation and achievement of strategies and effective business processes. As strategy develops and evolves, so internal structures must flex and change to fit in with the requirements and demands.

Summary

Now you have studied this chapter you should be able to:

●   Explain the difference between organizing and organization;

●   Discuss the relationship between structure and processes;

●   Evaluate the different approaches to structuring an organization – functional, matrix etc.;

●   Assess the impact of centralization and decentralization.

References

Child J (1984) *Organizations: A Guide to Problems and Practice*, 2nd ed. Chapman

Fayol H (1949) *General and Industrial Management*, Pitman

Mintzberg H (1979) *The Structuring of Organizations*, Prentice Hall

Mullins L J (1997) *Management and Organizational Behaviour*, Pitman

Urwick L (1952) *Notes of the Theory of Organizations*, American Management Association

Weber M (1947) *The Theory of Social and Economic Organizations*, Free Press

8

THE INTERNAL ENVIRONMENT – ORGANIZATIONAL CULTURE

Chapter 7 discussed the formal element of organizations in terms of organizational structure. This chapter moves on to consider the more informal or covert aspects of the organization, focusing on the concept of culture.

Objectives

After studying this chapter you should be able to:

● explain the meaning of organizational culture;

● identify the sources from which an organization develops its culture and the factors that might influence an organization's culture;

● classify different types of organizational culture;

● compare the different models and types of culture;

● evaluate the contribution of culture to organizational performance.

1 The Concept of Organizational Culture

The concept of organizational culture is important because it exerts a strong influence on organizational strategies, structures and systems and overall performance. It can shape the behaviours and actions of individuals in the workplace and is often referred to as 'the glue' that holds the organization together. The culture of an organization is also subject to the influences of external environmental changes.

This chapter will begin by considering the different definitions and types of culture, the major dimensions and the influences which impact on the development of organizational culture. It will then describe some of the different ways organizational culture can be analysed and consider the relationship between culture and organizational effectiveness.

2 What is Culture?

All organizations will have their own unique culture but it is a complex phenomenon which is difficult to define. Many definitions of culture can be found:

● 'the deeper level of basic assumptions and beliefs that are shared by members of the organization, that operate unconsciously and define in a basic 'taken for granted' fashion an organization's view of itself and its environment'. Schein (1992)

● 'a set of values, often taken for granted, that people in an organization understand. It reflects the way work is performed; and what is acceptable and not acceptable; and what actions are encouraged and discouraged'. Moorhead and Griffin (1992)

● 'organizational culture consists of the behaviours actions and values that people in an organization are expected to follow'. Pettigrew (1979)

Drawing together the common themes from the above definitions of culture it would appear to refer to the underlying values, beliefs and codes of practice that make an organization what it is. What is clear is that the culture of an organization will impact on how people react and expected to behave, and in turn will affect people's willingness to change.

Culture is then what distinguishes one organization from another and is symbolic of what the organization is really like. Handy (1993) simplifies the complexities of these different definitions is by suggesting that culture is 'the way things are done around here'.

3   Different Levels of Culture

Culture can be said to exist at a number of different levels within the organization, from the core beliefs and values to the visible manifestation of artefacts. Schein (1992) provides a model depicting the four major elements of corporate culture:

1. Basic assumptions – which represent the deepest level of cultural awareness and guide individuals' behaviour, determining how they should perceive, think and feel about things.

2. Values are often taken for granted and tell individuals what is regarded as important in the organization and what sort of behaviour is desirable. The more strongly based the values the more they are likely to affect behaviour. Values do not have to be articulated in a written form, but rather reinforced by the behaviours of management. However, some organizations do publish a set of 'Cultural Values' which are supposed to provide a blueprint for working practices. For example, a department of Barclays Bank developed cultural values to underpin their activities; these include:

    ● Respectful – 'people are assets too' – recognize and value the difference in people; balance work and family needs; be supportive; value all contributions; listen to what people say; provide opportunities for growth.

    ● Professional – 'quality counts' – be honest, have integrity; respect your own time and that of others; present the right image; do what we say we will do; be responsible for our own actions.

- Innovative – 'all ideas are worth a hearing' – develop ideas; be willing to change; challenge the norm; encourage creativity; make a difference.

3. Norms guide individuals on how they should behave in a particular situation and represent the unwritten rules of behaviour. They tell people what they are supposed to do, say and believe, and are passed on by word of mouth or behaviour. This can be conveyed by how managers treat staff, and the importance attached by them to status and level of formality.

4. Artefacts are the visible and tangible manifestations of culture and include observable behaviours, structures, systems, policies, procedures and physical aspects of the organization. Some of the physical signs of culture are more visible than others, for example:

- the working environment setting, e.g. design, reception area, building and layout;

- corporate image in brochures, literature, etc.;

- customer relations;

- methods of communication;

- degree of freedom for staff;

- what the company stresses as important, e.g. Marks and Spencer plc traditionally stressed their high-quality goods.

One way of depicting the constituents of culture is using the organization iceberg model by French and Bell (1990). The part of the iceberg which is visible above the water can be characterised by the goals and strategy of the organization, the structure, systems and procedures, the products and services, all of which will both influence and be influenced by culture. The greater part of the iceberg, which is submerged, is concerned with the values, attitudes and beliefs, norms of behaviour, leadership style and behaviour all of which combine to make up the 'culture'.

In trying to explain how the culture of an organization can be described and understood Johnson and Scholes (1997) developed the framework of the cultural web, which brings together the different aspects of organizational culture. The main elements are:

- Stories – what people talk about in the organization to each other and outsiders in terms of important events and personalities and the mavericks who deviate from the norm, what matters in the organization and what constitutes success or failure;

- Routines – what are the normal ways of doing things, how do members behave towards each other, what are the procedures;

- Rituals – the special events the organization emphasizes in terms of what is particularly important; what does the organization highlight and reward, for example sales achievement, quality, innovation. These signal what is important and valued;

- Symbols – what are the symbols of the organization, for example logos, titles, company cars, travel arrangements (business class, first class etc.);

- Power structures – who are the most powerful individuals or groups, who makes the decisions, who influences the decisions;

- Control systems – the measurement and reward systems which denote what is important to monitor and focus activity on;

- Organizational structure – which reflect the power structure, who reports to whom on an informal and formal basis.

The culture of an organization should help people by providing shared meanings and signals, on how work is to be done, and how employees are to relate to each other and to other stakeholders such as management, customers and suppliers. However, culture exists at a number of different levels, for example at national level, organizational level, departmental level and team level. Thus, within an organization culture is not a uniform phenomenon. The organization will be made up of sub-cultures, for example the bank branches may have their own sub-cultures which are different from the sub-cultures in call-centres, processing centres and head-office departments.

4 Development of Organizational Culture

Both the structure and culture of an organization will develop over time and will be influenced by a complex set of variables, including:

- the history and nature of the business, the reason the organization was formed, the age and the values of the first owners;

- the external environment;

- the nature of the management and staff in the organization;

- the organizational goals and objectives;

- the structure, whether it is centralized or decentralized;

- the nature of the business environment;

- the size of the business;

- the life stage of the organization, whether it is in its youth, maturity or decline;

- the nature of the organization's business.

So although Abbey National, Barclays, Lloyds TSB, HSBC and NatWest could be considered to operate in the same business areas and have the same corporate status in terms of being plcs, it is their own unique culture that will differentiate them from each other, derived from the variables described above.

5   Classifications of Culture

There are a number of different models that can be used to classify or describe the culture of an organization (or part of an organization). Handy (1993), developing the ideas of Harrison (1992), suggests four different types of culture, which he also classifies in terms of 'Greek gods':

a.   Power or Club culture (Zeus).

b.   Role culture (Apollo).

c.   Task culture (Athena).

d.   Person culture (Dionysus).

a.   Power culture

Usually the power (club) culture, represented by the god Zeus, is based on personalities and is highly dependent upon one or a small group of people, often dynamic entrepreneurs, who keep the control of all the functions and make all the decisions.

The structure is best depicted as a web where power resides at the centre and all authority and power emanate from one individual. The organization is not rigidly structured and has little bureaucracy and few rules and procedures. People have to get on well with each other, hence organizations are like clubs of like-minded people who work on personal contacts rather than formal liaison.

This culture can react well to change because it is adaptable and informal and is excellent for the speed of decision-making. Small entrepreneurial organizations typify this type of culture and examples in the financial services sector could include investment banks and broking firms.

b.   Role culture

The role culture, referred to as Apollo, can be depicted as a Greek temple, drawing strength from the pillars which represent functions and divisions such as finance, marketing, human resources which are joined at the top where 'heads' form management boards. Everything is based on logical order and rationality and has a 'proper' place.

There are formal structures, rules and procedures which makes bureaucracy the major characteristic of this culture, with rigid structures and clearly defined roles and reporting relationships. The formal rules and procedures, which must be followed, ensure a smooth and efficient operation.

There is a clear hierarchical structure with each stage having clearly visible status symbols attached to it. Each job is clearly defined and the power of individuals is related to their position in the hierarchy; individuals are not allowed to overstep the boundaries of their authority.

There is a tendency for decisions to be controlled at the centre with communications, systems and procedures formalized.

This type of culture functions best in a stable and predictable environment because it is slow to change and react. While this perhaps typified the culture of the large banks, say, twenty years ago, it is still perhaps the dominant culture of some financial services organizations today.

c.   Task culture

The goddess Athena symbolizes task culture. It is job- or project-oriented, and can be depicted as a net with the culture drawing resources from various parts of the organizational system and power residing at the intersections of the net.

The emphasis in this culture is upon teams of people to achieve objectives and tasks and is one where the needs of the task and achieving results dominate, rather than the systems and procedures. Generally people working within a task culture find themselves in a management matrix where they will be working simultaneously for more than one boss. One of the bosses will have responsibility for the tasks being performed, while the other may be responsible for the 'personnel' role.

The power and influence tends to be based on specialist knowledge and expert power rather than on position in the hierarchy. Creativity is encouraged and job satisfaction tends to be high because of the degree of individual participation and group identity.

Task cultures have evolved so that organizations can respond to change more speedily and are most appropriate where flexibility and adaptability is needed. The principle concern is to get the job done. The culture thrives in situations where problem solving is key and relies on team leaders, coordinators and experts. This type of culture is becoming increasingly appropriate for activities in financial services organizations.

d.   Person or existential culture

Handy uses Dionysus to depict the person culture, which is formed when individuals work separately to serve their own interests but have a common need or work to a common purpose. In this culture the individual is the central focus – that is, the organization's purpose is to serve the interests of the individual within it.

Characteristic of this type of culture is where there is a collection of individuals who have come together, often on a professional basis. There is no real structure, very little central control, few interactions between participants and the pressure for the individuals to conform to an organizational norm is limited. This type of culture can be difficult to manage.

The organization is geared to satisfying individual member needs and this culture may be found when a group of individuals join together to derive the benefits from economies of scales by sharing office space, equipment and clerical support. Examples of a person culture may be found in a Barrister's Chambers or doctors' group practice, Independent Financial Services Advisers, etc.

Each of the cultures described has advantages and disadvantages and it is not possible to say that one culture is better than another. Pure forms of cultures in an organization are rare. In reality organizations need a mix of cultures for different activities and processes. The mix chosen is what makes organizations different and what makes them successful is getting the right mix at the right time.

Financial services organizations could traditionally be described as possessing a role culture, i.e. bureaucracies. However, many are now setting up task sub-cultures in order to achieve organizational goals. For example, in the areas of information systems development people are working as cross-functional project teams because this is essential for building and implementing new systems.

Another categorization of culture presented by Deal and Kennedy (1982) consists of four cultural profiles, based on their examination of hundreds of organizations and their environments. They suggest that corporate culture can be determined according to two factors:

– the extent of the risk connected with the activities of the organization;

– the speed of feedback on the outcome of employees' decisions.

The four generic profiles resulting are:

● tough-guy macho;

● work hard, play hard;

● bet your company;

● process.

● The *Tough-guy macho* (high risk, fast feedback) type culture reflects tough, individualistic and high risk-taking organizations. This type of organization is likely to be an entrepreneurial firm run by the owner. The organization is made up of people working as individuals who take high risks and receive quick feedback on whether their actions were right. Financial stakes are high and the focus is on speed, resulting in a high-pressure environment. Examples of this type of culture are to be found in the stock-market dealing, entertainment businesses, management consultancies and advertising agencies.

● *Work hard, play hard* (low risk/fast feedback) cultures are where the team is all-important and the customer is the key to success. Employees take few risks and any risk is relatively low. An example of this type of culture could be found in the retailing industry.

● *Bet Your Company* (high risk/low feedback) cultures are characterized by a slow feedback with decision cycles taking years, for example in pharmaceutical research. However, decisions are large-scale with high risk and the focus is on the future and investing in it. Examples of this type of culture would include investment banking and oil companies.

● *Process* (low risk/slow feedback) cultures are where technical performance is of critical importance and there is a need for order and predictability. The emphasis is on how to do something. This type of culture is perhaps characteristic of traditional insurance, banking and financial services organizations.

6 Culture – The International Dimension

As the financial services industry operates at a global level and faces international competition, an understanding of national culture has become increasingly important. Cultural practices vary between different countries and will impact on how organizations operate. Hofstede (1990) developed a model to explain national differences by identifying 'key dimensions' of common culture in the value systems of all countries. The dimensions are:

● Power distance which measures how far superiors are expected to exercise power. For example, in a high power-distance culture the boss will decide with no participation from employees.

● Uncertainty avoidance is the extent to which cultures prefer clarity or are prepared to accept novelty. This will affect the willingness of people to change rather than obey rules.

● Individualism/collectivism is concerned with where individual achievement is more important than collectivism where the interests of the group are put first.

● Masculinity/femininity dimension suggests that masculine cultures place an greater emphasis on assertiveness, performance, possessions, status and achievement whereas feminine cultures place greater importance on quality of life, sympathy and service.

A country's culture can be analysed using a scale from high, medium to low for each dimension. For example the UK could be described as low to medium on the power dimension, low to medium on uncertainty avoidance, high in terms of individualism and high on masculinity.

The features of a country's culture have important implications for managing cross-border mergers, where problems can arise because of the different ways companies are run as a result of cultural differences. This point is very relevant to financial service organizations who seek to grow through mergers and acquisitions with foreign companies, for example NAB takeover of Yorkshire Bank, Clydesdale Bank and Northern Bank.

However, it is important to remember that cultures in society are not permanent and as mentioned earlier, all cultures have sub-cultures and a range of complex and interrelated factors influence organizational culture. The national culture is just of one of these influences.

7 Culture and Organizational Effectiveness

There are different views on the nature of the relationship between culture and organizational performance. Some researchers believe that culture plays a major role in determining organizational performance, can improve an organization's ability to implement new business strategies, and contributes to organizational effectiveness and excellence and to overall competitive advantage.

This view is based on studies of Japanese and American management methods, for example, Ouchi (1981), Pascale and Athos (1981) The findings from the research suggested that the relative success of Japanese companies in the 1980s can be partly explained by their strong corporate cultures which emphasize humanistic values and concern for people which may extend beyond the boundaries of the organization. American companies adopting this type of management practice are referred to as Theory Z organizations. There are many contradictions surrounding the concept of the Japanese culture and management techniques, however, the characteristics of Theory Z as described by Ouchi include:

- commitment to employees, offering long-term employment, often for a lifetime;

- relatively slow process of evaluation and promotion;

- development of company-specific skills, and moderately specialized career paths;

- implicit informal control mechanisms supported by explicit formal measures;

- participative decision-making by consensus but individual ultimately responsible;

- broad concern for welfare of subordinates and co-workers as a natural part of the working relationship.

Peters and Waterman's (1982) research, which led to the excellence literature publications, also indicates the positive benefits of having a strong corporate culture. Their research on what makes an 'excellent' organization identified seven attributes as characterizing the corporate cultures of 'successful' firms:

1. A bias for action and a bias for getting things done.

2. Close to the customer by listening to and learning from the people the organization serves.

3. Autonomy and entrepreneurship, innovation and risk-taking is an expected way of doing things.

4. Productivity through people, treating staff as a source of quality and productivity.

5. Simple form and lean organization, in other words, simple structural forms and systems.

6. Hands-on, value-driven management with top management keeping in touch with 'front lines'.

7. Stick to the knitting, that is staying close to what you know and do well.

The work of Peters and Waterman has received widespread attention, but criticisms have been made of their research findings. For example, there are some problems with the methodology of their research, which critics state suffers from a lack of rigor which has led to doubt over the validity of the findings. A major flaw in the work of the excellence literature, and other research advocating specific cultural attributes for achieving excellence, is that it would suggest that there is one culture which is best for all kinds of organizations. This is contrary to the growing body of research (Schein 1992 and Chandler 1962) which suggests a contingency approach to organizational culture. This proposes that the corporate culture should support the strategy of the organization, which must be uniquely tailored to the competitive situation. Thus, organizations having different strategies and operating in different competitive situations should have their own unique culture, influenced by the characteristics of marketplace, strategy, size and market position of the organization.

8 Managing Organizational Culture

The culture of the organization is an important influence on organizational change. Strong organizational culture can be a strength or a weakness in terms of implementing and managing change. Although culture is built up over a period of time, a major change in an organization's situation may be impossible to handle within the existing culture. Any major new strategy will alter the 'way things are done' and some cultural change will be inevitable. There are signs that the organizational culture may no longer be appropriate, for example Braddick (1991) suggests the following could be such signs:

- no clear vision of the future;

- no widely shared beliefs or values;

- strong contrasting values held in different parts of the organization;

- leaders encourage 'divide and rule' by providing disagreement and division within the business;

- no central drive;

- internal focus, with politics and administrative detail at the expense of the workplace;

- short-term focus;

- high labour turnover, absenteeism and complaints;

- sub-cultures flourish;

- lack of emotional discipline, outburst of anger and frustration.

There is considerable debate as to whether changing such a deep-rooted phenomenon as corporate culture is possible because it involves changes to values and assumptions. It is easy for organizations to drift back to the customary way of 'doing things'. In pursuit of bringing meaning to the concept of culture it is necessary to distinguish between the *objecitivist/ functional* view of culture with the *interpretative* perspective. In essence, the former views culture as a variable which can be used to explain the characteristic differences between organizations and suggest that changing culture may be a challenge, but it is not insurmountable. The latter sees culture not as being a variable of something the organization *has* but rather culture is something the organization *is*. In other words, organizations *are* cultures and thus changing culture implies large-scale, wholesale change of everything in the organization.

The literature on deciding if *cultural change* is a real possibility suggests that an organization must make choices on whether to:

● ignore the culture;

● manage around the culture;

● change the culture;

● change the strategy to *fit* the culture.

In reality there is often a compromise between the above choices and to modify culture, in the context of broader change, education and persuasion is needed. This can alter attitudes and values, and along with changes in systems and structures, bring about the desired changes in behaviour.

As with the management of change generally there is no one recipe for the successful management of cultural change; however there are some guidelines. The organization when managing cultural change needs:

● clear strategic vision and managers who can communicate this vision to others;

● top management commitment;

● symbolic leadership;

● the setting of high standards and insistence on achievement;

● publication of successes;

● rewarding those who make important contributions and termination of deviants.

Where cultural change does occur it is, in reality, an extremely difficult and long-term process.

Summary

Having studied this chapter you should be able to:

● define the concept of culture;

● describe the frameworks that can be used to analyse culture;

● explain the factors that influence the development of corporate culture;

● discuss the different types of culture;

● explain the relationship between culture and organizational performance;

● assess the challenges to managing cultural change.

References

Braddick W A G (1991) *Management for Bankers*, 2nd ed. Butterworths

Chandler A D (1962) *Strategy and Structure: Chapters in the History of Industrial Enterprise*, MIT Press

Deal T E & Kennedy A A (1982) *Corporate Cultures: The Rites and Rituals of Corporate Life*, Addison-Wesley

French W L & Bell C H Jr. (1990) 'Organization Development': *Behavioural Science Interventions for Organization Improvement*, 4th ed. Prentice Hall

Handy C (1993) *Understanding Organizations*, 4th ed. Penguin

Harrison R (1992) 'Understanding Your Organization's Character', *Harvard Business Review*, May-June

Hofstede G, Neuijen B, Ohayv D & Sanders G (1990) 'Measuring Organizational Culture: a qualitative and quantitative study across twenty cases', *Administrative Science Quarterly*, Vol. 35

Johnson G & Scholes K *Exploring Corporate Strategy*, 5th ed. Prentice Hall Europe

Moorhead G & Griffin R W (1992) *Organizational Behaviour*, 3rd ed. Houghton Mifflin

Ouchi W (1981) *Theory Z: How American Business Can Meet the Japanese Challenge*, Addison-Wesley

Pascale R T & Athos A G (1981) *The Art of Japanese Management*, Simon & Schuster

Peters T J & Waterman R H (1982) *In Search of Excellence*, Harper & Row

Pettigrew A M (1979) 'On Studying Organizational Culture', *Administrative Science Quarterly*, December

Schein E H (1992) *Organizational Culture and Leadership*, Jossey Bass

9

GROUP DYNAMICS AND TEAMBUILDING

Objectives

After studying this chapter you should be able to:

● describe the meaning of groups;

● explain the reasons why groups are formed;

● distinguish between the different types of groups that exist in organizations;

● discuss the characteristics that influence group cohesiveness and performance;

● explain the communication processes for groups;

● evaluate the effectiveness of group decision-making;

● discuss activities involved in teambuilding;

● analyse the nature of group conflict.

1   The Importance of Groups

Success within the service sector depends, to a large extent, upon the ways in which people, as individuals and in groups, are managed.

The CIB Management and Organization in Financial Services Syllabus

Groups are an integral part of the work organization. People rarely work in isolation in organizations; most interact with others and most work activities need some coordination through group work. So if an organization is to function effectively and efficiently good teamwork is needed.

The overall success of organizations operating in the financial services sector is significantly influenced by the interactions of a number of different groups, who may facilitate or inhibit the attainment of organizational goals. The changing nature of structures and tasks, including flatter hierarchies, reductions of layers of middle management and moves to more employee involvement, mean that there is a greater emphasis on groups and project teamwork. Being an effective team player is a key competence essential to most job roles in the industry.

Groups exert a major influence on organizations, and this influence can be both positively and negatively directed at achieving organizational goals. Effective group working can also have both positive and negative effects on an individual's satisfaction and performance, and on task aspects of productivity and quality, and ultimately the achievement of organizational goals.

It is clear that today's managers must have a good understanding of the nature and impact of group dynamics, i.e. the psychological process that occur in groups, in order that groups can be used more effectively to accomplish organizational goals. To be successful, members of groups must work together as teams sharing a sense of unity and purpose. However, group performance is both complex and dynamic, with a number of different variables influencing and constraining the behaviour of the group and its members.

This chapter will start by providing a definition of groups followed by an investigation of the different types of groups and the characteristics of effective groups. The managerial implications of groups will then be explored, with reference to communication, decision-making, team building and managing group conflicts. The terms 'groups' and 'teams', for the purpose of this chapter, are used interchangeably.

2 What is a Group?

There is no single, all-embracing and accepted definition of groups. The definition provided by Schein (1988) is a popular one and combines some of the common characteristics of other definitions. He states that:

A psychological group is any number of people who:

- interact with one another;
- are psychologically aware of one another;
- perceive themselves to be a group.

A useful framework for analysing the characteristics of groups is provided by Adair (1986), who suggests a work group to be:

A collection of people who share most, if not all, the following characteristics:

- a definable membership;
- group consciousness;
- a sense of shared purpose;
- interdependence;
- interaction;
- an ability to act in a unitary manner.

Essentially, a work group is where there are more than two people who share goals and interact with each other over time, collaborate rather than compete, and individuals perceive themselves as being members of the group.

3   Why are Groups Formed?

There are a myriad reasons why groups are formed in organizations but in broad terms these can be divided into the achievement of work tasks, and the need to fulfil social needs.

Groups are formed as a consequence of the formal organizational structure and arrangements of the work activities. For example, certain tasks can be performed only through the combined efforts of individuals working together. They enable tasks to be completed more efficiently because of the benefits of multiple viewpoints and specialist knowledge/expertise.

They are also formed with a view to making boring and routine work more palatable and interesting in order to enhance job satisfaction. Groups can be thought to fulfil social needs, and can be formed to provide an outlet for companionship, support, role identity, affiliation and recognition, and to give a sense of belonging to individuals. These reasons can all be identified with the human relations approach to management. Simplistically, this gives recognition to the importance of group values and norms when providing guidelines on generally accepted behaviour and providing potential sources of motivation and job satisfaction.

Furnham (1999) provides the following analysis on why people join groups:

Security	Groups provide safety in numbers, protection against a common enemy
Mutual benefits (Goal achievement)	By joining together, group members can work to ensure attainment of shared goals and benefits
Need to be social	Groups satisfy the basic need to be with others, to be stimulated by human companionship
Self-esteem	Membership in certain groups provides people with opportunities to feel good about their accomplishments and to identify with others from the same group.
Mutual self-interest	Banding together, people can share their mutual interests

4   Types of Groups in Organizations

There are many different distinctions and classifications of types of groups but most research makes the distinction between formal and informal groups. This is an important distinction in terms of the management of groups because of the different agendas in terms of task and social needs, both of which will influence the behaviour of individuals.

Formal Groups

The division and organization of work activities into different sections gives rise to the formation of formal groups in the organization. Formal groups are deliberately created by the organization to perform specific tasks and are part of the formal organizational structure. This type of group is created with the explicit objective of achieving organizational goals and objectives, and is governed by organizational rules, regulations and job descriptions. Objectives and roles of the members of the group will be predetermined, i.e. leaders are appointed and processes articulated.

Formal groups can be permanent or temporary. A permanent group may be a section or department in an organization. Although the formal group is a permanent feature of the organizational structure there may be changes in terms of the actual membership. A temporary group could be a task or project group consisting of employees who work together to complete a specific task after which the group will be disbanded. This type of group is common in matrix organizational structures.

Informal Groups

Informal groups develop in a more spontaneous way but can have a significant impact on the way people work. They are often based on personal relationships, friendship or common interests, where membership is voluntary. They are not explicitly set up by management and do not figure in the formal hierarchy, but, rather, they are formed to satisfy needs beyond those of doing the task such as the need to sustain friendship, the need to for affiliation and to enhance one's own personal status.

Informal groups develop across or outside the formal structure of the organization, and although they tend to be with people of the same status (that is horizontal), vertical and mixed groups can also be formed.

Informal groups can work to support or obstruct the achievement of organizational goals. The potential problems of informal groups arise from them serving a counter-organizational function, for example by resisting changes to work.

The benefits of informal groups include the fact that they provide social satisfaction for individuals, and they can aid the communication process in terms of providing informal information channels. However, these informal 'grapevines' can result in unnecessary anxieties for individuals because unfounded rumours can sometimes develop.

Groups can also take different forms according to the needs of the organization. Holbeche (1998), for example, identifies the following types of teams:

1. *Senior management teams* who are responsible for determining the strategic focus of the organization and for putting the overall business needs ahead of any one function or department.

2. *Project teams* who are brought together for a specific business project, and bring skills and expertise from different business functions. They are essentially multi-functional,

and usually have a temporary existence. Team members will still report to their line manager and return to their original role once the project work is completed.

3. *Process teams* have become popular in financial services organizations where business process re-engineering (BPR) projects have meant the need for greater collaboration between different areas of the organization handling different parts of the process. Process teams are therefore created to ensure the smooth operations of managing various processes, for example, service improvement teams

4. *Self-directed teams* are teams who work together without any direct supervision, and who have developed as organizations have downsized and reduced the levels and numbers of managers. This type of team is responsible for making its own decisions, setting its own goals and organizing its own work.

5 Factors Influencing the Behaviour and Performance of Groups

There are many interrelated variables that influence and constrain the behaviour of groups, and contribute to the effectiveness of group working. The different factors impacting on group behaviour and performance can be considered under the headings of:

- cohesiveness of group members;
- group norms and values;
- group formation, development and maturity;
- group roles;
- group communication structures.

Cohesiveness of group members

Cohesiveness, in the context of groups, can be defined as how much members of the group like each other and want to remain members (Shaw 1981), and can be determined by the strength of commitment by individuals to the group and its goals. An effective group would be where the performance of the 'team' comes first and the individual comes second.

There are many different sources of cohesiveness:

- the level of contact and interaction between members of the group (both physical and functional distances);
- shared goals in terms of agreeing the group's purpose and direction;
- similarity and compatibility of attitudes and values of group members (factors influencing the homogeneity of the group include shared backgrounds and interests, and similar attitudes and values);

- members are supportive of others;

- group size – it is hard to be prescriptive about the optimum size of a group but cohesiveness is difficult to achieve where a group exceeds 10 to 12 members. As a group increases in size problems emerge in terms of communications, coordination and supervision, and a large group may end up splitting into smaller units;

- organizational factors such as management and leadership style and organizational culture;

- goal congruence – the group's goals should be compatible and aligned with the organization's goals;

- performance-related norms, for example, in terms of output, quality and cooperation.

The relationship between performance and group cohesiveness can have both a positive and a negative impact on productivity. A highly cohesive group may be considered to be desirable because the theory is that satisfied workers will lead to higher performance. This brings benefits to both the individual, in terms of a more enjoyable work climate, and to the organization in terms of high performance and achievement of objectives. With a highly cohesive group, factors such as lower absenteeism, lower turnover, good communications and participation and fewer problems with intra-group conflict are evident. This underlies the content theories of motivation, based on the assumption that there is a direct relationship between job satisfaction and job performance.

The negative aspects of cohesiveness emerge when there is conflict between the norms and values of a highly cohesive group and those of the organization.

Group norms

Group norms are the standards or ideas to which the group will conform. They can be formalized and written, or implicit and unwritten, inferred from observation of behaviour. Each group will evolve a unique set of norms that reveals its nature, with no two groups developing the same set of norms. Norms develop on issues such as the task, process, social arrangements and allocation of resources.

The concepts of group norms and values have implications for the manager because they will directly affect organizational performance, work practices, and the achievement of work targets. The Hawthorne studies provide some research evidence on the potential negative impact of group norms on the performance of the task. In the Bank Wiring experiments it was shown that group performance norms on output were stronger in influencing individual performance than financial incentives for greater output. The experiments revealed that the output performance norm of the group was lower than in fact the group was capable of producing. The outcome was that the organization was not achieving its full potential in terms of productivity.

Action was taken by the group to ensure that conformance to 'task' norms occurred and the 'proper' behaviour of individuals was observed. Deviant behaviour resulted in the withdrawal of communication, or social pressures being exercised by isolating the non-conformist (ostracizing) and binging (a hard blow on the upper arm). Behaviours not tolerated included over performance ('rate buster'), under performance ('chiseller'), reporting to the supervisor any information that might be harmful to the group ('squealer'), and being officious (that is a person with authority over group members should not take advantage of his or her seniority).

The work by Asch (1952) illustrates that group norms do not only affect behaviour but can also exert a significant influence on the judgement of individuals, not always to the benefit of the organization. This well-known study involved asking groups of individuals to compare a series of standard lines with various alternatives. They were then asked to state which of the alternative lines was the same length as the standard line. In each group all but one of the members were in collusion with the researcher and offered the same incorrect answer. In over a third of cases the genuine member of the group was swayed by the responses of other members, conforming to the norm. The result was of course wrong. In other words they succumbed to group pressure. Those who did not conform to the group pressure did state, after the experiment, that they experienced stress and discomfort.

In order that the organization can take advantage of the positive attributes of a cohesive group, the manager needs to be in a position to influence norms by selling task norms at the group formation stage.

Group development

The level of group performance is also affected by the manner in which groups come together. Although a number of people can be brought together to undertake a task, it cannot be assumed that the group will immediately work together effectively. To build an effective team it is important to acknowledge that it must be allowed to progress through the developmental stages and to go through a period of growth.

Tuckman (1965) describes a general model of group formation which suggests that to be effective, a group must progress through a number of stages, which have a linear relationship. He identifies the successive stages of group development as forming, storming, norming, and suggests that it is only when these stages have been successfully passed through that the group can concentrate on the attainment of its purpose and on performing the task.

Forming This period involves the initial formation of the group and brings together a number of individuals who establish parameters and formulate the initial objectives of the group. This stage is a period of testing individuals in terms of acceptable behaviours and codes of conduct, before roles begin to emerge. Members are attempting to create their identity within the group.

Storming This period can be characterized as a period of internal conflict and high emotion. As people begin to know each other so they start to present their views to the group and disagreements and arguments begin to occur. This may lead to conflict and hostility, and even the collapse of the group.

If this stage is successfully passed through then new objectives and operating procedures for the group can be established with more meaningful structures and procedures.

Norming

As the conflict is resolved, so new guidelines and standards of behaviour will be established. Group cohesion develops, and norms of what is acceptable behaviour are set which will govern members' behaviour.

This stage is important in establishing agreed standards of performance. However, these can work against effective organizational performance, as for example in the case of the Hawthorne experiments discussed earlier in the chapter.

Performing

When the group has successfully progressed through the three earlier stages it will have created the cohesiveness to operate effectively as a team. At this stage the group will finally be able to concentrate on the achievement of its objectives and will be at its most effective because energies are focused on the task.

Tuckman suggested that the effectiveness of a group may be adversely affected if time constraints are put on each stage of progression. However, more recent research suggests that Tuckman's model, which presents the different stages as a linear progression, is too simplistic. For example, it is assumed that any intra-group conflicts have been resolved at the storming phase. In reality these conflicts often resurface later on in the life of the group, having a detrimental impact on group performance.

The permanence and stability of group members is important in terms of group development and maturity. It does take time for group spirit and unity to develop, so group cohesiveness is more likely where members of the group are together for a reasonable period of time. Constant and frequent changes of group membership can have an adverse effect on group performance. Therefore, where changes do occur, with individuals leaving and new members joining, the group should be allowed to go through the group formation process before it can be fully effective.

Group roles

A factor that will influence the performance of a group is the roles individuals play, which will start to emerge in the forming stage of group development. The development of an effective group should involve the identification of distinct roles for members

Situational factors, such as the requirements of the task and style of leadership, and personal factors, including values, attitudes, motivations, ability and personality, will influence an individual's role within a group. The role will determine the 'expected' behaviour of that individual. The implication of this is that an individual may play a role in one work group that is different from a role in another group.

One of the advantages of teamworking is that a group can combine all the necessary qualities for success, which an individual alone cannot possess. Research by Belbin (1981) was based on the hypothesis that a balance of skills and expertise is needed for the formation of an effective team. He identified a number of roles which are essential for effective performance:

Coordinator	Controls the way a team moves towards achieving the group objectives, making best use of available resources, and recognizing and ensuring that best use is made of each team member's potential. Typical features: calm, self-confident and controlled but reasonably extrovert.
Implementer	Turns plans and ideas into practice and carries out plans efficiently and systematically. Tends to be hardworking and have a common-sense and practical approach, usually conservative, dutiful and predictable in nature but also hard working and self-disciplined.
Completer/Finisher	Makes sure that the team is protected as far as possible from mistakes and searches for the work that needs more attention. Characteristics: has a sense of urgency about things, always conscious of deadlines. Conscientious, anxious, paying attention to detail, tends to be a perfectionist.
Monitor /Evaluator	Analyses problems, and evaluates ideas and suggestions, so that they can then make an informed decision and perform well in a quality role. Typical features: unemotional, clever, detached, prudent, and shrewd in one's judgement.
Planner/Innovator	Good source of ideas for the group and is imaginative and creative but may need to be encouraged by other members to contribute. Tends to be individualistic in nature and serious-minded but knowledgeable.
Resource investigator	Explores and reports on ideas, developments and resources outside the group, and excels in conducting negotiations. Characteristics: extrovert, enthusiastic and curious, have good social skills and enjoys exploring anything new.
Shaper	Shapes the way team effort is applied, directs attention to objectives and priorities, and seeks to impose a structure on discussions and their outcomes. High achiever usually outgoing but impatient, dynamic, has drive and likes to win.
Team worker	Supports members and promotes team spirit. Characteristics: responsive, and sensitive but may be somewhat indecisive, socially oriented.
Specialist	Provides specialist skills and knowledge and has a dedicated and single-minded approach. Can adopt a very narrow perspective and can sometimes fail to see the whole picture.

To be effective, the team should have a balance of all these roles. Some members will adopt a primary role and others may have what Belbin refers to as a back-up team role as well as their primary role. While the different roles have both positive qualities but also weaknesses, other members of the team should compensate for the weaknesses.

It is important that role definitions are clear because inadequate or inappropriate role definition can lead to role conflict, and this can have a detrimental impact on the behaviour of individual members and the group. Role conflict can emerge in different forms, including role incompatibility, role ambiguity, role overload/underload and role stress.

a)   Role incompatibility may arise where contradictory expectations are made on an individual and where people feel 'caught in the middle'.

b)   Role ambiguity arises when people are unclear about their duties, responsibility and authority. For example, if an individual has insufficient guidance on his or her job description.

c)   Role overload occurs when an individual is at one extreme inundated with work and therefore finds it impossible to perform the expected roles well. At the other extreme role underload is when an individual feels the role is undemanding and they have capacity to undertake more roles.

d)   Role stress can arise because of the conflict between the different demands made on individuals by other people, and can cause tension and inability to perform.

Communication Structures

The levels of interaction within a group will influence group behaviour, group performance and the satisfaction derived by individuals. A key factor on the level of interactions is the structure of channels of communication. Research by both Leavitt (1951) and Shaw (1964) investigated communication networks in terms of problem solving, member satisfaction and leadership when different systems of communication were imposed on the group. Five different structures of communication networks were identified: the wheel, the chain, the Y, the circle and the all-channel. These different networks are illustrated in Figure 9.1.

Figure 9.1: Communication networks

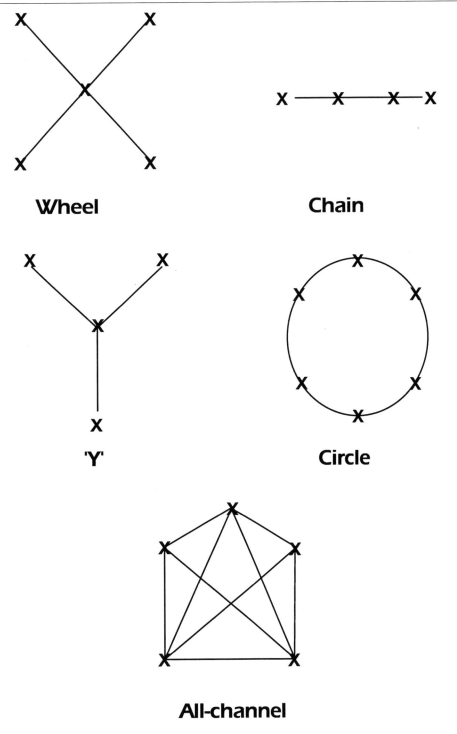

The basis of this research was to examine performance depending upon the different levels of freedom of communication and the degree of centralization of leadership.

Referring to the different structures identified in Figure 9.1, the wheel is the most centralized network with the link person at the centre of the network acting as the coordinator for activities and information flows and restricting communication access. The circle is an example of a more decentralized network with decision making involving some degree of member participation. The all-channel involves full discussion and high levels of interaction among members and is the most decentralized network. The Y and the chain are intermediate forms. The more centralized channels restrict communication access, whereas the decentralized channels provide the maximum flow of information.

The research findings revealed that simple problems are best solved, and with fewer mistakes, by centralized networks, for example the wheel. However, more complex tasks were found to be more effectively performed by the less highly centralized groups, such as the circle or all-channel networks where everyone communicates with everyone else.

The researchers concluded that the greater the amount of inter-connectiveness of the communications network the higher the levels of satisfaction. So although the central person in the wheel network experiences high levels of satisfaction, for members on the periphery the wheel is the least satisfying network.

However, in reality any of the systems could have an adverse effect on the motivation of group members. Consideration must be given to the preference of group members for a particular network. The nature of the task must also be taken account of, as well as the physical location of a group.

The managerial implications of the research are that if a work group is faced with a variety of tasks and objectives then no single network will be effective. For example, although the wheel is effective and efficient in the accomplishment of simple tasks, it can result in low job satisfaction and the low motivation of group members.

6 Group Decision-making

There are some clear advantages of group decisions which Mullins (1989) identifies as:

- the pooling of resources;
- more knowledge and expertise available;
- interaction that can provoke future thoughts/ideas (snowballing effect).

In addition, where members are involved in decision-making they are more likely to be committed to the decisions and their implementation. Although group decision-making does offer many benefits for both the organization and individuals, there are certain situations when individuals working alone may be more efficient. This is because group decision-making:

- is more costly;

- is time consuming;

- can create conflict or be a compromise decision;

- lacks confidentiality;

- tends to be more risky.

Whereas individual decision-making tends to be:

- cheaper;

- quicker;

- confidential;

- risk aversive.

A number of the disadvantages of group decision-making can be examined by reference to the concepts of 'groupthink' and 'risky shift phenomenon'.

- **Groupthink** relates to the exclusion of divergent views in discussions that can diminish the decision-making capability of the group. It is more likely to emerge in long-term, highly cohesive groups that are isolated from external pressures. Consensus behaviour dominates, and diminishes creativity and innovation in preference for conformity. In such situations there is the demise of alternative actions.

- **The 'risky shift' phenomenon** relates to the view that some groups will take greater risks than an individual would because individuals can hide behind the anonymity of the group (Stoner 1961). Coexisting with 'risky shift' is the notion of 'cautious shift', which suggests that decisions may be made in a cautious direction.

The consequences of both 'risky shift' and 'groupthink' can lead to poor decision-making and can have a dysfunctional effect on group performance.

There are also psychological pressures resulting from individuals working closely together whereby the group's emotional impact can affect individual behaviour and judgement. It is suggested that when acting alone, an individual will have a greater reality orientation and be more efficient intellectually rather than operating within the stultifying effects of group interaction. This supports the findings of the research undertaken by Asch (1952), discussed earlier in the chapter.

The factors that will ultimately influence whether decisions are made by either the group or by an individual are often interrelated, and will be determined by issues such as:

- the urgency and time available;

- the need for specialization;

- the need for confidentiality;

- whether it is a routine/non-routine decision;

● the cost implications of group decisions.

7 Work Environment and Organizational Factors

The work environment and other contextual factors can also impact on effective group performance. These could include:

● the physical work environment;

● organizational culture;

● technology and task design;

● group autonomy;

● leadership style;

● reward systems;

● performance feedback;

● training and consultation;

● external threats.

If groups are to work effectively together the different human resource policies such as the reward systems, performance measures and feedback mechanisms must be designed to complement group work rather than operate against it by focusing on the individual .

The nature of technology and work systems will influence group behaviours and performance, with new information systems leading to new patterns of work organization and the structure of groups. This is characteristic of changes occurring in many financial services organizations where new technologies have significantly changed work processes. Effective team working is crucial to the activities of, for example, centralized processing centres and telephone call centres.

8 Encouraging the Performance of Groups

Managing the dynamics of groups is complex and more challenging then managing individuals. When encouraging a group to perform more effectively the manager plays a crucial role. Building on the actions proposed by Braddick (1991), a manager should seek to:

● establish clear objectives for the group, since a common purpose will unite the group. However, objectives must be realistic and time scales for achievement given;

● good planning, to ensure the group has clear targets and members are involved in the process, thus building commitment. The manager should ask whether priorities established are realistic and relevant, and whether future direction is established with steps to get there identified;

- structure, the group should be well structured with tasks organized effectively with all members clear as to what is required from them;

- motivate the group, the members of the group need to be recognized and feel that they are making a contribution to performance. Attention should also be given to developing team spirit and comradeship;

- decision-making, where appropriate decisions should be made jointly through group participation encouraging inputs from all members;

- provide feedback and evaluation, the group needs to know their progress so they can be given coaching or training if appropriate. Feedback should be honest but constructive;

- ensure resources and external support are available, this includes both physical and financial resources;

- provide effective leadership, both in relation to the task orientation but also in supporting individual group members;

- openness, in terms of encouraging constructive problem solving rather than a blame culture. The group should be open and honest in communications between themselves, and should communicate appropriately beyond the team;

- rewards, the group should be rewarded and successes should be celebrated.

One model focusing on the group and the individual developed to achieve effective performance is that proposed by Adair's action-centred leadership. This model suggests that effectiveness revolves around the balance between concern for the task, concern for the group and concern for the individual. The manager must be aware of three critical needs: to achieve the task, to build the team, and to develop each individual.

Indicators that a group or team is working well include both qualitative and quantitative measures. Cooperation, belief in common goals and aims, commitment to the group, support of individual members, good communications, participation by all members, and conflicts resolved by the members themselves are examples of qualitative measures, and suggest that a group is working well.

In addition, the more quantitative benefits of lower levels of labour turnover, accident rates, absenteeism, errors and complaints may be evidence that a group is working effectively together. The positive outcome for the organization is higher levels of productivity and the achievement of targets.

9 Team-building

The notion of team building is developed from work on organizational development, which is essentially concerned with trying to fulfill the twin objectives of organizational goals and satisfying individual needs. Thus, team building can be defined as 'the process of enhancing the effectiveness of the team'. Attention is focused on both work procedures and interpersonal relations. Enhancing the effectiveness of a team requires attention to characteristics such as cohesiveness, norms, group development, roles and interactions, along with communications, involvement and decision-making. In other words to all the factors already discussed.

Team building is concerned with encouraging team spirit and a feeling of belonging. In achieving this team members should be encouraged to support and help each other. Team meetings and team briefings are important activities in developing team spirit. Effort should be focused on integrating group cohesiveness and norms with productivity and commitment to the task. Team-building activities should be developed to take advantage of the benefits of strong group cohesiveness while using tactics to minimize any negative impact.

Many financial service organizations are making conscious attempts to develop managerial teams, investing in team-building training activities. A whole range of techniques can be used to encourage team development and the bonding of members, some of which are based on non-work task exercises, for example Outward Bound courses. Individuals are provided with the opportunity to learn more about themselves and their impact on others. The desired outcome of these activities is to develop effective and high performance teams with the ultimate goal of improving organizational performance.

The membership of a group is not static, so team building must be a continuous activity. This has implications for the indoctrination and socialization of new members to the ways of the team, specifically the team's values, norms and expectations. The indoctrination is necessary to reduce role ambiguity, to increase the feeling of security and to create more behavioural uniformity. Bowditch and Buono (1990) identify indoctrination as a three-stage process starting with anticipatory socialization, followed by organizational or group encounter and finally acquisition of group norms and values. Successful indoctrination will have a positive influence on an individual's productivity and commitment to the group.

10   Managing Group Conflict

Wherever there is interaction between individuals and groups it is inevitable that conflict will emerge; this can have positive and negative consequences. Members must work well as a team but also each group must work well with other groups. Two broad categories of conflict can be identified, intra-group conflict and inter-group conflict:

1. Intra-group conflict arises when there are hostilities *within* the group, and where disagreements and differences between members occur. This type of conflict may emerge in the 'storming' stage of group formation proposed by Tuckman (1965) because of factors such as opposing norms and values, deviant goals and objectives, and disputes over roles.

    Intra-group conflict may also occur where membership of the group is diverse, for example with reference to gender, culture, age etc. Diversity is a very topical issue, with debates centering on whether a diverse group is more or less effective than a homogenous group. Managing diversity is challenging and will be discussed as a theme in its own right in Chapter 19.

2.   Inter-group conflict is concerned with conflicts between different groups or teams, for example, departments and sections in the organization.

Rather than focusing on eliminating conflict, which given the dynamics and nature of the work organization is probably unattainable, managers should decide what actions they can take to minimize conflict. Emphasis should be on:

● the setting of a superordinate goal. This is one all groups can aim for and one that will require increased communication;

● relatively greater emphasis being given to total organizational effectiveness;

● high levels of communication between groups;

● bringing the leaders of groups into interaction, and also encouraging a high degree of interaction between members of different groups through project working and also through inter-department social activities;

● frequent rotation of staff between sections and departments should be encouraged in order to stimulate a higher degree of understanding;

● the reallocation of tasks and responsibilities;

● inter-group training;

● locate a common enemy, such as a competitor or possibly another area/department in the organization;

● avoid win-lose situations, because groups should not have to compete for scarce resources and rewards should be shared between departments.

Inter-group conflict should not always be considered to be necessarily dysfunctional. Indeed it should be promoted in certain situations to encourage healthy competition. Inter-group conflict may be desirable in some instances, for example to develop a team with low group cohesion. Each group becomes more tightly knit and elicits greater loyalty from its members. The group also tends to become more highly structured and organized, as well as more task orientated. A number of financial services organizations have encouraged inter-group competition, for example by setting up sales league tables on performances between teams both within and between branches and rewarding the best performers. However, actively encouraging competition between teams must be carefully managed to avoid potential negative outcomes, such as a lack of cooperation and communication between groups. This could ultimately lead to the ineffective operation of the task for the organization. If a team is in the losing situation this can result in members finding ways to attribute the failure to others and the group can splinter, with intra-group conflict surfacing.

Many staff surveys suggest that while groups usually rate themselves highly on intra-group communication and cooperation, scores are often lower for inter-group communication and cooperation.

Summary

Now that you have studied this chapter you should be able to:

- Define the term 'groups';

- Explain why people form groups in the work organization;

- Distinguish between different types of groups;

- Discuss the characteristics of effective groups;

- Analyse the benefits and disadvantages of cohesive groups;

- Explain communication structures for groups;

- Evaluate group decision-making;

- Describe how the manager can encourage effective group work;

- Discuss the activities that can be used to encourage team development;

- Analyse the different forms of group conflict and recommend actions to minimize conflict.

References

Adair J (1986) *Effective Teambuilding*, Gower

Asch S E (1952) 'Effects of group pressure upon the modification and distortion of judgements', *Readings in Social Psychology*, Swanson, Newcombe and Hartley

Belbin R M (1981) *Management Teams: Why They Succeed or Fail*, Butterworth Heinemann

Belbin (1993) *Team Roles at Work*, Butterworth Heinemann

Bowditch J L & Buono A F (1990) *A Primer on Organizational Behaviour*, Wiley

Braddick W A G (1991) *Management for Bankers*, 2nd ed., Butterworths

Furnham A (1999) *The Psychology of Behaviour at Work, The Individual in the Organization*, Psychology Press

Handy C B (1986) *Understanding Organizations*, 3rd ed., Penguin

Holbeche L (1998) *Motivating People in Lean Organizations*, Butterworth Heinemann

Leavitt H (1951) 'Some Effects of Certain Communication Patterns on Group Performance', *Journal of Abnormal and Social Psychology*, Vol. 46

McKenna E (1994) *Business Psychology & Organizational Behaviour: A Student's Handbook*, Lawrence Erlbaum

Mullins L J (1996) *Management and Organizational Behaviour*, 4th ed., Pitman

Schein E H (1988) *Organizational Psychology*, 3rd ed., Prentice Hall

Shaw M E (1964) 'Communication Networks', in *Advances in Experimental Social Psychology*, Vol. 1, New York Academic Press

Shaw M E (1981) *Group Dynamics: The Psychology of Small Group Behaviour*, 3rd ed., McGraw Hill

Stoner J A F (1961) 'A Comparison of Industrial and Group Decisions Involving Risk', Unpublished, School of Industrial Management, MIT thesis, quoted in Brown R (1965) *Social Psychology*, New York: Free Press

Tuckman B W (1965) 'Development Sequence in Small Groups', *Psychological Bulletin*, 63

10

LEADERSHIP AND THE ROLE OF THE MANAGER

Objectives

After studying this chapter you should be able to:

● define the different aspects of the manager's role;

● analyse the role of management authority, control, power and empowerment in organizations;

● explain the different theories of leadership and management style;

● critically evaluate the different approaches to leadership and management style.

1   What is the Work of Managers?

As has already been established in Chapter 6, management is a key activity in the organization. During the twentieth century there has been a massive expansion in terms of the number of white-collar workers and managers, and the development of those industries (e.g. technical or professional) that employ managerial skills.

It is through management that the work of employees can be directed towards organizational goals. It is also through management that the different aspects of an organization are brought to fruition. The manager's role within the organization is therefore made up of a number of different aspects including:

● responsibility for the individual

● responsibility for the group that is formed by these individuals

● responsibility for the tasks that the manager is assigned to carry out

● responsibility for achieving the organizational goals assigned

As there are many different levels within the organization, so there are various managerial/ supervisory levels. A senior manager may be primarily concerned with the long-term future direction of the business, whereas a branch or departmental manager will be most concerned with achieving weekly or monthly goals.

The nature of managerial work involves the performance of three key roles:

● securing resources (meeting clients, developing the business, etc.);

● managing projects or work teams;

● supervising or undertaking professional and technical work.

These have been commonly referred to as 'Finders, Minders and Grinders'. Each term reflects a role, so finding is securing the resources necessary to deliver business objectives, minders is the effective management of those resources and grinders is the completion of the technical aspects of the role.

Managers usually fulfil some aspect of all of these roles. The criterion for promotion to a supervisory/managerial position is often based on a high level of technical knowledge. However as managers become more senior within the organization so the requirement to be involved in technical work often diminishes. Future roles may demand more interpersonal and project management skills.

This established career path has several implications. Many individuals have greater interest in the technical aspects of their work, and have no interest and sometimes little ability in developing broader managerial skills. However, they can often feel pushed into a managerial role because the organization offers only limited progression for technical specialists.

What then are these broader managerial skills that are required by organizations at the different levels?

2 Managerial Skills

The skills required of a manager to deliver his or her role fall into three broad areas:

1. *Technical skills* – these are generally job-related but tend to reduce in importance as individual progresses up the managerial ladder.

2. *Conceptual or process skills* – these include business planning, decision-making, financial control and analysis, change management and risk management. These generally increase in importance the more senior/strategic the role.

3. *Interpersonal or people skills* – these include team working, motivation of self and others, leadership and interpersonal communication.

Many organizations use these broad categorizations of skills as a basis for management development and selection. A term, which has been used to describe the combination of these skills, is competencies. It has been defined by Boyatzis (1982) as:

> *An underlying characteristic of a person, which results in an effective or superior performance in a job.*

The concept of competencies embodies the ability to transfer skills and knowledge to new situations within an occupational area and so refers to technical knowledge as well as cognitive and interpersonal skills. These are explored more fully in Chapter 15.

3   The Manager's Role – The Traditional View

As well as categorizing the broad skill areas required of a manager, it is also possible to define the roles he or she will be involved in carrying out.

The earliest attempt at defining these roles was by Henri Fayol. Many writers appear to agree with Fayol's view on six main roles or functions for managers, which include forecasting, planning, organizing, coordinating, commanding and controlling. These are examined in more detail below.

Forecasting

Most managers need to look ahead and anticipate events as part of their job. The extent to which they are required to do so varies according to their level of responsibility in the hierarchy. At the lower levels they are more concerned with the implementation of strategy and operational issues rather than devising strategy themselves. In such cases, forecasting takes the form of deciding on possible future action to meet a target – i.e. how many staff are needed at what times to deliver the sales and service targets in a department.

Forecasting implies both proactive and reactive approaches. A proactive approach is required when a manager examines and tries to anticipate the demands of the economy, customers, competitors and business development areas. This could be described as looking for opportunities.

A reactive approach could be described as looking for threats. Some UK financial services organizations have had reactive forecasting, for example, and have needed to respond quickly to threats like telephone banking and insurance systems by introducing their own systems in response to the strategies and initiatives of their more proactive competitors.

Planning

Strategic planning has already been discussed in Chapter 3, so this section is concerned with the nature of managerial planning. Planning implies that an organization is:

- breaking down duties
- devising a programme of objectives
- allocating the work.

It calls for forecasts, and demands that managers look ahead and anticipate future events.

Planning involves a series of eight well-established stages:

1. Determine the aims of the job.

2.   Estimate and secure the resources required.

3.   Identify key result areas and the key tasks within them.

4.   Define success criteria.

5.   Set standards of performance.

6.   Define short-term goals and first steps.

7.   Set individual targets

8.   Set up monitoring and review systems.

Problem-solving

This involves the manager identifying difficulties, preferably before they arise, and planning action to cope with the issue. Again there is a series of well-defined stages in the problem-solving process, which have some similarities to the stages in planning:

- selecting and defining the problem;

- gathering data about the situation;

- examining the situation to identify failings and irrelevancies;

- developing the new improved situation;

- installing the plan in action;

- maintaining the plan and modifying it where deviations have occurred.

Organizing and co-ordinating

The complex requirements of activities today means considerable organization and co-ordination of all resources is necessary. It is crucial where a project is involved, because all activities should proceed in a coordinated way. As activities increase across functional and departmental boundaries, so there is an increasing emphasis on coordination and project management skills.

Controlling and monitoring

This activity describes monitoring events and taking steps to bring them into line with plans. It presupposes that plans are already in place, otherwise there is nothing to control or aim for, or to measure performance against. From the plans, targets are derived and performance can be measured against these targets. Appropriate action can then be taken to eliminate the variance or to adjust the plan so that it reflects what can be achieved. Controlling activities can occur by:

1.   Timing events;

2.   Checking key areas are completed;

3. By establishing any variance;

4. By assessing finance.

Communication

As already mentioned communication and interpersonal skills are an essential part of a manager's role. There needs to be effective communication with peers, superiors, subordinates and customers and suppliers if objectives are to be achieved. Communication as a topic area is fully discussed in Chapter 13.

4 Managerial Roles – Alternative Views

Other classifications exist which also attempt to describe the essential functions of a senior manager's job. Mintzberg (1979) classified the essential functions into ten different roles and divided a manger's role into three major groups:

1. Interpersonal roles – emphasizing the relationships with others.

2. Informational roles – emphasizing the gathering and dispersion of information.

3. Decisional roles – emphasizing taking and implementing decisions.

These functions are illustrated in Figure 10.1, below.

Figure 10.1: Mintzberg's managerial roles

Interpersonal Roles

Figurehead
Leader
Liaison

Informational Roles

Monitor
Disseminator
Spokesperson

Decisional Roles

Entrepreneur
Disturbance Handler
Resource Allocator
Negotiator

Interpersonal roles

These arise from the manager's status, authority and relations with others. The manager is a figurehead representing the organization and its policies. He or she is a leader, responsible for staffing and for the motivation of subordinates. There is also a role to play in liaison with others outside the manager's own unit.

Informational roles

The manager has an important communication role to play in the organization. Information must be monitored so that the manager can understand how the organization operates and the influence of the environment.

The manager also acts as a disseminator of information, passing on information. The manager acts as a spokesperson communicating information to other departments, or to different levels in the organization, and outside the organization to suppliers, etc.

Decisional roles

These involve the manager in making decisions about the future of the organization and the department. In an entrepreneurial role the manager initiates and plans controlled change by solving problems, and by taking action to improve the existing situation. The manager can also act as a disturbance handler reacting to situations and unpredictable events. The resource allocator role involves the manager using formal authority to decide where effort will be expended, and making decisions about the allocation of resources. The negotiator role involves the manager negotiating activities with other individuals or organizations, for example a new agreement with a supplier, and emphasizing the need to get things done.

Mintzberg (1979) suggests that to some extent this is an arbitrary division of a manager's role, and that the manager's work does not always divide itself neatly into these categories. It is merely one way of trying to group the manager's duties. An alternative approach could be the finding, minding, grinding categorization referred to earlier

Although the manager's role encompasses all these activities, they vary between seniority and function. Interpersonal and decisional roles are perhaps most likely to be found at the senior level, informational when the manager is acting as a middleman.

5   Leadership

A debate exists as to whether the terms 'leader' and 'manager' are interchangeable. It could be argued that the job of a manager normally involves the leadership of some employees, but not all leaders are managers. To be an effective manager one must develop good leadership skills.

Because leadership is a key aspect of effective management, research has been devoted to exploring why some leaders are effective and others ineffective.

Four major perspectives to this issue can be discerned. They correspond broadly speaking to four historical phases:

● trait or qualities approach (end of the 19th century and beginning of the 20th century);

- style of leadership approach (from the mid- to late-20th century;
- contingency/situational approach (from the 1970s onwards);
- functional approach (the most recent).

6   Trait or Qualities Approach

This was the first attempt to explain why some people are successful as leaders and others are not. It focuses on the individual occupying the post, and assumes that leaders are born and not made.

It suggests that leaders have certain qualities or traits which are innate and not easily developed or acquired, and that this distinguishes them from their followers. Attention should therefore be directed to selecting as leaders those people who possess these qualities, because the characteristics cannot be developed or encouraged through training. Can we predict good leaders because of the qualities displayed by the individual early in life. etc.?

However, researchers have found it difficult to identify the traits likely to lead to leadership effectiveness. Among the many that have been suggested are size, energy, integrity, decisiveness, knowledge, wisdom and imagination.

The problems with this approach are several:

- it may be that effective leaders learned to develop these qualities after becoming leaders, and that the ability to respond to different situations is the key trait;
- there is not much agreement among researchers as to which characteristics are most important (McKenna 1991);
- this approach does not help in the development and training of future leaders.

7   Styles of Leadership Approach

During the 1950s a new explanation of leadership effectiveness began to emerge. This suggested that certain leaders were effective because of the behavioural style they adopted, and it recognized that managers cannot merely rely on position in the organization to exercise leadership. This is known as the style approach. The styles they can adopt range from autocratic to democratic. McGregor (1960) summed up these two extremes in his Theory X (authoritarian) and his Theory Y (democratic).

The traditional or authoritarian approach to leadership is expressed in Theory X:

1. The average person has an inherent dislike of work.

2. Because of this most people must be coerced, controlled and threatened with punishment to get them to put forward adequate effort towards the achievement of organizational goals.

3. The average person prefers to be directed, wishes to avoid responsibility, has relatively little ambition and wants security above all.

A modern approach to leadership is expressed in McGregor's Theory Y, a democratic approach which he believed was more appropriate for today's manager:

1. Work is as natural as play or rest.

2. The average person not only accepts but seeks responsibility.

3. In modern industrial life people's potential is only partly utilized.

4. External control and the threat of punishment are not the only means of bringing about effort towards organizational objectives.

A number of other theorists support this style approach.

Tannenbaum and Schmidt (1973)

Tannenbaum and Schmidt developed a continuum of leadership behaviour along which various styles were placed ranging from 'boss-centred' (authoritarian leadership) to 'employee-centred' (democratic leadership), as illustrated in Figure 10.2. The continuum also included the degree of authority used by a manager and the degree of freedom for subordinates. This continuum of styles could be summarized by the phrase 'tells, sells, consults, joins'. At one end of the continuum leaders try to distribute power in decision-making using consultation, participation and delegation. At the other end the amount of decision-making by the supervisor or leader increases.

Figure 10.2: Tannenbaum and Schmidt model

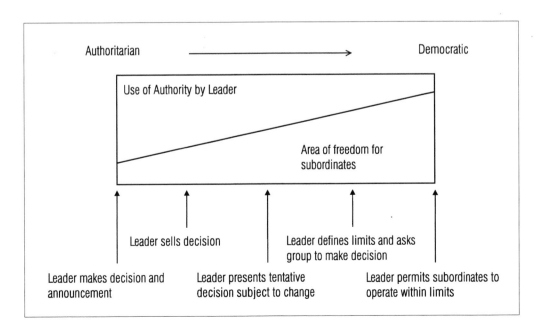

Later developments of the style approach were more sophisticated and involved trying to account for the complexity of the situations the leaders find themselves in.

Blake and Mouton Managerial Grid (1984)

Blake and Mouton saw leadership as being two-dimensional – concern for the employee and concern for the task – and placed the different styles on a grid illustrated in Figure 10.3.

The most effective leaders are those who rate highly on both dimensions, and who exhibit a concern for production and for people. Blake and Mouton found evidence that the supportive styles, i.e. concern for people scoring five or more were related to lower labour turnover, less inter-group conflict and high group satisfaction.

Figure 10.3: Blake and Mouton grid

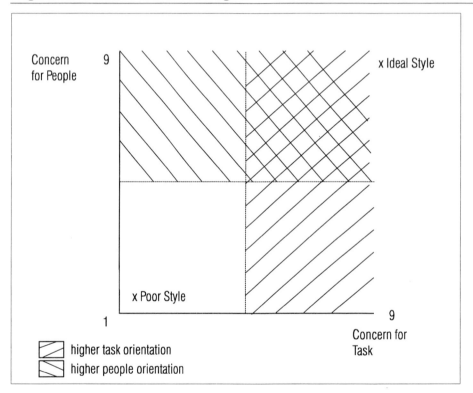

The style approach suggests that a leader is successful because he or she adopts the right style for the situation faced. Generally this view supported the idea that the democratic style was the most successful.

8   The Contingency or Situational Approach

More recent views on effective leadership belong to what is termed the contingency school, and develop from the concept that the most effective leaders have the ability to adapt their style according to the situation. Perhaps one of the most influential theories within this group is Fiedler's contingency theory.

Fiedler's contingency theory (1967)

Based on studies of a wide range of group situations, Fiedler explored the relationship between leadership and organizational performance. To measure the attitudes of a leader Fiedler classified a leader's orientation in terms of whether he or she enjoyed working with others, and were then said to have a high least preferred coworker (LPC) score, or whether he or she was more production-orientated with a low least preferred coworker score (LPC).

A questionnaire was issued to potential and existing leaders which, when completed, indicated whether they enjoyed working with others (a high LPC score) or whether they disliked working with others (a low LPC score).

Fiedler also attempted to identify key features in the situation including:

1. *Position of power* where the more formal the leaders' positions the greater the range of rewards and punishments at their disposal. In such positions power can then be judged as strong or weak.

2. *Task structure*, where a high degree of task structure gives a more favourable situation for the leader because it means he or she can more easily monitor and influence the subordinate's behaviour.

3. *Leader member relations*, which asks whether the relationship between leaders and their followers is good.

All of these factors are combined in Fiedler's contingency model and indicate which situations are favourable to a particular type of leader.

When a situation is very favourable (with good leader-member relations, a structured task, and a strong position of power) or very unfavourable (with poor leader-member relations, unstructured task, and a weak position of power), a task-orientated leader (low LPC score) with a directive, controlling style will be more effective.

When the situation is moderately favourable then a participative approach (a high LPC score) will be more effective.

Fiedler concluded that any leadership style may be effective depending on the situation. However, since some leaders may find it difficult to change their style, effectiveness can still be improved by changing the leadership situation. The position of power, task structure and leader-member relations can all be changed to make them compatible with the characteristics of the leader.

Hersey and Blanchard (1973)

Another model within the contingency school is the Hersey and Blanchard situational theory.

This model is based on consideration of relationship behaviour and task behaviour. It suggests that the effectiveness of the leader is also affected by the willingness of the person the leader is attempting to influence.

Hersey and Blanchard suggest that leaders engage in:

- supportive behaviour which is concerned with the development needs of employees;

- directive behaviour which is concerned with directing and steering but allows the employee to perform independently.

A successful leader will select a style that is appropriate and which is based on the level of development of the employee.

9   Functional Approach

This approach is the most recent and focuses on the function of leadership. It also views leadership in terms of how the leader's behaviour affects and is affected by the group he or she manages. This approach believes that the skills of leadership can be learnt and developed by concentrating upon the functions that lead to effective work performance. John Adair (1979) uses a functional approach in his guidance on how to train leaders which is known as action-centred leadership.

The effectiveness of the leader is dependent on meeting three areas of need within the work group:

- the need to achieve the common task;

- the need to maintain morale and build a team spirit;

- the need to meet the needs of the individual and the group.

This is illustrated in Figure 10.4.

Figure 10.4: Adair's action-centred leadership

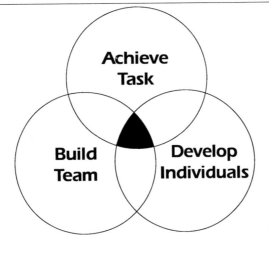

The action by a leader in any one of these areas of need will affect one or both of the other areas. The most effective leader will be the one who can meet all these needs and maintain a balance. This approach by Adair was also explored in Chapter 9 when examining groups.

10 Recent Trends

The most recent trends in terms of leadership theory seem to group all the approaches described above into one category which is regarded as providing a transactional view of leadership. The newest approach assumes that a transformational view to leadership may now be the most effective for the circumstances organizations face.

The transactional approach or more traditional approach to leadership assumes that a leader enters into transactions or relationships with subordinates and explains the requirements in terms of the contributions and the rewards the subordinates could receive. This situation can apply in circumstances of stability where established processes and systems are available to deal with this exchange and transaction.

However, in a turbulent environment with the advance of technology and ever-changing products and circumstances, leaders need to have vision and to be creative, innovative and capable of inspiring others to share their dreams. Leaders need to take calculated high risks, to establish high standards and to challenge the existing structure. Bass (1990) lists the characteristics these leaders need as charisma, intellectual stimulation and consideration of the emotional needs of each employee.

In addition, it has also been found that vision, creativity, and the selection and training of talented people is also desirable.

Changing environments mean that theorists have once again looked at the traits and characteristics of effective leadership rather than just the style that leaders may adopt in a given situation.

Associated with the leader's position in the organization are a series of terms such as power, control and authority, and it is these aspects of the managerial and leadership role that the final section of this chapter examines.

11 Power

Power is closely connected with leadership and management. However, it is a difficult term to define because of its constantly changing, complex and intangible nature. Power can mean the extent of control and influence, but it can also mean the type of influence. It is used to refer to the system of rewards and penalties of a formal and informal nature that will ensure compliance to an organization's activities and policies.

For instance, has someone chosen to follow a course of action against their better judgement because of the power held over them, i.e. they were threatened, or because they understood the advantages of such a path?

The complex nature of power is also indicated by the use of a number of similar terms, for example authority, control and influence. These words are often used interchangeably, but in academic terms they have different meanings. Power is a subjective term in the sense that it is not always used but the fear lies in its anticipated use. In other words, it can be a threat.

Foucault (1979) emphasized the disciplinary notion of power as a process. Other writers have tried to define the sources of power and therefore its nature. Weber (1947) perceived the power of managers as coming from the owners of the business and was exercised by managers on their behalf. Similarly departments or groups can wield power.

Etzioni (1975) and French and Raven (1959) have similar definitions of the sources of power:

- *institutional* – this rests on external social and economic structures;

- *reward* – the ability to give rewards;

- *coercive* – the ability to punish;

- *legitimate* – based on the leader's position, and acknowledged by the recipient of authority;

- *referent/charisma* – admiration for the power holder;

- *expert* – this emphasizes the specialist knowledge or skill, and is crucial to the organization's survival.

12 Empowerment

Over the last decade the term empowerment has been much used in organizations. Many companies have tried to introduce or support empowerment programmes as a way of improving competitiveness and dealing with customer requirements more effectively.

It is difficult to find a definition that encompasses the various forms empowerment has assumed. Empowerment implies giving an employee the opportunity and authority to take more responsible decisions and a greater say in the operation of the business. The aims of empowerment can be summarized as:

- increasing an organization's effectiveness through quicker decision-making;

- more responsiveness to customer needs;

- cutting costs through the reduction of management layers;

- coping better with the rapid changes required;

- enabling staff to be more creative and make greater use of skills.

Empowerment is also perceived to offer benefits to employees:

- it can provide greater opportunities for development;

- it can give greater responsibility to the individual for achievement.

Despite these advantages, problems can be created by introducing empowerment because it strips out a layer of management and redistributes the power to former subordinates. Empowerment can also cause a withdrawal of resource by reducing the number of managers and investment in training, and other human resource systems are needed to support its development. There can also be problems in ensuring consistency of standards across the different business units and departments that have been empowered. Resistance from senior staff may also result because they perceive a loss of individual power as a result of empowering subordinates.

13   Authority

Authority as a term used in organizations is closely related to power, and is the subject of research and study by many writers, including Max Weber as already mentioned in Chapter 6. It is usually associated with the position held in an organization and as a type of social control means that others accept the power of senior officials.

Authority is a legitimate means of social control and, according to Weber (1947), there are three types:

- *charismatic* – based on respect and admiration;
- *traditional* – established by custom and rule;
- *rational* – legal occupancy of senior positions. This is widely used in modern work organizations, especially bureaucracies.

The similarity in terms and definitions often make it hard to distinguish authority from the concept of power, especially where the power emanates from the position of the leader or his or her personal charisma.

14   Control

As mentioned by Fayol (1949) organizational achievement and structure implies that control has to exist to direct and coordinate work, especially since not all employees in the organization share the same corporate goals. There has been much discussion about the conflict between managerial control and workers' resistance, for example the writings and research on employee relations. Child (1984) emphasized two managerial tasks, control and integration, which are the basic structures of authority and the division of labour.

There is the issue of control to maintain direction in the organization versus control stifling initiative and adaptation. There are often situations where major policy decisions are centralized; there are also situations where operations are delegated in order to maintain control but also to encourage initiative.

Part of the key to control is understanding individuals and assigning to them the type of work they enjoy. Control is therefore the interface between behaviour and the process of management (Mullins 1997).

Control through assessment and remuneration is explored in Chapter 18, and control through financial and accounting systems has been examined in Chapter 5.

Summary

Now you have studied this chapter you should be able to:

- explain the role and functions of a manger;

- discuss how managers can be most effective in terms of their management of employees;

- evaluate the different approaches to effective leadership;

- understand the meaning of the terms power, empowerment, authority and control.

References

Adair J (1979) *Action Centred Leadership*, Gower

Bass B M (1990) *Bass and Stodgill's Handbook of Leadership*, Free Press

Blake R R & Mouton J S (1984) *The Managerial Grid*, Gulf Publishing Company

Boyatzis R (1982) *The Competent Manager*, John Wiley

Etzioni A (1975) *A Comparative Study of Complex Organizations*, Free Press

Fayol H (1949) *General and Industrial Management*, Pitman Publishing

Fiedler F E (1967) *A Theory of Leadership Effectiveness*, McGraw Hill

Foucault M (1979) *Discipline and Punishment*, Penguin

French J R P and Raven B (1959) 'The bases of social power' in D Cartwright ed. *Studies in Social Power*, Institute for Social Research

McGregor D (1960) *The Human Side of the Enterprise*, McGraw Hill

McKenna E (1991) *Business Psychology and Organizational Behaviour*, Lawrence Erhlbaum

Mintzberg H (1979) *The Structuring of Organizations*, Prentice Hall

Tannenbaum R & Schmidt W H (1973) 'How to choose a leadership pattern', *Harvard Business Review* May-June, pp 162-175

Weber M (1947) *The Theory of Social and Economic Organization*, Free Press

11

MOTIVATION

Objectives

After studying this chapter you should be able to:

● Describe the main theories of motivation;

● Understand the limitations of theoretical approaches to the motivation of colleagues;

● Recognize the interrelationship between motivation and reward within organizations;

● Describe how job design can help the motivation of staff

● Choose approaches to the motivation of colleagues.

1   What is Meant by 'Motivation'

In relation to 'motivation' a manager is concerned with either or both of two things:

a)   the reasons why a human being acts in a certain way, and

b)   how to channel the efforts of colleagues towards the achievement of organizational goals.

It is important to recognize that motivation impacts on the relationship between the manager and many categories of 'colleague'. The colleague is most often – and readily – identified as a subordinate – but the term, in relation to 'motivation', could also include peers, bosses, customers and other stakeholders. For the purposes of this chapter, for the sake of simplicity, motivation will be explained in the context of the boss/subordinate relationship.

The concept of motivation – as an area for management – is fundamentally dependent upon two assumptions:

a)   that the subordinate is prepared to contribute his or her effort, and

b)   that it is possible for that effort to be channelled in a particular direction.

Although both of these assumptions are open to question, it is helpful, initially, to proceed on the basis that they hold true for most people for most of the time.

2   Classical Approaches to Motivation

Early ideas on motivation stemmed from the work of theorists such as Adam Smith, author of *The Wealth of Nations*, a fundamental treatize on Economics. These ideas held that the prime motivators of man – remembering that in the early days of the industrial society work was predominantly a male occupation – were the pursuit of self-interest and the maximization of economic gain. In a practical sense these ideas were key to the scientific management principles expounded by Taylor, Urwick and the Gilbreths who held that 'the principal object of management should be to secure the maximum prosperity for the employer, coupled with the maximum prosperity of each employee'. (Taylor, 1947)

The principles of scientific management underlay Henry Ford's development of production-line approaches to manufacturing but the need to motivate personnel through maximizing their economic gain from their contribution of effort to a defined and repetitive task tended to be overlooked. This in itself is not surprising because these methods of manufacturing came into vogue around the time of the Depression – when economic gain could be equated with having a job – and the production-line approach is susceptible to careful cost management.

There are dangers in the modern world of work of reproducing the adverse effects of Fordism in the development of call centres which, once they are established, are frequently managed on the basis of controlling costs (through standardized responses and call-length targets) as opposed to a basis of providing a valued service to a customer or a basis of motivating a workforce.

3   Human Relations Approaches to Motivation

In the second half of the 1920s ideas about motivation that could operate as a counter-balance to the 'economic gain' approach began to be developed, most memorably through an investigation that became known as the Hawthorne Studies. These, at least in their later stages when they were conducted by researchers led by Elton Mayo, Professor of Industrial Research at Harvard, applied something akin to the 'scientific method' to a study of the effects on productivity of changes in working conditions. The generalized conclusions from the studies included the ideas that:

- the need to belong to a group and to have status within that group is a significant motivational factor – possibly more important than straightforward economic incentives, and

- informal groups at work develop their own norms and are thus significant determinants of employee behaviour.

The importance of the studies lay in the fact that they were based more on empirical observation than theoretical perception and that they revealed that the influences on an individual's deployment of effort were far more complex than Taylorist approaches suggested. They thus served to shift the focus of thought on motivation away from economic gain towards less tangible 'social' factors.

This dichotomy of approaches to motivation was neatly encapsulated by McGregor (1960) in which he contrasted 'Theory X' with 'Theory Y'.

Theory X assumes that man is lazy, basically immature, shirks responsibility, dislikes work and needs a combination of incentivization and threat in order to perform well.

By contrast Theory Y holds that man has a psychological need to work and thrives when given responsibility and the opportunity to achieve.

4   Maslow's Hierarchy of Needs

Abraham Maslow was, in a sense, a disciple of McGregor: having held a professorship at Brandeis University he returned to industry and studied the operation of Theory Y in a Californian electronics factory. He recognized that Theory Y was both too simple to explain fully what was involved in human motivation and that an overemphasis on Theory Y risked ignoring the beneficial aspects which were inherent in Theory X – namely the satisfaction of man's needs for structure and elements of certainty.

From this basis Maslow constructed his idea of the 'Hierarchy of Needs' which postulated that man – a needs-driven animal – was motivated to satisfy needs within five broad categories, always paying attention to the lowest unsatisfied level of need. Thus it was only after an individual's basic physiological needs had been satisfied – including needs for warmth, food, and sexual fulfilment, then for a safe and structured environment – that higher order needs for love, affection and a sense of belonging, esteem and self-actualization would operate as motivational factors. In this way Maslow was able to introduce a greater complexity to the social as opposed to economic factors that could influence man's choices in relation to his contribution of effort.

5   Herzberg's 'Two Factor' Theory

That these non-economic factors were important was given greater credence by the work of Herzberg (1968). This work was founded on an analysis of the feelings (expressed through completion of a questionnaire) of a statistically significant number of professionals who were asked to describe times when they felt exceptionally good about their work and times when they felt exceptionally bad about it.

This research disclosed that there was one group of factors that tended to predominate when the respondents were dissatisfied at work and a quite different group of factors that were evident when the respondents were more positive about their work.

Herzberg labelled those factors which led to feelings of satisfaction (which included achievement, recognition, responsibility, personal development and satisfaction in the nature of the work itself) 'motivators': those which were prevalent when the respondents were dissatisfied he labelled 'hygiene factors'. These included working conditions, company policy, salary, status and job security.

Most employees spend a significant part of their working lives operating – in motivational terms – at a 'level of nil-dissatisfaction'. If, during these periods, a hygiene factor becomes significant (for example, a change in company policy) the employee is likely to withdraw effort (in terms of quantity and/or quality) rather than contribute greater effort.

Herzberg himself indicated the connection between his ideas and those of Maslow by identifying that man has two sets of needs – those of an animal for food warmth, safety, security and the avoidance of pain, and those of a human for personal psychological growth, development and self-realization.

6   John Hunt – Motivational Profiles

Professor John Hunt of the London Business School (see *Managing People at Work*) further develops the complexity that is now evident in the non-economic motivational factors by identifying that the motivation profile of an individual will change in accordance with age, personality and circumstances.

Hunt built up a substantial database from responses to a 'Work Interests Schedule' which measured the relative importance to the individual of five areas of concern:

- Body
- Structure
- Relationships
- Significance (which has subsets of Recognition and Power)
- Fulfilment

He found that for the most part of their working lives most of his respondents were relatively more concerned with the 'higher order' areas of concern (relationships, significance and fulfilment) and thus had motivational profiles akin to the following:

Table 11.1: Motivational profiles

Relative Concern for . . .

BODY   STRUCTURE   RELATIONSHIPS   SIGNIFICANCE   FULFILMENT

This pattern was disrupted – significantly – during two sets of circumstances, which he labelled ' Mating' and 'Amateur Parenthood'. Mating relates to the period in life when respondents were making serious efforts to find a life-partner when, not surprisingly, relative concern for relationships and body increases – and concern for the other areas correspondingly decreases.

Similarly, when the first child is expected (and this applies to both sexes) relative concern for body, structure and relationships increases.

The significance of 'age' as a factor affecting the motivational profile is most clearly shown in males around the age of 45, at which point it is not uncommon for relative concern for body (which may manifest itself as a drive for fitness, or an engagement with participative sport, or an interest in food and wine as well as a straightforward concern for health) and relationships to increase while relative concern for significance and fulfilment decreases. This is a feature of what has come to be known as the 'mid-life crisis' which represents a period of reassessment of life-goals.

Not everyone experiences this phenomenon – many continue with the generally upward profile, seeing significance and fulfilment as of relatively greater concern. These differences are possibly explicable by the differences in the personalities of those concerned.

7   Expectancy Theory

The idea that there is no universally applicable model for 'motivation' is one that has become more appealing as the world of work has become both more global and more complex.

A useful model to deal with motivation as being particular to individuals is given by expectancy theory developed as a result of the work of Vroom, Porter and Lawler during the 1960s.

This deals with the relationship between 'effort', 'performance' and 'outcome' as shown below:

Table 11.2: Expectancy model

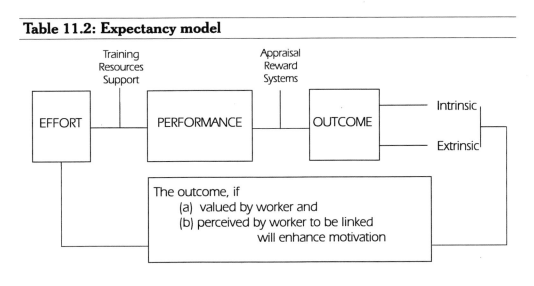

In essence expectancy points out that what the employee can contribute can be categorized as 'effort'. In today's world 'effort' would be defined to encompass all the attributes (skills, training, experience etc.) which the employee can bring to a task. In accordance with the theory, the employee will be prepared to contribute greater effort (in either or both of quantitative and qualitative terms) if he or she believes that this will lead to a desired outcome (such as a bonus) – or conversely that the absence of that increased effort will lead to an undesirable outcome (such as the termination of employment or lack of promotion).

The great contribution made by this theory is twofold.

Firstly it moves thinking away from the search for common motivational factors and focuses on what may be brought to bear by a manager to channel the efforts of individual subordinates. Secondly it highlights the importance of the links between 'effort'(what the subordinate can contribute) and 'performance' (what the organization wishes to manage) and between 'performance' and 'outcome'. The manager's responsibility is thus not only to strengthen the link between the outcome and the effort (e.g. by ensuring that the anticipated bonus materializes, or by recognizing the contribution of the subordinate) but also to ensure that there are no barriers that hinder the effort contributed by the subordinate from producing the performance desired by the organization (e.g. by ensuring clear targets are agreed, training given and necessary resources marshalled etc.).

8 Is 'Motivation' Worth Bothering about?

It could well be argued that, from the philosophical point of view, there is no justification for managers concerning themselves with attempting to motivate their subordinates.

At one end of the philosophical spectrum is the idea of determinism, which contrasts with the belief that man is possessed of free will.

Determinists hold that all 'events' are 'effects' – i.e. necessitated by earlier events. Thus everything that happens is an effect of a prior series of effects – one link in a chain of causation which is itself solid. As a result nothing which happens comes about because of or is influenced by any independent input. In the second epilogue to *War and Peace*, Tolstoy expounded his ideas that all actions taken by any man are predetermined by his character, upbringing and his experience of life up to the point of taking the action. Accordingly anyone knowing the complete history (but only someone knowing the complete history) of that man will be able to predict the action he will take. In this sense all that we do is predetermined.

By contrast the doctrine of free will suggests that all human actions are the results of the continued exercise and re-exercise of choice on the part of those taking the action. The implication of man having free will is that, although actions **may** be constrained by events from the past – i.e. are predetermined – this is not an unavoidable consequence of existence because we can each of us recognize that we have a choice and can exercise that choice in such a way as to free ourselves from the shackles of a determinist chain of causation.

For the manager as motivator both concepts – of determinism and of free will – are equally depressing. If the balance of truth is in favour of determinism then, although a motivator may be able to influence another person, this would only be one of a vast number of elements in the chain of causation leading to that person's action. Conversely, if man is possessed of free will then any influence that a motivator has is continually liable to be countermanded by subsequent choices made by the subject of the motivation. Neither of these prospects is encouraging if the objective of the motivation is to channel effort towards the achievement of particular goals.

In all probability, man's actions are neither fully free nor fully predetermined. There may be occasions when the range of possible actions open to us is severely constrained and the action that we actually take is a more or less inevitable consequence of the events we have experienced since conception (or at least since birth!). At other times we may be able to recognize the possibility of a completely unencumbered choice. On most occasions, however, we will probably find that our range of options is limited – or to put it the other way round – our freedom to act is constrained.

If this proposition is true, the theories and models of motivation outlined above may become more useful – but it is important to note that they will not necessarily be equally applicable in all circumstances. The key – in relation to motivation in the workplace – lies in a more careful analysis of why motivation is of importance.

9   Motivation Within Organizations

Most expositions of ideas on motivation are presented as if they seek to answer only one question – 'Why does man act in a particular way?'. In relation to the management of people at work in organizations it is probably necessary to answer three questions:

> 'Why does man work?'
>
> 'Why does man work for an organization?', and
>
> 'Why does man work hard for an organization?'

Looking at motivation in the light of these questions it is relatively easy to see a fit with the theories and models.

Maslow and to a lesser extent Hunt provide answers to the first of the questions. If man did not work then it would be difficult for him to deal with his basic physiological needs because work provides the means – either directly or indirectly through earning a medium of exchange – to supply warmth, shelter, food and whatever is necessary to attract a mate.

Man may have to work but does not have to work for an organization. Nevertheless working with other people –something that is readily accomplished consistently by working for an organization – enables man to satisfy needs for belonging and concerns for relationships. A combination of the ideas of Maslow regarding the need for some form of associative relationship and the experience of the Hawthorne experiments point to the power of the attraction of working within an organization as a motivational tool in itself.

Maslow's next order of needs contemplates that man – having established himself within a group – becomes 'egregious man' seeking to differentiate himself from the common herd and establish some mark of distinction. It is here that Herzberg's research indicates how esteem needs can be satisfied – partly through achievement within the job itself and partly through that achievement being recognized as worthy.

Herzberg is again helpful in answering the question 'Why do I work hard?' – which is often a matter of the intrinsic satisfaction of a job well done and recognized as such. The withdrawal of recognition – or failure of a boss to give it when the subordinate feels that it is due – is, in an organizational context, one of those aspects of 'company policy' that can be cited as a hygiene factor causing the subordinate to fail to work hard for the organization.

Although the general theories are helpful in gaining an understanding of the rationale that underlies the ways in which subordinates contribute their effort to an organization, it is expectancy theory that provides managers with a tool with which to encourage a high quality of contribution from the employee.

Part of the reason why expectancy is particularly useful lies in the way in which it can combine with the usual organizational systems for performance management, budgeting, training and appraisal, in order to provide supportive links between effort, performance and outcome.

The resources allocated during the budget setting process and enhanced by the provision of appropriate training can support the link between effort and performance. The link between performance and outcome is supported by any system that determines and clarifies what performance is required of the employee. Finally it is probably through the appraisal system that the link between outcome and the future effort of the employee is best managed both by recognizing the merit of past performance and requiring that attention is paid to the development needs of the appraisee.

10   Job Design and Motivation

Job design

The application of motivational theories has led to an increasing interest in job design and the effect of this on motivation and work performance. New job design tries to accommodate personal and social needs at work through the reorganization and restructuring of tasks. It therefore helps in enhancing personal satisfaction and makes best use of people (an expensive resource today). The content theories of motivation, especially those of Herzberg, assume a direct relationship between job satisfaction and improved performance. The process theories recognize the complexity of individuals and consider the relationship between satisfaction and performance in more detail.

The level of job satisfaction can be affected by a wide range of variables including: the individual (personality, education, etc.), social factors (the relationship between coworkers, groups, etc.), cultural factors (underlying attitudes, beliefs and values), the organization (its nature and size, formal structures) and the environment (economic and social factors).

In Chapter 6 the issue of employee control over the environment was explored and how methods of work advocated by the classical school could increase feelings of alienation and powerlessness. Much research work carried out in the 1960s and 1970s tried to develop new job designs and to increase the personal satisfaction of the employee derived from work, making the best use of people as a resource. In order to increase satisfaction these new job designs should emphasize, according to Hackman and Oldham (1980), three key areas:

- work should be experienced as meaningful, worthwhile and important;

- workers must experience that they are responsible for the work outcome and accountable for the products of their efforts;

- workers must determine how their efforts are working, the results achieved and whether they are satisfactory.

These three features are most likely to be achieved if there is present in the core activities of the job:

- *skill variety:* the degree to which a job requires the worker to perform activities that challenge a variety of skills and abilities;

- *task identity:* the degree to which a job requires the completion of a whole piece of work with a seen outcome;

- *task significance:* the degree to which the job has a perceivable impact on the lives of others;

- *autonomy:* the extent to which the worker has freedom in scheduling work and determining how it will be carried out;

- *feedback:* the degree to which the worker gets information about his or her efforts from the work or supervisors;

- *development:* the opportunity to develop in the job.

There was a major research study carried out by the Department of Employment into job design in the UK during the 1970s, which was entitled *On the Quality of Working Life*. The research involved establishing evidence about desirable task characteristics aimed at increasing job satisfaction and motivation. It suggested:

- combining tasks to create a coherent whole job, either using independent tasks or related ones, so that their performance makes a significant contribution to the job holder;

- providing feedback on performance both directly and through others;

- providing a degree of discretion and control in the timing sequence and pace of work and effort;

- including a degree of responsibility for outcomes.

Within the job there should be an opportunity for learning and problem solving within the individual's competence. It should be seen as leading towards a desirable future and provide opportunities for development in ways that are relevant to the individual. The job should also enable workers to contribute to the decisions that affect their jobs, while providing adequate resources and support and ensuring that goals and expectations are clear.

Within these criteria a number of different forms of new job design have evolved, including job rotation, job enlargement, group working and job enrichment.

Job rotation

This is perhaps the most basic form of individual job design. Job rotation involves moving a person from one job or task to another. It helps to add variety and relieve boredom in the short term because it offers a wider range of tasks to perform. Normally the tasks are very similar and once a routine is established a worker can become very bored again. Job rotation may add to the range of skills a person possesses, but they are not usually skills at a different level.

Some theorists would claim that it is not really job design because it does not attempt to restructure jobs, but rather gives a worker the opportunity to do different tasks.

Job enlargement

This emerged during the 1940s and 1950s as a response to high task specialization. It offers employees a greater variety of operations with longer cycle times, and it requires a wider range of skills. There is normally an enlargement of tasks horizontally as well as greater latitude given to workers to determine methods and procedures.

It is not always a popular technique when employed in organizations. Workers may view it as increasing the number of routine boring tasks, and as a means of increasing productivity and reducing the number of employees.

Job enrichment

The basis for this concept lies in Herzberg's two-factor theory of motivation. Motivators are intrinsic to the job and offer the opportunity for achievement, recognition, advancement, etc. Motivators determine the extent to which a person is satisfied by a job.

Job enrichment offers vertical job enlargement. Workers are given greater autonomy over the planning, execution and control of their own work. It increases the complexity of work and provides a more meaningful and challenging job. It would mean, for example, not only assembling a product but also pacing the work, receiving feedback on the product and checking its quality. It emphasizes greater control for the employee. As with job enlargement, some employees view this as worker intensification, rather than as an explicit organizational strategy of developing and motivating staff.

Group working

This emphasizes the achievement of the group through its work. The group assumes greater responsibility for the effective performance of the work. Specific goals are set, but the members decide how the goals are to be achieved and have greater choice and wider discretion over the planning and control of their work as a group. This technique ensures that the technological process is integrated with the social system and so becomes a socio-technical method.

The organization's choice of job design will ultimately depend on its philosophy and structure. Is it person-centred or job-centred? Does it aim to achieve technical efficiency or individual satisfaction through work? How much organizational control and managerial direction can be surrendered to individual authority and responsibility? These and similar factors will determine an organization's approach to job design and whether any change in redesign is truly possible.

More recently greater emphasis has been placed by organizations on autonomy and feedback rather than on other core dimensions of job design. Many organizations have introduced empowerment, and so given greater authority for action to employees. The area of empowerment has been explored in greater detail in Chapter 7.

Before focusing upon the extrinsic reward systems used by organizations and how they are implemented, the next section will examine the procedures that allow an organization to establish relative criteria for the value of a job. These processes are termed job evaluation systems.

Summary

Now that you have studied this chapter you should be able to

- Critically evaluate ideas on motivation;

- Recognize factors impacting on personal motivation;

- Recognize the relationship between 'reward' and 'effort';

- Choose approaches to enhance the prospect of motivating others.

References

Taylor FW *Scientific Management* (1947) Harper and Row

McGregor *The Human Side of Enterprize* (1960) McGraw-Hill

Herzberg F (1968) 'How Do You Motivate Employees?' *Harvard Business Review,*

12

MANAGEMENT OF STRESS

Objectives

After studying this chapter you should be able to:

● Explain the mechanism of stress;

● Describe strategies and tactics for the management of stress;

● Understand the significance of roles in relation to stress management;

● Choose approaches to the management of personal stress.

1 Definition

Stress is a concept that is known to engineers, doctors, psychologists, chemists, biologists and no doubt many others including managers; each group will come up with its own definition of what constitutes stress, but there is no universal easily accessible definition. In the world of management it is probably easiest to think of stress as being present when an individual has 'more than [s]he can cope with'.

It may also be sensible to recognize that 'stress' and 'pressure' are not synonymous. It is not unusual for the criteria for selection for a job to include 'an ability to work under pressure' – but they are unlikely to require 'an ability to work under stress'. In this sense 'pressure' is positive whereas 'stress' has only negative connotations. That having been said, working for long periods under relentless pressure may be stressful.

Stress results from the interaction between elements that are outside the individual – which are labelled 'stressors' – and elements that are inside the individual – initially the individual's capacity to deal with the stressors (which is probably fundamentally dependent upon the individual's personality) and secondly the body chemistry of the individual.

The influence of personality is important in that different people react to stressors in different ways. What may be a major catastrophe for one individual may be only a mild irritant to another.

The fact that the interaction between a stressor and the individual manifests itself at a chemical level within the individual's body is particularly important: the reason why stress leads to ill health stems from the fact that this interaction in an individual who is stressed produces surges of hormones within the body (principally adrenaline and noradrenaline, the 'fight or flight' hormones) which in turn lead to irreversible effects on body cells

2   Stressors

The stressors that operate in our lives are likely to be different from one individual to another but they will fall into one of four broad categories:

OVERLOAD   whereby the individual has too much work to do or too many 'roles' to play;

UNDERLOAD   whereby the individual has too little work to do or too few 'roles' to play;

FRUSTRATION   whereby the individual is unable to control his or her own environment to the extent of being able to achieve objectives; or experiences stress within the roles he or she is expected to carry out;

CHANGE   whereby the individual finds that the stability of his or her existence is disrupted by things beyond his or her control

In this context a 'role' is a bundle of expectations of a relationship with another person – i.e. what you expect of the other person and what the other person expects of you. A discussion of the significance of roles in relation to the management of stress appears later in this chapter (see sections 7 - 9 below).

The effect of the operation of a number of stressors on the life of any one individual is cumulative, so that an apparently trivial incident may provoke a traumatic reaction because it is the latest in a long chain of stressors.

It is perhaps important to recognize that stressors are part of the fabric of everyday life – at least in Western societies. Two psychologists, Holmes and Rahe (1967), produced a rating of different life events – from those that occur regularly (e.g. Christmas and holidays) to those that one encounters rarely if at all (e.g. being sacked, going to jail, suffering bereavement). Each of 42 different life events was given a score determined by the likelihood that it would operate as a stressor. The highest score (100) was given to the death of a spouse, while Christmas was assigned a score of 11. Holmes and Rahe reckoned that the effect of a life event could persist for 18 months to two years and that an accumulated score of 150 or more gave a 50% chance of a major health breakdown within a two-year period.

Consider the following events and scores:

Event	Score	
Separation from long-standing partner	65	
Major change in financial circumstances	38	
Taking on a relatively large mortgage	31	
Major change in living conditions	25	
Total	159	

Notice how these life events seem to go together in the sense that if two long-standing partners decide to go their separate ways, the other three events will probably become part of the life of at least one of them. Already the score exceeds 150 and there are another 37 life events identified by Holmes and Rahe as having the propensity to act as a stressor which can add further to this score.

The importance of this research lies in the ability that it gives us as individuals to anticipate and manage the stress levels in our lives. Broadly speaking the strategy should be that if there is an impending major change in life at work – new job, new boss, new responsibilities etc. – it makes sense not to seek opportunities for change in life outside work, and *vice versa*.

3   Personality

The effect of personality was most readily explained by Friedman and Rosenheim who suggested that mankind could be divided into two types:

- Type 'A' – people who were competitive, thrusting, dynamic, impatient, sensitive to pressure, tense, and

- Type 'B' – people who were patient, relaxed, calm, saw lengthy time horizons and were 'laid back'

Type A personalities are easily identified as the lifeblood of corporate existence – the self-starters with the entrepreneurial spirit eager to win business etc. The trouble is that their behaviour has been associated in several research studies with unhealthy symptoms (smoking, excessive drinking, high blood pressure and high cholesterol). One study of American men in their forties identified that those with Type A personalities had 6.5 times the incidence of coronary heart disease in comparison with Type B men.

4   Symptoms of Stress

The ways in which we as individuals exhibit symptoms of stress vary. The British Medical Association booklet *Coping with Stress* cites the following as being among the common reactions:

Feeling of being under pressure	Inability to relax
Feeling mentally drained	Feeling frightened constantly
Irritability	Conflict
Aggression	Inability to concentrate
Increased tearfulness	Increased fussiness
Increased indecision	Impulses to run and hide
Fear of fainting	Fear of failure
Lack of enjoyment	Fear of social embarrassment
Change in appetite	Change in sleep patterns
Increased headaches	Indigestion
Constipation	Diarrhoea
Back pain	'Butterflies' in the stomach
Nausea	Weakness in the limbs
Muscle tension	Tiredness
Sweating	Fidgeting

Notice that many of these reactions are contradictory, and that they are not the exclusive province of stress – each can be the symptom of some other disorder. This implies that recognizing stress both in ourselves and in others is not easy – but the clues are likely to lie in **significant behavioural changes over time**.

5 Managing Stress – Strategies

AWARENESS Be aware of what for you constitutes a stressor; and of what your typical reaction to stress is. If you know how you typically react then you can watch for that or those reactions and from them determine what it is that stresses you.

DIET A sensible diet is helpful both in limiting the chances of succumbing to stress-related diseases and in limiting the effects of such illnesses. The main principles are to eat to maintain a sensible body weight; to eat fewer fatty foods; increase dietary fibre; eat more cereals, pulses, fruits and vegetables; eat less sugar and salt. A watch should be maintained on the consumption of caffeine through drinking coffee and tea.

FITNESS It is preferable to maintain a reasonable level of fitness by taking some exercise on a regular basis – a 20-minute session, three times a week is what is recommended as adequate. The principle of the approach to the exercise is that it should stimulate the heart (therefore leave you moderately 'puffed'), address suppleness and build up muscle tone in those muscles – apart from the heart – that are important to you, principally the leg muscles.

BALANCE   Getting an appropriate balance between the various areas of life is particularly important. You have responsibilities to your family, to other close relationships, to your employer but most of all to yourself. Stress often arises when the balance between these areas goes astray, and it is therefore important for each individual to sort out what really matters in his or her life. These priorities may, of course, change at different stages in life.

SUPPORT   One of the most effective ways of managing stress is to ensure that there is strong and reliable social support available with whom daily problems can be articulated. This is most often found within family relationships, but if these are not available friends and mutual support groups may provide what is needed. The key contribution made by the supporter is simply listening to what is said – there does not need to be any attempt to solve problems because the major benefits flow from the simple articulation of one's feelings about the events which crowd into one's life and which may act as stressors.

ABUSE   Tobacco and drugs of dependence are not helpful in combating the effects of stress and should be avoided completely. The consumption of alcohol should be carefully managed. It now seems well established that moderate consumption of alcohol increases an individual's chance of avoiding stress-related illness – in comparison with those who avoid alcohol completely and those who indulge immoderately. This then begs the question 'What is moderate consumption?' For males the suggested intake is 28 units per week and for females 21 units. A unit of alcohol is equivalent to one measure of spirits, one glass of wine or half a pint of beer. For a strategy of moderate consumption to be effective, the consumption should be spread more or less evenly through the week (rather than saved up for a binge at the weekend) and days of consumption should be interspersed with alcohol-free days.

6   Managing Stress – Tactics

As noted above some pressure in our lives is probably beneficial because it enhances our performance; therefore it is useful to acquire techniques that help to control the boundary between pressure and stress.

Among the best ways of doing this are:

BREATHING   Watch sports players who are about to perform some important individual feat, for example a goal kick at rugby. As part of the preparation the kicker will generally take a couple of deliberate deep breaths. The effect of this is calming mentally in that the concentration is on the breathing – momentarily at least – and stimulating physically in that more oxygen is being made available both for the muscles and the brain. The same technique can be applied to any anxiety-provoking situation, e.g. an important interview, presentation or exam!

RELAXATION   This involves the deliberate attempt to relax muscles by initially tensing them and then allowing them to relax completely. Again there is a twin benefit in that not only is there a general release of tension within the muscles but also, because there is a need to concentrate on the exercise, the mind relaxes. It is a useful technique for coping with that modern stressor the tailback!

ASSERTIVENESS Much stress is caused because of our tendency to give too much credence to the rights of other people over the rights of ourselves. Thus when the boss dumps work on us late in the afternoon we accept it and subsequently castigate ourselves for having acquiesced and perhaps missed an opportunity to do something else. Also we tend to criticize ourselves for not seizing opportunities to project our own viewpoints. Assertiveness teaches that in situations such as these we have a choice – and as long as we positively exercise that choice (which may mean that we choose not to say anything, or we choose to accept the work from our boss) we are less likely to move into a spiral of self-criticism and thus are better able to manage stress.

7   Roles

One of the key points to recognize in relation to the management of stress is that stress does not arise only as a result of an individual having to undertake too much **work**. Underload is also a potential stressor and both overload and underload can refer to 'roles' as well as work.

Remembering the definition of role as a bundle of expectations of a relationship, think for a moment about the roles played by a typical individual. These may include:

manager, subordinate, supplier, customer, colleague, adviser, counsellor, mentor (in relation to the world of work),

plus: child, parent, spouse, friend, confidante, sibling, neighbour, team member, club/association member etc. (in the world outside work).

It is often a useful exercise to identify and chart the role set of an individual – identified for these purposes as the 'focal individual'. This means representing diagrammatically all those people with whom the individual has more than merely trivial interactions. At its most sophisticated such a chart – with the focal individual at its centre – shows the people who are of greatest importance to that individual relatively close to the centre and those who consume more of the individual's 'energy' relatively large. When such an exercise is undertaken it is often quite surprising how many relationships are identified and how they are seen by the individual in terms of importance and energy consumption.

The importance of this in relation to the management of stress is twofold.

8   Role Stress

Firstly, there are problems that are inherent within the roles which, as individuals, we are required to fulfil. These (which are most likely to fall within the 'frustration' category of stressors) can be classified as follows:

ROLE AMBIGUITY	This arises when there is uncertainty in the minds of people within the role set as to precisely what the role of the focal individual is at any particular time. At work this often manifests itself as uncertainty about the scope of responsibility or about others' expectations of the focal individual's performance. These frequently need to be addressed through the incorporation of greater clarity into the role definition.
ROLE INCOMPATIBILITY	This arises when the expectations within the role set are well known but incorporate inconsistencies. For example when there is a clash between the corporate management style and the natural management style of the focal individual – or between the organization's ethical philosophy and the individual's ethics. Role incompatibility can be managed by the individual making a decision as to which of the incompatible elements he or she should give priority or by seeking a resolution to the incompatibility from the parties involved.
ROLE CONFLICT	This occurs when it is necessary for the individual to carry out more than one role in the same situation. The expectations in relation to each of the roles are quite clear but they conflict with each other. An example is where a role at work may require the individual to be present until a particular task is completed on the very evening when, in the role of parent, the individual is required to be at a child's school performance. Role conflict can be managed by 'compartmentalization' so that particular roles are consigned to particular areas of the individual's life – e.g. 'Between Monday and Friday

I will give the organization what it demands but my weekends will be devoted to my family'. Another approach is to assign priority to particular roles so that when there is a role conflict the decision as to which to pursue can be made in accordance with these priorities.

9 Role Overload and Underload

Secondly, individuals can become stressed by virtue of an overload or an underload of roles.

Role overload can arise from the sheer volume of roles that an individual is required to carry out – the clearest example of this is within the job of a school teacher who, within a large school, may have to live up to the expectations of more than 1,000 pupils. Role overload can also arise from an individual having too many **significant** roles to fulfil at any one time. For example the individual may need to satisfy the expectations of a demanding boss, a problem teenage child, an elderly parent needing care and attention and a partner energetically pursuing a career. Faced with a role set including important and 'energy-consuming' roles such as these, it is easy to imagine how stress can ensue unless the competing expectations can in some way be managed.

Not everyone appreciates that stress can also arise as a result of underload – either of work or of roles until the possible effect of the loss of a role or roles which are of importance to the individual is recognized. The most obvious example of this is bereavement, particularly of an elderly spouse who was probably the single most important relationship in the life of the surviving focal individual. Retirement or redundancy both lead to significant decreases in the amount of work and the number of roles impacting on the life of the individual such that the whole approach to life may require adjustment – and one of the possible reactions has frequently been found to be a breakdown in health.

10 Social Perspective

We are often told that within Western society many days of work are lost to stress-related illness and that stress within the workplace is increasing. It is questionable that this is in fact the case because there is little by way of data to justify these conclusions. Particularly within the financial services industry there has not been a trend of increased deaths in harness, ill-health retirements, deaths shortly after retirement, absence through illness – i.e. the usual indicators of an increase in stress levels.

Although to some extent this may result from a want of sound statistical data it is also probably fair to say that as a society our management of stress is improving at three levels.

a.   More and more organizations are taking an enlightened attitude to the management of stress because it is recognized that in times of unprecedented change, work becomes more stressful and therefore the more that individuals are able to manage their own stress the more likely it is that they will avoid stress-related illness.

b.   Managers are similarly more sensitive to the possibility of stress within their own work teams and are prepared to adjust approaches in order to prevent pressure from escalating to stress and thus to ensure that overall productivity remains high.

c.   Individuals are now more aware – possibly as a result of organizational education programmes – of the causes and effects of stress and of the means of managing stress within their own lives.

The work of, for example, Holmes and Rahe helps people to be able to anticipate the effect upon their personality of the various life events identified as potential stressors. Similarly they are aware and can apply the strategies and tactics for managing stress.

Summary

Now that you have studied this chapter you should be able to:

- Participate knowledgeably in discussions relating to stress management;
- Critically evaluate stress management programmes;
- Be in control of personal stress.

References

T Holmes and R Rahe *The Social Readjustment Scale* (1967) Journal of Psychosomatic Research, 11. Pergamon Press

13

COMMUNICATION AND NEGOTIATION

Objectives

After studying this chapter you should be able to:

- Describe the process of communication;

- Identify barriers to effective communication;

- Plan how best to deal with these barriers;

- Describe organizational approaches to communication;

- Recognize the drawbacks of structures of communication within groups and between individuals;

- Distinguish between 'bargaining' and 'building a wise solution';

- Recognize how personality impacts on interpersonal negotiation;

- Develop strategies for effective negotiation.

1   The Process of Communication

Communication has been defined as 'The process whereby messages are transmitted from one person to another' (Williamson (1981)). At its simplest this can be represented diagrammatically as

Sender ➡   Medium of transmission   ➡   Receiver

Not surprisingly the actual process of communication is not as simple as suggested by this diagram because the message to be transmitted never starts life in a form that is acceptable to the medium of transmission. If it did then there would be no need for a medium of transmission because the message could be relayed directly from sender to receiver.

This means that before the medium of transmission can be accessed the message has to be translated – or encoded – into an acceptable form (for example 'words'); similarly before the receiver can access the message it has to be decoded. A further complication arises because it is improbable that the process of encoding, transmission and decoding is instantaneous and therefore there is the possibility of 'interference' – often referred to as 'noise' – distorting the message.

2 Barriers to Effective Communication

Barriers can arise within each of the elements in the communication process.

The sender may distort the communication by:

- not being clear as to what has to be communicated;

- ineptly choosing words that do not accurately reflect the idea/concept he or she wishes to convey;

- choosing words that intended recipients cannot understand;

- choosing words that provoke – wholly or partly – an emotional response in the recipient[s];

- choosing an inappropriate medium (e.g. text messaging instructions that would benefit from discussion);

- sending mixed messages simultaneously (e.g. by there being incongruence between the verbal message and non-verbal signals, both of which are available to the receiver).

'Noise' may corrupt the communication by:

- physically impairing the receiver's ability to receive the message – or the sender's capacity to receive feedback;

- physical failure of the medium of transmission (e.g. disruption of a telephone network or system downtime);

- limiting the encoding/decoding capabilities of the sender and receiver (e.g. the classic, probably apocryphal, but illustrative example from the First World War when allegedly the radio message 'Send reinforcements, we're going to advance' was interpreted as 'Send three and fourpence, we're going to a dance');

- obscuring the message within a welter of other communications (e.g. having to deal with a very large number of voice mail and e-mail messages following the return from holiday).

The recipient may contribute to communication difficulties by:

- not being in an appropriate state to receive the message (e.g. because of concentrating on some other task);

- not wishing to receive a message from that sender (e.g. bills!);

- filtering out elements of the message he or she does not wish to deal with;

- having a mind set that does not admit of the substance of the message – and therefore prevents the receiver from appreciating the sender's standpoint.

The above list is illustrative of the many difficulties that can impede accurate communication. It implies that both sender and recipient should take steps to give every chance that these barriers can be overcome.

3 Overcoming Barriers to Communication

The sender should:

- have a definite, clear objective: others will have a far greater chance of understanding the communication if the sender has articulated – at least internally – what he or she wants to achieve by the communication;

- plan the communication: it is better if, at the outset, the sender has thought about **what** is to be communicated; to **whom** it is to be communicated and **how** it is to be communicated;

- ensure that all elements of the communication (words, tone, non-verbal signals, medium, environment etc.) fit with each other and with the subject matter of the communication;

- think about the receiver[s] and the situation in which he or she will be when the message is received;

- anticipate reactions to the message and cater for these – if appropriate – within the message or choice of medium;

- practise;

- seek and work with feedback from recipients.

The receiver should:

- be aware of the contribution he or she is making to the communication by way of feelings about the sender and/or medium and of the prejudice which, inevitably, he or she brings to the receipt of the message;

- listen attentively, or – more broadly – receive the message actively rather than passively;

- check out anything that is not clearly understood;

- give feedback to the sender so that the sender can ascertain that what has been communicated is what was meant to be communicated.

4 Communication within Organizations

There are few organizations within the financial services industry that do not depend to some extent on the speed and accuracy of their communications to maintain their competitive edge.

The restructuring of the industry has to a large extent been founded upon the introduction into the commercial world of information technology which has both enhanced the communication capability of organizations within the industry and hindered the development of those organizations which were unable, quickly, to adjust their systems to meet the demands of the modern customer.

Financial institutions had grown in the past partly by virtue of their capacities to run elaborate paper-based communication systems. The advent of information technology, coinciding as it did with deregulation of the industry, disadvantaged the traditional institutions in two ways:

a)   they were unable, quickly, to found business strategies on electronic communication methodologies partly because of entrenched patterns of thinking and partly because of the sheer size of their potential databases;

b)   the emergent IT industry was unable to supply them with products that would meet their future requirements while preserving their existing data unscathed and accessible.

As a consequence, although having embraced the technological revolution wholeheartedly, many financial service institutions find themselves lumbered with less than ideal communication systems and the prospect of a continuing massive investment requirement to bring and keep their approaches to communication up to date.

The importance of this observation is twofold. In the first place much of the research undertaken on communication within organizations predates the advent of extensive use of information technology. Secondly any generalist description of communication systems will be of limited applicability having regard to the prevalence and dynamic nature of communications technology.

That having been said, there are some fundamental points that can be made about organizational communication.

5   Media of Organizational Communication

Given the definition of communication it is unproductive to restrict thinking about organizational communication to traditional media – such as memoranda, e-mails, telephone systems etc.

Among the media in general use within large organizations are:

Advertisements	General décor	Performance indicators
Annual reports	House magazines	Policy statements
Budget statements	Information circulars	Press leaks
Business objectives	Job descriptions	Procedures manuals
Cascades	Meetings minutes	Rule books
Clear desk policies	Mission statements	Strategy papers

Codes of behaviour	Notices	Technical circulars
Dear colleague letters	Operational plans	Training sessions
Evaluation reports	Pay cheques	Video and audio conferencing

This list even ignores the medium which, by all accounts, is the most popular means of communication within organizations, namely the 'grapevine' – the loose network of connections (or the network of loose connections) between employees whereby information – particularly in the form of gossip, rumour and tittle-tattle – is passed rapidly around the organization.

The fact that the grapevine peddles gossip etc. does not in any way demean its value as a method for rapid – and often accurate – dissemination of information. Gossip etc. generally incorporates elements of truth with the addition of embellishments which usually tend to move its substance further from reality. Once this concept is grasped then it becomes relatively easy to distinguish between the elements of the gossip that are potentially substantial and those that are mere persiflage – provided that two key points are known:

a) the source of the rumour – and hence his or her reliability, and

b) the proximity of the source to the part of the organization with which the rumour is concerned.

In an organization with modern communication systems the possibility of broadcast messages through e-mail or text messaging means that the use of the grapevine can become ever more efficient – but far less fun!

6 The Direction of Communication

The grapevine is an example of lateral communication within an organization. Information within an organization can also flow vertically both upwards and downwards.

Downward channels tend to reflect the hierarchy of the organization and are used to facilitate the information flows from the top or centre of the organization (or part of the organization) to staff.

Katz and Kahn specify five elements that may bear upon the importance of downward communication to the organization:

1. Job instruction: subordinates are informed as to what they are expected to do.

2. Rationale for the task: the subordinate's task is placed in context by virtue of its relationship to other tasks that are being accomplished within the organization.

3. Procedures and practices: the ways in which task elements are to be performed are communicated to the workforce.

4. Feedback: whereby individual workers get to know how the organization views their performance.

5. Ideology: securing the emotional involvement of the employees is an important element of downward communication.

From this list it can be seen that downward communication is by and large concerned with either the 'big picture' (ideology) or with the microcosm of the employee's task (elements 1 to 4). This dichotomy has probably been reinforced by moves in the 1990s to 'downsize and empower' largely by removing middle management which, on the Katz and Kahn analysis, has no specific function to play in respect of downward communication.

Traditionally middle management did have important roles to play in relation to upward and lateral communication.

Upward communication can fall into one of two categories – 'hard' or 'soft'. The hard category is concerned with the vital information that senior management needs in order to ensure that strategy can be delivered. This is the information that is generally gathered through the organization's budgetary and management information systems (see Chapter 5).

The soft category is what in Braddick's (1987) words 'helps senior managers to estimate the motivation and morale of people lower down the organization and to have some feeling for the likely responses to possible changes'. Middle management at least had the potential to provide a conduit for communication of these aspects up to senior management. Where middle management no longer exists, there is an additional premium placed either on more formal upward communication channels – e.g. appraisal and exit interviews – or on effective human resource management systems to ensure that appropriate staff with appropriate attitudes (and only such staff) are in place to meet the challenges set by senior management.

Lateral communication also provided a rationale for the existence of middle management, particularly in bureaucracies. This was because much of the communication across departmental or functional boundaries was channelled up through the management hierarchy and across the organization at middle-management level. This communication was, however, generally paper-based. The advent of networked communication systems facilitated speedy communication between a sender and a number of recipients located in disparate parts of the organization. It also meant that new protocols for communication had to be devised which could match the speed of decision-making to the speed of communication without overburdening key recipients.

7   Negotiation – Introduction

There are three aspects of what may be termed 'negotiation' with which managers are likely to become involved:

a. working on behalf of their team, unit, department, division, organization etc. to secure an advantageous position generally in relation to the use of a resource or resources – 'bargaining';

b. again working on behalf of their team etc. but this time working with another team, unit, department, division or organization in order to arrive at a position which is mutually advantageous – 'building a wise solution', and

c.   at the interpersonal level, seeking to secure a commitment from another person to act in a certain way.

Each of these aspects of negotiation requires an approach that is different from that required by the other two, but this distinction between approaches is rarely appreciated.

8   Bargaining

		The other side	
		Win	Lose
Our side	Win		✔
	Lose		

The above diagram represents the traditional view of what negotiation is about: it is confrontational and the essence of successful negotiation is to win. If one of the parties to the negotiation is to win then the other party will be the loser – the failed negotiator will have put his team, unit etc. in a disadvantageous position.

In reality this model is encountered more at the stage of planning the negotiation than at the stage of assessing the outcome of the negotiation. This outcome is more likely to fall into one of two categories:

● Lose/lose – neither side makes any concessions that are acceptable to the other side and as a result neither side gains any advantage from the process – there is a breakdown of negotiation;

● Each of the two sides scores a series of 'wins' in different aspects of the negotiation with the result that both sides feel satisfied at the end – although in all probability both sides have conceded more than they originally planned to do.

This indicates another key aspect of bargaining, namely that it will probably involve concessions: it is vital that this point is appreciated when the bargaining is being planned.

The idea that bargaining should be planned suggests that there are distinct stages that apply to the process. These are:

1.   Planning

2.   Statement of initial positions

3.   Clarifying points identified in the statement of initial positions

4.   Bargaining itself

5.   Closing.

Planning – The homily 'To fail to plan is to plan to fail' is particularly applicable to bargaining given that an essential ingredient to the process is concession. Planning should incorporate anticipation of the other side's position and arguments; an appreciation of the strengths and weaknesses of our side's arguments and an analysis of the aims of the bargaining from the point of view of which of the aims are essential and which are merely desirable. The model below illustrates that in the planning stage thought should be given to what will load into the area of concession – i.e. desirable as opposed to essential objectives.

Planning further involves attempting to identify those issues that the other side is likely to raise and securing the information which will be necessary to enable those issues to be dealt with.

| Our side | Most desired outcome | Area of Concession | *Bargaining area* | Least desired outcome |
| Other side | Least desired outcome | *Bargaining area* | Area of Concession | Most desired outcome |

Statement of initial position During this stage the two sides state clearly and without too many arguments what they require from the negotiation.

Clarifying Having listened to the other side's initial statement it will probably be necessary to explore precisely what is meant by some of the terms used or within some of the objectives that have been stated. It is particularly important that this should be done both at an early stage and thoroughly. A possible consequence of not clarifying is that eventually an agreement is reached on what both sides have assumed to be the key areas while an issue which is important to one side has been overlooked or sidelined only to re-emerge at a late stage as a significant stumbling block to overall agreement.

Bargaining itself Sensible ground rules for this stage include:

● Remain flexible

● Do not revisit areas where agreement has already been reached

● Work to a definite and agreed deadline

Research into the behaviours of skilled negotiators suggests that the following should be avoided:

● Things that will irritate the other side – for example trite phrases such as 'our fair and reasonable offer': more generally evaluative words (e.g. 'fair' and 'reasonable'). These are avoided because they imply the opposite about the other side and impose value judgements on the substance of the negotiation with which the other side, almost by definition, cannot agree.

● Defend/attack spirals: these start with mild insults aimed at the other side's offer, tactics, behaviour or personalities, which then expand into less than mild insults which, with vituperative responses from the other side, lead to a trading of insults which move the process away from the object of the negotiation.

- Counter proposals: it is better to deal with the proposal put forward by the other side than to implicitly reject it by proposing something else.

- Multiple arguments: a natural tendency is to think that the more arguments in favour of a proposition the better, however arguments are not likely to be equally strong and putting forward many arguments means that some of them will be relatively weak and can therefore be attacked more readily by the other side. Skilled negotiators tend to select their strongest argument and rely upon it.

Among the behaviours favoured by good negotiators are:

- Flagging: making it clear to the other side what it is you are about to do – e.g. 'I think it best if at this point we summarize'.

- Testing understanding: check that anything which is apparently agreed means the same to both sides.

- Motives commentary: explain to the other party why you want a particular outcome from the exercise – this avoids them attributing possibly incorrect motives to you.

Closing When an agreement has been reached it is vital that it is summarized in words that are agreed by both sides. Any areas where there is not an accord should be revisited in order to ensure that the entire process is not vitiated. It is sensible to confirm that your side will produce and circulate notes of what has been agreed.

9 Building a Wise Solution

The concept of building a wise solution is frequently thought of as being represented by the following diagram:

		The other side	
		Win	Lose
Our side	Win	✔	
	Lose		

In common parlance this is 'going for a win/win position'. It is however counterproductive to think in these terms when contemplating building a wise solution. This is because the possibility of 'win/win' implies the possibility of 'win/lose', which should be no part of the process of discovering the wise solution.

The essential difference between bargaining and building a wise solution is that bargaining is founded upon what is known as 'solution-driven thinking'. Thus each side preparing to bargain recognizes that there is a problem (in the broadest sense), derives a solution to that problem which favours that side and then seeks to gain the other side's agreement to that solution.

When faced with a problem that is complex – and this is frequently the case when negotiation is needed – there are at least two things that are not known at the outset; (a) what is the solution and (b) how to move from the problem to the solution. This implies that when faced with a problem, particularly a complex problem, it is better if the process of moving from problem to solution is not founded upon 'solution-driven thinking' because, apart from all other considerations, this may mean that the solution eventually agreed is not the most appropriate one in all the circumstances.

The idea in building a wise solution is to move away from solution-driven thinking and the confrontation of bargaining in order to derive a mutually beneficial result – or, at least, a result that best meets the interests of all parties.

Parties to this approach meet with a view of coming to a complete understanding of the problem they face before attempting to derive a solution. Having understood the problem, a solution is built that addresses each of the elements of the problem in a way that does not disadvantage either party vis-à-vis each other.

By way of illustration, consider an organization which has hitherto provided in-house catering for its staff and now wishes to outsource this operation.

One approach to the problem of outsourcing the service provision would be to draw up a specification of the service required that is published to possible suppliers who are invited to submit, competitively, proposals as to how the specification would be met. From these suppliers one is chosen and a deal then negotiated between the supplier and the organization in which the organization seeks to secure the least cost disadvantage to itself.

Once the supplier is installed the management of the relationship with the organization passes from the catering supplier's sales/negotiating function to its service function – which is required to make a profit from the operation and therefore finds ways and means (portion control and cheaper ingredients for example) to find the required margin within the price that was negotiated.

The above represents the bargaining approach. If, as an alternative, a building a wise solution approach is taken the catering supplier would be identified far earlier in the process of developing a specification (this can still be done on the basis of competition between potential suppliers). Subsequently the supplier would work with the organization in developing the specification that will form the basis of the catering contract and the organization would discover through dialogue with the supplier the implications on the level of service of any decisions taken with regard to the price paid. Thus the organization appreciates the problem from the supplier's viewpoint and eventually derives a solution the consequences of which for its own personnel are fully understood.

10   Interpersonal Negotiation

In managerial situations many human interactions that involve one party acting in accordance with the wishes of another are based upon the power relationship between the two parties. Where, however, there is no power relationship, or the power vested in the two parties is equivalent, it may be necessary for there to be some element of negotiation in order for the two parties to act in accord.

A useful model for interpersonal negotiation divides humanity into three categories, as illustrated in the following diagram:

Figure 13.1: Interpersonal negotiation

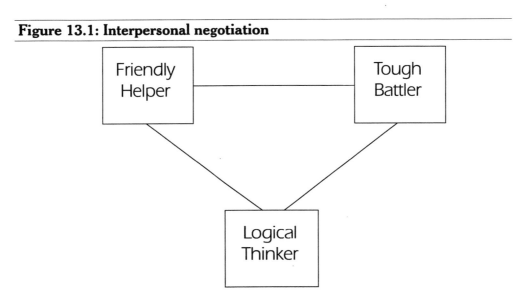

Each category requires a different negotiating approach, as indicated by the label attached to the category.

Friendly Helpers are best approached from the basic position 'I have a problem and I need your help in resolving it ...';

Tough Battlers are best approached from the basic position 'I need your abilities to make this happen ...', and

Logical Thinkers are best approached from the basic position 'All things considered the rational thing for us to do here is ...'.

The key to using this model is to know the party whose commitment you wish to harness well enough to be able to identify the category into which he or she fits and then to plan an appropriate approach. Where the other party is not so well known it may be necessary to plan all three approaches and test them to ascertain which one is going to work.

Summary

Now that you have studied this chapter you should be able to:

- Understand the process of communication;
- Recognize and overcome those elements that impede effective communication;
- Critically assess organizational communication systems;
- Describe the processes involved in negotiation.

References

Braddick (1987) *Management for Bankers* Butterworths, London

14

HUMAN RESOURCE STRATEGY: HRM AND ITS RELATIONSHIP WITH BUSINESS STRATEGY

Objectives

After studying this chapter you should be able to:

- distinguish between the terms personnel and HRM;

- discuss the different perspectives of HRM;

- describe the main ideas underpinning HRM;

- explain the relationship of HRM with business strategy;

- discuss the implications for HR policies of pursuing alternative strategic directions;

- explain the roles of the HR specialist and the line manager;

- analyse the changing employment relationship and psychological contract in the financial services sector.

1   Human Resource Management – An Introduction

The turbulence within the financial services sector is reflected in the more flexible ways in which, from a strategic viewpoint, organizations seek to manage their human resources.

The CIB Management and Organization in Financial Services Syllabus

Human resource management (HRM) has received widespread attention as the new term for managing people. HRM has moved up the management agenda, on the one hand elevated to a strategic position on the basis that people are a critical resource and can be viewed as route to achieving competitive advantage. On the other hand there have been some significant changes in the employment relationship, in particular the intensification of the search for efficiency, resulting in a strong downward pressure on costs, and particularly labour costs.

This chapter will explore the nature of HRM by looking at the traditional role of personnel and how HRM differs. It will go on to examine the strategic nature of HRM, and will finally consider the changing employment relationships and the psychological contract financial services organizations. The subsequent chapters will then consider, in greater depth, the different HR systems in terms of competencies, HR planning, recruitment and selection, training and development, career planning, reward systems, and the HR environment, examining specifically flexibility and diversity.

2 The Traditional Role of Personnel Management

HRM and personnel management are both concerned with the organizational processes that are directed at attracting, retaining and developing talented individuals and, as such, include the design, implementation and management of 'people policies' associated with:

● recruitment and selection;

● human resource planning;

● training and development;

● performance management;

● appraisal;

● rewards.

Both are involved with industrial and employee relations, for example negotiation and application of agreements on remuneration and working conditions, and other terms of employment. However, in order to determine how HRM and personnel management are different it is necessary to consider the historical role of personnel. Although the practice of personnel management has varied enormously across organizations, traditionally the personnel function developed from a welfare role. The personnel manager has been that of arbitrator or person in the middle, and was primarily concerned with managing the interface between the organization and the individual.

Some of the characteristics of personnel include:

● supportive/paternalistic role;

● operates at a tactical level;

● fire-fighting activity;

● short-term perspective;

● reactive (e.g. reacting to changes in the external environment, such as employment legislation, labour market conditions, trade union actions and other environmental influences);

- designing efficient systems to ensure equitable policies for selection, rewards, discipline, dismissal, redundancy;

- administration and implementation of 'people' policies.

There are many definitions of personnel but fundamental to most is that people have a right to be treated as human beings while at work, and that they will be effective only when their job-related needs are met and personnel activities should be directed at achieving this.

3 The Nature and Philosophy of Human Resource Management

There are still many debates on whether or not HRM represents something 'different' to personnel. The term HRM has, however, been in use for the last 30 or 40 years. In the UK, HRM came into prominence in the mid-1980s when many industries, including financial services organizations, were facing an increasingly complex and turbulent environment. Organizations started to recognize employees as a key strategic resource, which could be utilized in pursuit of gaining competitive advantage.

The characteristics and philosophy of the HRM concept remain ambiguous. Beardwell and Holden (1997) suggest that four broad perspectives exist on HRM:

1. HRM is merely a renaming of the personnel function with nothing to distinguish it from personnel.

2. HRM represents a fusion of personnel management and industrial relations, and therefore creates a new management discipline and function that takes a **holistic** approach to the management of people.

3. HRM represents a resource-based approach that stresses the potential of the **individual** employee in terms of an investment rather than a cost, and focuses on the role of the individual rather than collective employment models.

4. HRM can be viewed as part of the strategic business function in the development of business policy. Thus it is concerned with matching employment policies to organizational strategies.

The above definitions and perspectives suggest that HRM can be viewed as a strategic approach to acquiring, developing, managing and motivating people, with policies that should match the organization's business strategy. It is concerned with creating a positive culture and encouraging the commitment of employees to the goals, objectives and values of the organization. This links to the two principal thoughts on HRM. One has its roots in business strategy literature and the other has strong links with the human relations school, emphasizing the need for personal development in order to gain the commitment and motivation of employees.

Storey (1992) distinguishes between the 'soft' and 'hard' dimensions of HRM. 'Soft' HRM stresses the 'resource' part of HRM with a focus on employee development, communication, motivation and leadership, i.e. the human relations approach. The 'hard' form of HRM is concerned with managing the human resource in a rational way, as for any other economic factor: 'employees are just another figure in the input/output equation' (Armstrong 1994). This version tends to emphasize business and management needs rather than the needs of the individual.

Although HR strategies should be developed to support the achievement of business objectives, it must be recognized that people cannot be treated just like any other resource. People are individuals and have their own needs and expectations that may or may not be consistent with those of the organization. So HRM must be both *business* and *people* oriented. HRM practitioners are often torn between the hard (management) and soft (developmental) aspects of HRM. This can be applied to the financial services sector where hard HRM has been in evidence in terms of the downsizing and de-layering activities of organizations, while at the same time a soft approach has been used to provide a high-quality service.

Contrasting HRM with personnel, some researchers propose HRM is 'resource' centred, directed mainly at management needs for human resources to be provided and deployed to achieve business objectives. Personnel management is more 'workforce' centred, i.e. personnel is more likely to take into account the views and aspirations of the workforce and is not totally identified with management interests.

4   The Aims and Characteristics of HRM

The aims of HRM, according to Armstrong (1994), are:

- To enable management to achieve organizational objectives through people;

- To utilize people to their full capacity and potential;

- To foster commitment from individuals to the success of the company through a quality orientation in their performance and that of the whole organization;

- To integrate human resource polices with business plans and to reinforce an appropriate culture;

- To develop a coherent set of personnel and employment policies which jointly reinforce the organization's strategies for matching resources to business needs and improving performance;

- To establish an environment in which the latent creativity and energy of employees will be unleashed;

- To create conditions in which innovation, team-working and total quality can flourish;

- To encourage willingness to operate flexibility in the interests of the 'adaptive organization' and the pursuit of excellence.

There are a number of characteristics of HRM that can be discerned, which Armstrong (1994) goes on to identify as:

- it is a top management-driven activity;

- the performance and delivery of HRM is a line management responsibility;

- it emphasizes strategic fit, in other words the integration of business strategy and personnel strategies;

- it involves the adoption of a comprehensive and coherent approach to employment policies and practices;

- great importance is attached to a strong culture and to strong values;

- it lays great emphasis on the attitudinal and behavioural characteristics of employees;

- employee relations are unitarist rather than pluralist, individualist rather than collective, and involve high rather than low trust;

- the principles of the organization are organic and decentralized with flexible roles and reliance on teamwork;

- rewards are set according to performance, competence or skill.

The above is just one model of HRM. However, there are many variations on how it might manifest itself in an organization which will be contingent on the type of business and nature of the environment. Therefore, HRM may be applied differently in different companies.

A number of assumptions underpin the features of HRM:

1. People are the most important assets an organization possesses. Organizations exist to deliver value to their customers and it is the human capabilities that distinguish successful organizations from the rest. This could be said to be especially true for financial service organizations.

2. Organizational success is better achieved if people policies are linked with and make a contribution to business objectives. This will enable management to achieve organizational objectives through its workforce and develop a coherent set of personnel and employment policies that jointly reinforce the organization's strategies for matching resources to business needs and improve performance. Because HRM is of strategic importance, it should be considered by senior management in the formulation of business objectives and strategies.

3. Corporate cultures, values, organizational climate and managerial behaviours exert an influence on achievement. Culture must be managed, starting from the top, to get values accepted and acted upon. The culture should be aimed at achieving flexibility, creating commitment and innovative teamwork, and focusing on reducing total quality management in the pursuit of excellence. HR policies should be integrated with business plans to reinforce appropriate culture or to modify an inappropriate culture. Commitment must be fostered from the individual because his or her performance is fundamental to

the success of the organization.

4. Continuous effort by senior managers and line managers is required to encourage organizational members to work together towards the achievement of common goals. There are common interests between employers and employees and as such adversarial confrontation should not exist.

The assumptions described above are embraced in another theory of HRM proposed by Guest (1987). He presents HRM as a particular approach to employee management and identifies four dimensions of HRM: integration, high commitment, flexibility/adaptability and quality:

1. Integration 'is the ability of the organization to integrate HRM issues into their strategic plans, to ensure that the various aspects of HRM cohere and for line managers to incorporate an HRM perspective into their decision-making'.

2. High commitment 'is concerned with both behavioural commitment to pursue agreed goals and attitudinal commitment reflected in a strong identification with the enterprise'.

3. Flexibility 'is primarily concerned with what is sometimes called functional flexibility, but also with an adaptable organizational structure with the capacity to manage change and innovation'.

4. High quality 'refers to all aspects of managerial behaviour, including management of employees and investment in high-quality employees, which in turn will bear directly on the quality of goods and services provided'.

Some would argue that the different theories do not adequately address the complexities of HRM, and that there are inherent tensions. Legge (1989), for example, comments on some of the problems with integration:

● if an organization is operating in diverse product markets, can it have a company-wide mutually reinforcing set of HRM policies;

● if the business strategy dictates the choice of HRM policies, some strategies will dictate policies that fail to emphasize commitment, flexibility and quality.

5   Integration of HRM with Business Strategy

There is increasing interest by business strategists in the human resource and this is one reason why the vocabulary has changed from personnel management to human resource management. As Armstong (1994) proposes 'Human Resource Management is a strategic and coherent approach to the management and organization of an organization's most valued asset, the people working there, who individually and collectively contribute to the achievement of its objectives for sustainable competitive advantage'.

This implies that the successful achievement of business objectives depends upon the effective use of human resources, along with financial and physical resources and therefore HR initiatives should be aligned with the strategic objectives of the organization.

The key to successful integration of HRM with business strategy is based upon:

● understanding how business strategy is formed;

● understanding the key business issues that have an impact on HR, for example, growth or consolidation, increasing competitive advantage through quality;

● developing a performance-oriented culture, through empowerment, involvement and team working.

To achieve this, a good fit is needed between business strategy and human resource strategy so that the latter supports the former. In practice there are difficulties in achieving this 'fit' for a number of reasons:

1. The diversity of strategy for different sections of the organization means that HR strategies must vary. This has implications for setting consistent HR policies throughout the organization. One of the key difficulties of managing HR at a strategic level for many financial services organizations is that HRM policies are often set at head office level for the whole organization or group, but these may not be appropriate or fit with the HR strategies required for specific business units.

2. The changing and evolving nature of business strategy which makes it difficult to develop relevant HR strategies.

3. The absence of clearly written and transmitted business strategy, which exacerbates the problems of clarifying the strategic business issues which HR strategies should address.

4. The qualitative nature of HR issues can conflict with business strategy that is often quantifiable (e.g. market share, profitability, etc.). Some HR areas are quantifiable, for example resourcing, but it is more difficult to measure the impact of complex variables such as commitment, good employee relations, morale, etc.

5. Financial orientations can be incompatible with the policies described as imperative to the practice of HRM.

6. Tensions between 'soft' and 'hard' HRM. As a strategic activity HRM can be 'hard' in that people will come first only when it is economically advantageous to pursue such a strategy but it could be argued that equally important is managing the 'softer' people issues. The softer aspects are critical to encourage greater employee participation and the liberation for employees from bureaucratic systems, thus giving individuals greater autonomy and responsibility.

The 'Investors in People' standard (IiP), which many financial services organizations are seeking to achieve, explicitly links business strategy with the management of people. This is best summed up in the statement provided by Investors in People UK: 'An Investors in People makes a public commitment from the top to develop all employees to achieve its business objectives. Every business should have a written but flexible plan which sets out business goals and targets, considers how employees will contribute to achieving the plan and specifies how development needs in particular will be assessed and met. Management should develop and communicate to all employees a vision of where the organization is going and the contribution employees will make to its success, involving employee representatives as appropriate'.

6   Developing an HR Strategy

Human resources are a key resource for financial service organizations: the skills and motivations of employees and the way they are deployed can be a major source of competitive advantage. As already discussed in Chapter 3 a critical stage in understanding the strategic capability of an organization is having sound knowledge of the resources available. The strategic intent for organizations can have an impact on all HR systems, for example the way staff are selected, appraised and rewarded. Of key importance is the close alignment of the different employment systems with business strategy. HR strategies should be directed, primarily, towards making business strategy work. This is a view supported by Guest (1989) who states:

> *The effectiveness of the organization rests on how strategies interrelate and how HRM issues are integrated into strategic plans – the various aspects of HRM cohere and line managers incorporate an HRM perspective into their decision-making.*

When deciding its business strategy an organization has a number of alternative strategic directions which it could take to achieve its corporate objectives. For each of the alternative directions there are different methods for development. Whatever method is chosen, there will be implications for HR policies. For example, an organization pursuing a policy of diversification could do so by either acquisition or internal development. Each would have ramifications for human resources. In the case of internal development, the organization would have to consider the human resource requirements in terms of the numbers of people, types and levels of skills. If new skills are required then the selection procedure may have to change.

In the case of diversification via a merger, a key consideration in assessing the suitability of this option would relate to the cultural 'fit' between the two organizations. Thus, different business objectives will have implications for HR policies in terms of:

● recruitment and selection;
   How can we acquire, retain or shed the right number and quality of people to meet the forecast needs of the organization or department?

● developing and training;
   How can we train and develop employees to ensure that they respond to change and the resulting demands for different skills and abilities?

● performance and reward management;

How can we ensure that we have a fully committed and well-motivated workforce, and that those worth retaining stay with the business and reward those who deliver the desired results?

The successful implementation of strategy and the management of change will also have implications for HRM. As already discussed in Chapter 4, HR policies must be developed to encourage and support organizational change.

The formulation and implementation of HR strategies, as for business strategy, must take account of both external and internal factors. For example, demographic factors are changing the shape of the workforce. There is a declining number of young people entering the workforce and organizations must consider their recruitment and selection strategies in order to attract young people and those from alternative groups such as women returners. Technological changes are also significant in that they are changing the structure of work. New employment legislation on areas such as equal opportunities and work time will also affect HR strategies.

Internal factors that impact on managing and developing human resource policies are:

- cultural change;
- maturing workforce;
- workforce diversity;
- job design;
- pressures on quality of life;
- pressure for education;
- continuous learning and skills development;
- redundancy;
- morale and motivation.

All of these factors are pertinent to what is occurring in the financial services sector.

7   Roles and Responsibilities within HRM

Although HRM is a strategic activity, the implementation of HR policies is often the responsibility of line managers at local level. An increasing proportion of line management time is taken up with 'people' management issues. Managers therefore need to develop skills that are not just technical and task-oriented but softer inter-personnel skills. They must be rewarded for the 'people management' activities of their role. Increasingly, these softer skills are becoming important key competencies needed for progress within the organization.

There is, of course, still a role for specialist HR staff who are needed to provide guidance and support on all matters relating to the employees, such as providing guidance on issues relating to employee legislation. Specialist HR staff may also take an active role in procedures such as recruitment and selection, training and development, and assessments for promotion decisions. The aim is to ensure that management deals effectively with everything concerning the employment and development of people (Armstrong 1995).

The various areas of HR activity in developing, revising or implementing policies to achieve business goals include:

1. **The Design of Jobs**. This involves analysing, designing and structuring, and will mean measuring and deciding upon the content of jobs in order to evaluate their worth and relationship with other jobs and functions. Job design is looked at in detail in Chapter 11.

2. **Recruiting and Selecting Staff**. This involves the planning and forecasting of the numbers and types of employees required both now and in the future, looking at the supply both in the organization and outside, and drawing up plans to close any gaps between demand for employees and supply. In addition it involves understanding the requirements for a job in terms of the competencies required to do it successfully. Finally, it involves choosing the most suitable candidate from those who apply using selection techniques as appropriate in the most reliable, valid and ethical way. Chapter 16 investigates HR planning and the processes involved in recruitment and selection.

3. **Developing Staff**. This involves determining the appropriate method of training or development and evaluating effectiveness. This will include analysing training needs at corporate, divisional or individual level. Job analysis and HR planning will assist in the process of defining what is required.

4. **Performance Monitoring and Appraisal**. Managing performance is concerned with the design and implementation of performance management and appraisal systems. Developing staff and performance management are explored in Chapter 18.

5. **Rewarding Staff**. The activities here will include measuring the value of jobs, their position in the organizational hierarchy, and monetary value. Administering pay systems and the development and implementation of the wider staff benefits packages is also included. Also under this heading the external market rates and influences must be understood. Chapter 18 explores in detail issues relating to performance management, and the appraisal and design of reward systems used in the financial services sector.

6. **Employee Relations**. This involves the communication, participation and involvement of staff, and includes relations with trade unions, staff representatives and consultative committees.

7. **Social Responsibilities.** This would involve ensuring that statutory obligations relating to the Health and Safety at Work Act and any other employee legislation such as equal opportunities are fully discharged. The legal implications are explored more fully in Chapter 2.

8. **Administrative Responsibilities**. In addition to all the above responsibilities, records of individual employees must be kept up to date within the scope of the Data

Protection Act. Guidelines on the policies and procedures for the conduct of affairs to ensure consistency and equability in their application across the organization must be developed.

8   The Changing Nature of the Employment Relationship

There is some evidence to support the view that HR does have a more strategic organization in financial services organizations. Linked with this change, there has also been major changes to the employment relationship.

During the period from the Second World War up until the early/mid-1980s, organizations operating in the financial services sector saw prosperity and growth. Employees could anticipate lifetime employment and career progression with a single organization. The culture tended to be one of 'the company will look after you'. However, changes in market conditions have provided the imperative for greater organizational flexibility and employee adaptability. Management practices have changed radically with the move away from a paternalistic culture to a flexible high-performance culture. Within this context, many organizations have moved away from the traditional HR policies which underpinned jobs for life and 'onwards and upwards' career progression.

With the introduction of flatter organizational structures, the focus is now on improving staff employability, based, in theory, on a flexible employer-employee relationship. Employability is concerned with developing the competitive skills to gain and retain jobs. The idealistic position would be where the employer and the employee both share the responsibility for maintaining and enhancing individuals' employability inside and outside the organization. The outcome will be employees who are constantly reviewing and updating their skills.

The assumption underpinning the concept of employability is that individuals will accept less job security in return for opportunities to develop new skills and expertise. It can be viewed by enlightened employers as having the dual benefit of encouraging employees to develop as a way of adding value to the organization, but also as a hedge against unemployment. However, and notwithstanding the growing literature on the subject, it is still the case that the concept of employability has yet to be implemented in financial services organizations on a wide scale.

Employability is tied up with the concept of 'the psychological contract' in that both are concerned with what employers and employees want and expect from each other, and the understanding people have regarding the commitment made between themselves and their organization. In other words:

●   the employer: What outputs they will get from the employees?

●   the employee: What rewards will be given for investing time and effort?

The rapidly changing economic climate in which financial services organizations now operate has meant there have been pressures for change on both sides of the psychological contract (employer and employee). Sparrow (1996) provides a useful summary of the old and new characteristics of the psychological contract, and Figure 14.1 identifies some of these factors.

Table 14.1: The changing psychological contract

Characteristics	Old	New
Change environment	Stable, short-term focus	Continuous change, intense competition
Culture	Paternalistic, time served	High performance where those who perform get rewarded
Focus	Security, job for life	Employability, lucky to have a job, no guarantees
Rewards	Paid on level, position, status, length of service	Paid on contribution linked to business strategy and objectives
Motivational currency	Promotion, onwards and upwards	Job enrichment, skills, competencies and personal development
Promotion basis	Expected, time served, technical competence	Less opportunity, horizontal/ lateral, new criteria for those who deserve it
Personal development	The organization's responsibility	Individual's and employer's responsibility to improve employability
Employee's key responsibility	Good performance in present job	Making a difference
Employer's key input	Stable income & career advancement	Opportunities for self-development
Employee's key input	Time & effort	Knowledge, expertise, adding value
Redundancy/ tenure guarantee	Job for life	Lucky to have a job, no guarantees
Trust employees organization possible	High trust and commitment to	Desirable, but expect to become committed to profession

Source: Adapted from Sparrow (1996)

The features of the psychological contract are central to the motivation of employees. The changes illustrated in the chart suggest that organizations are now more demanding of their employees and the paternalistic culture no longer dominates. Organizations are becoming more ambiguous places to work where people will be utilized only when they have the required skill. Individuals need to plan their own development and manage their own careers because jobs for life and job security are disappearing. Job enrichment and development of new skills will be the motivational currency rather than promotion. Pay systems will be based on an individual's contribution to the organization, for example through performance-related pay systems, not on grade, position or status.

It is argued that new psychological contracts are a necessary part of the transformation process to improve organizational performance capabilities. However, there is the suggestion that the 'new' contract can be conceived as a degradation of the employment relationship and trust, and it is predicted that the quality of the contract will deteriorate from the employee's perspective.

The Royal Bank of Scotland is an example of an organization that has instigated change in the psychological contact through its re-engineering programme, 'Project Columbus'. One outcome from the project has been a rationalization of grade structures where staff have had to reapply for redesigned jobs. The new job roles have been advertised on the basis of competencies rather than grade and without reference to pay (Hiltrop 1995).

Different psychological contracts may exist for different groups of employees in financial services organizations, for example:

a)   Senior managers will receive a high degree of support and investment, which is necessary to ensure that they stay, or to attract new high-calibre staff.

b)   Highly skilled staff/specialists (possibly contract staff) are capable of managing their own careers and thus maintaining employability outside the organization.

c)   Other more general staff receive a high level of role-specific training from the organization but limited general and personal development. They are expected to take the initiative in maintaining much of their employability.

All HR policies and processes will impact on the relationship between the employer and the employee. Any changes in the contract will have implications for HRM, for example:

● finding new ways to attract, retain and motivate employees;

● changes in management style;

● changes in roles;

● the building of cross-functional teams;

● creating challenging work experiences;

● provision of training;

● nurturing leadership talent;

● eliminating barriers to change.

The psychological contract must evolve, reflecting the changed business conditions and the expectations of people entering the workforce. However, some semblance of balance must be made in order that employees are not exploited.

Summary

Now that you have completed this chapter you should be able to:

- Contrast the terms HRM and personnel management;

- Explain the underlying features of HRM;

- Discuss the strategic role of HRM;

- Identify the different HR policy areas that must be considered in the development of business strategy;

- Explain the role and responsibilities of both specialist staff and line mangers with respect to HR activities;

- Define what is meant by the term employability;

- Analyse the changing nature of the psychological contract for financial services organizations.

References

Armstrong M (1994) *Human Resource Management*, Kogan Page

Armstrong M (1995) *A Handbook of Personnel Management Practice*, 5th ed. Kogan Page

Beardwell I & Holden L (1997) *Human Resource Management: A Contemporary Perspective*, 2nd ed. Pitman

Guest D E (1987) 'Human Resource Management and Industrial Relations', *Journal of Management Studies*, Vol. 24, No. 5

Guest D E (1989) 'Personnel and HRM: Can you tell the difference?', *Personnel Management*, January

Hiltrop J (1995) 'The Changing Psychological Contract: The Human Resource Challenge of the 1990s', *European Management Journal*, Vol. 13 No. 3

Legge K (1989) 'Human Resource Management: A Critical Analysis', in J. Storey ed., *New Perspectives on Human Resource Management*, Routledge

Sparrow P R (1996) 'Transitions in the Psychological Contract in UK Banking', *Human Resource Management Journal*, Vol. 6, No. 4

Storey J (1992) *Developments in the Management of Human Resources*, Blackwell

15

COMPETENCIES

Objectives

After studying this chapter you should be able to:

- determine the nature of competencies;

- identify the different types of competency;

- describe the advantages and disadvantages of competencies;

- explain the relationship between competencies and reward;

- discuss the role of competencies in relation to training.

1   Defining Competencies

There has always been a tension that exists when defining competencies. There is talk of core competencies, personal competencies, job competencies or occupational competencies. Where do skills, knowledge and abilities fit in? Indeed there has even been a debate about how to spell the term – is it competencies or competences?

One definition popularly used is that competency is 'an underlying characteristic of a person which results in effective and/or superior performance in a job' (Boyatsis, 1982 p21) and a later definition comes from the Training Commission in 1988 which states that competence is 'the ability to perform the activities within an occupational area to the levels of performance expected in employment'.

Both of these definitions suggest that *skill* level and *knowledge* need to be present in order to display the competency, otherwise it would be deemed to be a form of incompetence until the necessary skill and knowledge levels could be demonstrated.

Competencies are not in themselves new phenomena because the ideas behind them can be traced back to the work of McClelland in 1973 who suggested that, when recruiting, managers should assess competence rather than intelligence. This implies that it is not what a person knows that is important rather that what they actually do at work which matters.

There appears to be increasing use of competencies in financial service organizations, particularly in recruiting and developing people. One major financial services organization has defined the competencies it wishes to see displayed in the organization in the belief that this will enhance the performance and success of the organization *and* the individuals. These competencies are incorporated into the performance management system, so that individuals can gain feedback on the key competencies required to perform the work. In this way the individual and the appraisor can assess whether the competencies are relevant and are being performed in such a way as to obtain maximum performance. However it does mean that the competencies have to be very clearly defined so that all parties can direct their efforts in the most appropriate way.

The Different Types of Competency

Competencies can be applied in different ways. For example, it could be argued that competencies can be based on various factors such as: industry, organizational, job or role specific or personal. These will be explored in more detail.

Industry competencies

Cockerill (1989) provides examples of competencies developed for the financial services industry and the list is as follows:

- information search
- concept information
- conceptual flexibility
- interpersonal search
- managing interaction
- developmental orientation
- impact
- self-confidence
- presentation
- proactive orientation
- achievement orientation

Organizational competencies

These are described as the core competence of the organization providing the key to competitiveness. Examples of organizational competencies are:

Sony – miniaturization

Philips – optical media

Honda – engines and power trains

3M – pressure-sensitive tapes and coated abrasives

Citicorp – operating system providing 24-hour access to world markets

Continental Bank – intimate knowledge of customer needs and relationships with customers

Very often it can be seen that the core competency of the organization is closely linked to its mission and vision and value statements, thus reinforcing the purpose for the organization's existence.

It is clear from the literature available that there are many different lists of competencies and that there are many significant similarities between them

Job/role competencies

These are job specific, such as business planning and financial control, and are very functional and therefore quite clear about the behaviours and outputs expected

Personal competencies

These are skills and abilities demonstrated by an individual at an adequate level such as team working, motivation of self and others, leadership, communication. Personal competencies enhance an individual's marketability and can be cross-functional, so for example a good team leader would be welcome in a planning department, a finance department or an IT department.

The following list (Source: Marchington and Wilkinson (1997)) shows the many skills required for a manager to perform effectively:

- breadth of awareness and strategic perspective
- oral and written communication
- leadership decisiveness and assertiveness
- team working and ability to work with others
- analysis and judgement
- drive and persistence
- organization and planning
- sensitivity to others' viewpoints
- self-confidence and persuasiveness
- flexibility and adaptability

This list is not exhaustive and it may be useful to refer to the study pack in the appropriate student activity to explore some of the issues surrounding competencies.

When using competencies there are many considerations that need to be accounted for. For example one of the competencies for a manager taken from the above list is 'oral and written communication', but this needs to be clarified in much more detail for it to be applied usefully by individuals in organizations, not least because managers will be operating at different levels in organizations and different results and competencies will be expected. An example of how a competency could be defined at different levels in an organization is given below.

Competency: oral and written communication

Senior Manager
Articulate and able to communicate to large audiences in all situations, fully considering their needs. Is credible and persuasive and able to establish rapport quickly. Can quickly interpret and comment on written reports and feedback

Middle Manager
Able to communicate fluently to staff conveying information and ideas accurately. Uses appropriate body language which supports the message, and able to write reports that are well structured, clear and succinct.

Junior Manager
Able to talk clearly to team members and managers, and explain numerical and verbal information clearly. May use structured templates to assist with clear and unambiguous statements

2   Advantages of Competencies

There are many advantages for an organization that defines its competencies clearly. The overall aim of using competencies is to improve organizational and personal performance, and once in use it is claimed that competencies can achieve the following advantages:

- allows a degree of flexibility for the organization and the individual, facilitating horizontal movement, as well as vertical movement within an organization, but also enhancing the marketability for the individual and facilitating movement between companies – also this assisting career planning;

- encourages a widening and deepening of the skills for the organization and the individual, thus helping to establish and promote standards and benchmarking;

- evaluates the added value of the person, not the job, thereby permitting recognition for the competencies used to perform the job;

- competencies can be integrated with the HR systems of an organization thereby enabling a company to recruit the right competencies, train and develop in the right competencies, appraise the performance of the competencies, and align compensation systems with the aim of maximizing organizational success.

- can be used as part of a culture change incorporating behaviours and competencies to assess and reward what people actually do, e.g. Chase Manhatten Bank attempted to re-define the role of a manager from the traditional view of a manager (i.e. more senior, better privileges, higher status) to a more business-focused manager responsible for budget and cost management, achievement of targets and being an entrepreneur) (Case Study by Martin, S. (1995))

3 Disadvantages of Competencies

The main disadvantages of competencies also need to be considered and are set out below. These include:

- Keeping competencies up to date in a fast-changing environment may be difficult and require a lot of time, effort and cost. An organization must weigh up the cost benefits of the work involved to ensure it is justifiable

- Assessment of competencies can also be fraught with difficulties, because of differences in definition and interpretation.

- Managing the expectations of the users and clarifying how the competencies will be used in a consistent and fair manner across the organization.

For some observers, competencies raise questions which, until answered satisfactorily, will fail to inspire confidence, for example:

- Is it really possible to establish a list of generic competencies that are appropriate to all situations?

- How different is this list of competencies from the list of skills and abilities that have been traditionally documented and used in financial services organizations?

- What happens to individual flair and creativity if the individual performance varies from the stated and recognized competencies?

4 Competencies and Reward

Competence-based pay, or skill-based pay as it is sometimes called, is a relatively new way to reward individuals. This approach incorporates competencies into the overall reward system of the organization and individuals are paid depending on the standard or level of skill and behaviour demonstrated when performing the job. An obvious advantage of this approach is that it supports development, which is of benefit to both the individual because it enhances their personal skills repertoire and the organization where they are used. However a potential drawback is that the assessment depends on the ability, knowledge and evaluation skills of the assessor to ensure there is a sense of fairness and equity, not least because it directly impacts on the take-home pay of the individual!

5 Competency-based Training

The government introduced various National Vocational Qualifications (NVQs) which assess defined competencies linked to certain jobs; these competencies act as the building blocks for vocational training. In this way the intent was to make competency-based training more practical and appeal to a wider range of people than perhaps the more academic, examination style of attainment such as GCSEs or A levels.

There exists a framework of NVQs which accredit competencies so that an individual's performance at work can be considered along with traditional educational qualifications. Indeed NVQs have now established an alternative route to facilitate access to further and higher education, as demonstrated below:

Figure 15.1: Further and higher education

	Higher Degree		
	Degree	GNVQ 5	NVQ 5
		GNVQ 4	NVQ 4
	GCE Level	Advanced GNVQ	NVQ 3
		Intermediate GNVQ	NVQ 2
			NVQ 1
Age 16			
Age 14	Key Stage 4		
Age 5	National Curriculum		

(Source NVQ Monitor)

There are five levels of NVQ and these provide a clear route for development and career progression:

Level One recognizes competence in a wide range of work activities that are likely to be routine and predictable.

Level Two recognizes competencies in a broader range of work activity which may be more demanding and include some non-routine work.

Level Three recognizes competence in a broad range of work activities including complex and non-routine activities performed in many work settings. Usually includes the need to demonstrate a certain level of responsibility and autonomy and perhaps influence over others.

Level Four recognizes more complex technical and professional work activities performed in a variety of work contexts. It looks for a substantial amount of autonomy and responsibility and the influence over staff and the allocation of resources.

Level Five recognizes competence in a wide range of work activity in complex situations that require the demonstration of applying knowledge and techniques. There will be non-routine and unpredictable circumstances that arise and need to be dealt with. There is the need to demonstrate high levels of personal autonomy and responsibility for and allocation of resources. There is the need to analyse and diagnose, identify and formulate options and plan and implement solutions, evaluating them to ensure benefit for the organization.

6 Criticisms of NVQs

NVQs have been criticized by some commentators, and the main criticisms are given below:

- for not being as rigorous as similar systems in other countries;

- for promoting a conformist culture, accrediting insular activities and limiting creative debate (Macfarlane and Lomas (1994));

- that the range of assessment standards has been too variable. Prais (1989) suggests that NVQ standards are set too low, particularly when compared to other European countries;

- that overly bureaucratic procedures exist (Smithers 1993) resulting in a time-consuming process. Some have said that this factor has caused employers to lack confidence in the standards and has led to some employers developing their own competence-based systems;

- Heyes and Stewart (1994) suggest that NVQs do not overcome the skills gap as originally intended.

Despite these criticisms, GNVQ and NVQs are now widely accepted and recognized. Many large employers have incorporated the notion of competence as part of their employee development programmes, and some examples are now given below.

7   The Use of Competencies in Industry

The Management Charter Initiative (MCI)

The MCI is a government-backed initiative to help to ensure that organizations are committed to developing their managers so that Britain remains competitive with other countries. It is also an attempt to establish a recognized qualification route for managers, commencing with 'certificate level' for first-level managers, followed by 'diploma level' aimed at middle managers, thereby providing improved management education.

These levels contain key competencies, which need to be demonstrated by management while they are carrying out their duties. The emphasis is on 'output' rather than 'inputs', such as how many training courses an individual has attended.

Management Development Framework

The Management Development Framework is an example of how competencies were used in the Employment Service in the 1990s. It sets out broad competency statements for managers and supervisors. Individuals evaluated the importance of each statement to their particular job and then developed a training plan with their manager which contained their learning priorities and actions.

W.H.Smith

W.H.Smith is one company that has developed descriptions of competencies it looks for in managers (Jacobs, 1989). These include competencies such as leadership, planning and organizational skills and analytical ability. Leadership, for example, is described as an ability to direct group activities, ability to build an effective team, ability to involve all team members and the ability to provide help and advice when it is required.

Summary

Now you have studied this chapter you should be able to:

- distinguish between the different types of competency and give examples of each;
- explain the arguments for the advantages and disadvantages of competences;
- explain the relationship between competencies and reward;
- discuss the role of competencies in relation to training;
- discuss how the MCI and the NVQ systems use competencies;
- describe how organizations are using competencies.

References

Boyatsis RE (1982) *The Competent Manager*, New York, John Wiley

The Training Commission (1988) *Classifying the Components of Management Competencies*

Employment Service (1991) *Management Development Framework*

Martin S (1995) 'A futures market for competencies' *People Management* March, 20-4

Marchington M and Wilkinson A (1997) *Core Personnel and Development*, Institute of Personnel and Development p160

Cockerill T 'The kind of competence for rapid change' *Personnel Management* Sept 1989 pp52-56

Jacobs R. (1989) 'Getting the measure of management competence' *Personnel Management* June pp32-37

McClelland DC (1973) 'Testing for competence rather than intelligence' *American Psychologist*, 28 (1) pp1-14

Prais SJ (1991) 'Vocational qualifications in Britain and Europe; theory and practice' *National Institute Economic Review* May pp86-92

Smithers A (1993) *All Our Futures: Britain's Education Revolution*, Channel Four Television

Macfarlane B and Lomas L (1994) 'Competence-based management education and the needs of the learning organization' *Education and Training*, 36 (3)

Heyes J & Stuart M (1994) *Placing Symbols before Reality? Re-evaluating the Low Skills Equilibrium*, Personnel Review, 23 (5)

16

RECRUITMENT AND SELECTION

Objectives

After studying this chapter you should be able to:

- define 'recruitment' and 'selection';
- describe how organizations could use workforce flexibility;
- outline an approach to planned selection;
- describe a number of key aspects of selection;
- explain why selection is a difficult managerial activity.

1   Definitions of 'Recruitment' and 'Selection'

Recruitment is concerned with the relationship between an organization and the labour market and with the ways in which the organization seeks to attract potential employees in order to fulfil its human resource requirements.

Selection is concerned with the ways in which the organization chooses between current or potential employees in order to meet particular and specific resource needs. It should be noted that the techniques of selection may be applied in circumstances other than recruitment and promotion – such as selection for redeployment or redundancy. As part of the recruitment procedure, the organization needs to consider the different types of staff that may be appropriate to the job. There are a number of ways of examining the labour market and the structure of employment. One way in which this can be done is by exploring the structure of the internal labour market, the different categories of staff and the nature of their employment relationship. The next section will set out the various categories that offer labour market flexibility to financial services organizatons.

2   Flexibility in Financial Services

It is obvious in the trends that can be observed that strategic labour policies, i.e. in terms of resourcing and the type and levels of employees, are increasing in use. These strategies are currently directed at maintaining flexibility. The next section focuses on flexible labour policies in more detail, and the trends in the labour market, especially with regard to financial service organizations.

Why do organizations need flexible labour markets?

Financial services organization are constantly searching for solutions on how to respond to external environmental pressures and internal challenges of achieving cost containment while at the same time improving productivity. They are looking for methods of organizing labour resources in such a way that they are able to vary human resource input more easily. By doing this they will be better positioned to be flexible and responsive to the ever-changing marketplace and turbulent business conditions. As in most service industries, staff costs in financial services organizations represent the largest overhead. There is a clear need to identify alternative approaches to reshaping the organization's labour market and the structure of the workforce so as to facilitate the most efficient use of staff, achieving labour flexibility and reducing labour costs.

What does flexibility embrace?

Financial services organizations are employing flexible working practices so that they can adjust the size and mix of labour in response to changes in demand, thus ensuring that excess labour is not carried by the organization, and equally when there is the need to recruit labour with the right skills quickly the sources are available. Flexibility itself conveys the notions of adaptability, pliability and responsiveness to organizational change.

Within the context of **labour flexibility** four sources of flexibility dominate:

- functional flexibility
- numerical flexibility
- temporal flexibility
- financial flexibility

Each of these will be discussed in more detail.

Functional flexibility or task flexibility

This sometimes referred to as multi-skilling and is concerned with the ability to redeploy employees with appropriate training or retraining to different tasks and activities. Organizations can attempt to create greater flexibility by relaxing demarcations between different workers. It is suggested that the use of functional flexibility is increasing as skill boundaries are becoming less well defined due to the development of technology. Financial reasons in terms of the cost pressures on headcount may also lead to an increasing pressure to spread the available workforce over more tasks.

Functional flexibility could be viewed as a deliberate strategy to train and upgrade skill, either extending the job content horizontally (job enlargement) or vertically (job enrichment).

However, it could also be argued that at another level flexibility represents work intensification with workers undertaking a variety of tasks to meet shortages. Whichever perspective is taken, the overall aim of functional flexibility is to achieve greater workforce productivity within work-time, by altering the deployment of a workforce according to tasks required across function or hierarchy.

Numerical flexibility

This is where adjustments are made in the number of workers to meet the demands or fluctuations in output. It is generally taken to mean the ability to rapidly increase or decrease the numbers of workers employed. This can be achieved through the deployment of part-time staff and 'hire and fire' policies aimed at temporary staff.

Temporal flexibility or working time

This is sometimes subsumed under the numerical flexibility heading. Both forms relate to the volume of labour supplied. While most employees work standard blocks of time, the supply of work in not usually so regular, and is affected by seasonal pressures and varying customer demand. Temporal flexibility allows variability of labour time by varying patterns of hours worked in response to changing patterns of demand. This can be achieved through flexitime, shift work, overtime and annual hours arrangements.

Financial flexibility or wage flexibility

This covers both the ability to adjust labour costs, depending on the level of business activity, and the linking of wages to the state of supply and demand in the external labour market.

Financial flexibility can take different forms, and can include a payment system that links remuneration with performance, for example performance-related pay. The reward system could also be designed to encourage the development of functional flexibility through competence-based pay rewards for the acquisition and practice of new skills.

The flexible firm model

The flexible firm model identifies a framework for achieving the different forms of labour flexibility, and offers a set of suggestions whereby organizations may adopt one or more of the methods to achieve a more flexible approach to the supply and use of labour (Atkinson 1984, 1985).

The impetus for the model developed out of a need to respond to various external environmental pressures including the unstable operating conditions, intense competition, changing attitudes to work, demographic changes and skill shortages facing organizations in the UK. Other sociological influences promoting flexible working practices included the change in the labour supply, for instance the growth in the number of women who may seek or accept work on a part-time or temporary basis. The largely deregulated labour market has also facilitated greater flexibility.

The model is explained in Figure 3.3. At the centre of the circle are the core employees. Organizations will have a set of *core workers* who are full-time permanent employees supplying firm specific skills. The *core workers* will carry out the most important and most unique activities of the firm, and will have skills that are highly firm specific. It is necessary to have a core workforce within an organization so that there is continuity of employment and a level of experience from which it is possible to build for the future. The employment conditions for the core should encourage retention by providing training, career development opportunities and facilitate functional flexibility for those with skills critical to the business.

The first peripheral group is made up of labour that may be given the status of full-time employees, but are more vulnerable than the core workers. They enjoy less job security, have less access to career opportunities and tend to regard their positions as more of a job than a career. Flexibility is likely to take the form of numerical and financial flexibility. There is no need to achieve functional flexibility because their jobs need little or no training and tend to be less skilled. The relatively high labour turnover of this group contributes to quick and simplified numerical adjustments.

Figure 16.1: The flexible firm model

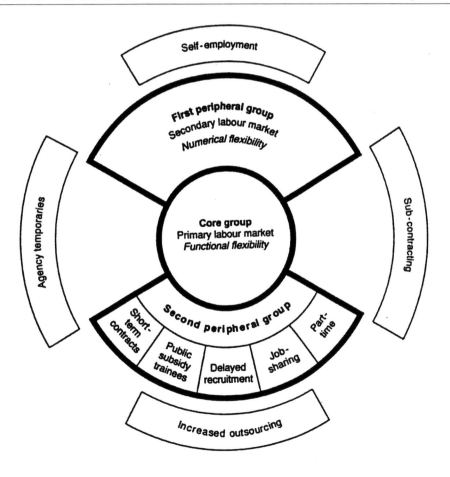

The second peripheral group is made up of staff employed on a part-time, temporary or fixed-term contract basis to supplement the numerical flexibility of the first peripheral group. However, this part of the model could be criticized for locating part-time workers in this segment. A growing number of organizations are operating job-share systems at management levels that represent core workers.

The third group consists of external workers who are not directly employed by the firm, for example, subcontractors, self-employed, agency workers and outsourcing.

The flexible firm model suggests that organizations will adopt different approaches to labour management for different sections of the workforce. The organization of a firm's labour markets and their division into separate components will mean that workers' experiences and the employer's expectations are increasingly differentiated (Atkinson and Gregory 1986).

Benefits and criticisms of the flexible firm

The benefits to the employer of the flexible firm include:

- reduced labour costs as a result of lower wage and non-wage employment of the periphery;

- the ability to tailor the size of the workforce to changing levels of demand, reducing costs of carrying excess labour and achieving 'lean production';

- increased productivity from core workers.

Criticisms have been made about the value and contribution of the flexible firm model. Critics have pointed to problems in defining the core and periphery. Adopting a more flexible labour force also raises problems for the management of human resources, for example:

- which function or area should be staffed in which way?

- which management styles should apply to which groups?

- how can commitment be generated from the different groups?

Having considered the main types of employment flexibility, the actual recruitment process can proceed, tailoring the recruitment method to the actual type of recruit required.

3   Recruitment

There are two basic approaches to recruitment:

a) the selection approach whereby the organization seeks to attract people with the attributes it assesses are necessary to carry out a particular, defined, set of tasks, and

b) the *classification* approach whereby the organization seeks to attract a sufficient number of recruits to match its headcount requirements with a view to designing jobs that will exploit their particular characteristics.

Within the financial services industry the classification approach will apply with regard to the annual recruitment of graduates and may apply when the organization is seeking senior management recruits.

There are several interfaces between the organization and the labour market:

a) general advertising – as a result of which the public – including current and potential customers and recruits – is kept aware of *inter alia* the organization's name and 'image';

b) specific advertising for defined jobs. Traditionally such advertisements are placed in newspapers chosen because they are read by relatively large numbers of potential recruits. There is now a tendency for organizations to explore other advertising media such as local radio and the Internet (see 16.15 below);

c) use of recruitment agencies which supply a service whereby they will provide the organization with potential employees either from their registered employment seekers or through their own advertising and contact systems;

d) use of executive search consultants who will seek to identify and interest potential recruits who are not necessarily currently seeking employment with the organization;

e) 'headhunters' – usually concerned with the search for senior executive recruits – who will work with the organization to analyse, define and, as appropriate, refine its requirements so as to be able to have a realistic chance to match them against those which are identified as being available within the labour market. Thereafter the headhunter will identify and, as appropriate, approach a field of potential appointees.

4   Selection

The essence of selection is to twofold:

a) to make the most appropriate decision on behalf of the organization, and

b) to comply with the law, regulation and best practice to ensure fair treatment.

There are two types of mistake that can be made in relation to the selection decision:

		Candidates for a position who ...	
		SHOULD be selected	SHOULD **NOT** be selected
Candidates for a position who ...	ARE selected	✔	A very costly experiment
	ARE **NOT** selected	A garden of missed opportunities	✔

These mistakes arise because the selection decision is fundamentally subjective in nature. Because mistakes are relatively expensive (including the recruitment, induction, training and exit costs of the failed selection and the recruitment etc. costs of the replacement selection) there is sense in taking all steps to ensure they do not arise. This is achieved in two ways:

a)   by following a defined procedure that has developed by way of best practice, and

b)   by seeking to increase the level of objectivity imported into that procedure.

Happily, adopting such an approach means that it is probable that the organization will also comply with the requirement for fairness.

5   Selection as a Planned Process

The process of selection comprises:

- Job analysis
- Job description
- Person specification
- Job advertisement
- Application form
- Long-listing and short-listing
- References
- Selection
- Decision
- Notification

6 ·   Job Analysis

Job analysis entails a rigorous examination of the job in order to determine in detail what it involves. The completed analysis forms the basis of the job description.

A structured approach is helpful and could comprise the following:

Objectives   What are the aims of the job? What value is added to the organization? Where does the job fit in to the work of the organization?

Responsibilities What resources are controlled by the jobholder? What effect does the jobholder have on resources controlled by others?

Decisions   What decisions does the job entail? Are they actual decisions, recommendations or authorizations/ratifications?

Relationships   What is the extent/nature of the relationships between the jobholder and bosses, subordinates, peers, other departments, customers (internal and external) and other stakeholders?

Environment   What is the nature of the geographical, physical, social and financial environment in which the job is done?

7   Job Description

From the job analysis a **job description** can be written: it should contain the following features:

Job title;

Job grade or evaluation;

Reporting lines – to whom does the jobholder report; who reports to the jobholder?

Main areas of responsibility;

Resources controlled;

Specific responsibilities – even to the level of key tasks;

Limits of authority;

Working conditions.

8   Person Specification

Having described the job the next stage is to describe by way of a **person specification** the person who will best be able to fill that job. A commonly used structured approach is Professor Alec Rodger's 7-point plan in which are specified, briefly, those attributes that are considered to be essential to enable the job to be done, or though not essential are desirable, or are likely to be contra-indications, i.e. they point to the lack of a capability to do the job.

The seven areas to which the plan directs attention are:

Physique, health and appearance

Attainments

General intelligence

Special aptitudes

Interests

Disposition

Circumstances.

Each of these areas is broken down into subsets – for example 'attainments' could comprise education, professional qualifications, accredited awards, experience gained and training undertaken.

The objective of the exercise is to use the labels provided by the 7-point plan as aides-mémoire to develop a framework relevant to the job against which to judge candidates during the long- and short-listing and selection stages.

9 Job Advertising

The content of the **job advertisement** is informed by the content of both the job description, which is used to inform the market of the work that is required of the jobholder, and the person specification – which indicates the personal attributes the organization looks for in the job holder.

In addition the advertisement should be:

> concise, accurate and attractive to suitable candidates. Conversely it should also seek to deter candidates who will clearly not be suitable from applying: this may be because the job really does require specific qualifications (e.g. a company secretarial position or a teaching post) or because the working conditions are not appropriate to all potential applicants (e.g. shift work, unsocial hours or a job requiring geographic mobility).

The advertisement should also contain the following information:

> Organization's name; organization's business; job location; the nature of the job; the title of the person to whom the jobholder reports; qualifications required; experience required; age range (if appropriate); salary range; further details of the remuneration package; promotion possibilities – if available; length of appointment; manner of application and the closing date for applications.

10 Application Forms

Any **application form** that is used – particularly in the case of large-scale recruitment, for example of school leavers – is likely to be standardized. When drawing up or choosing such a form the key point to remember is that it is likely to form the basis of both long- and short-listing procedures and a selection interview. It should therefore enable candidates

a) to provide information about themselves on the criteria on which listing will be based, and

b) encourage candidates to describe themselves in relation to the areas that can profitably be explored at interview to elicit evidence that the candidate either does or does not have the attributes sought for the job.

11 Listing

Long- and short- listing should be carried out against predetermined and relevant criteria drawn from the job description and person specification. In cases where there are large numbers of applicants the objective of long-listing is to eliminate from the field those candidates who cannot be considered seriously because they do not match the stipulated requirements.

The aim of short-listing is to finish with an appropriate number of suitable candidates to provide a competitive selection procedure so that there is a greater chance of choosing the most suitable person for the job. It is particularly important that short-listing is done as objectively as possible in order to ensure that there is no bias for or against any particular category of candidates.

It often happens at the listing stage that the organization has to begin to consider whether, and the extent to which it is prepared, to compromise on its requirements because the process to this point has not produced a field of suitable candidates.

12 References

Practice varies as to when in the process **references** are taken up. Clearly, if they are to be part of the informed decision-taking they should be available before the decision is taken and certainly before any unconditional offer of employment is made. The disadvantage of taking them before the selection procedures is that they require a contribution from an party external to those procedures who has no interest in meeting the selector's deadlines and who may indeed seek to frustrate the process (a current employer for example). The disadvantage of waiting until after the decision has been taken is that the references may disclose something about the candidate that should have been explored during the selection stage.

13 Selection Procedures

There are several techniques which can be used during the **selection** stage. These include:

Biodata analysis — Biodata is information about an individual which in a selection context can be compared with known information about current jobholders – both good and poor performers – and so provide an indication as to whether the candidate is likely to succeed or perform poorly in the job. If this technique is to be used then the application form – or the form from which the biodata is to be gathered – should be so drafted as to give candidates the chance to display information relevant to the job.

Telephone interviews — When a large number of candidates needs to be screened much expense can be saved by seeking standardized information in a standardized format through a telephone interview.

Aptitude tests — Aptitude tests are psychometric instruments designed to measure the performance of the person tested in such a way that it can be compared with that of others who have taken the test. As a predictor of success within a job it is vital to have information on current and past job holders both in terms of their performance in the job and their performance in the tests. If it can be shown that there is a correlation between a particular range of performance in

[a] test[s] and good performance in the job then the use of the test will increase the level of objectivity that can impact upon the decision.

Personality inventories Personality inventories seek to establish how an individual judges him- or herself on a number of dimensions in such a way as to enable the self-perceptions to be compared with those of a norm group.

Assessment centres Assessment centres aim to assess a group of individuals using a number of different techniques which are designed to be both comprehensive and integrated. The techniques used may include:

- *Group exercises* such as business games, group tasks and leaderless group discussions. Essentially such exercises should be designed to explore how the individuals react in a group but can also provide evidence of leadership, persuasiveness, oral communication, and inter-personal skills in general.

- *Role plays* in which candidates may be observed undertaking a particular, briefed, type of communication activity such as an appraisal interview.

- *In-tray exercises* in which candidates are faced with a number of problems to be dealt with in what is probably an inadequate amount of time. Such exercises can be designed to illustrate the candidates' approaches in a number of areas such as:

  grasp of detail; written communication; managerial style; analytical ability; approach to subordinates etc. In addition assessment centres frequently involve some or all of the other techniques outlined in this section.

Selection interviews The interview is the most widely used selection technique and it is extremely unlikely that a manager or an organization would want to appoint or employ someone sight unseen. The objectives of the interview are threefold:

a) to discover and explore evidence of the candidate's attributes or lack of the attributes required to do the job;

b) to leave the candidate with a good impression of the organization, and

c) to ensure that the candidate feels and recognizes that he or she has been treated fairly.

14   Decision and Notification

The aim of the selection process is to be able to reach a **decision** that is founded upon evidence relevant to the job in question, and well documented.

Notification should take place as soon after the decision as is practical. Naturally both successful and unsuccessful candidates must be notified and it is good practice to be prepared to discuss the reasons for rejection with the unsuccessful candidates.

15   Basis of Selection Problems

That the selection of personnel was an activity that was fraught with complications began to be recognized towards the end of the 1950s when a series of well-established experiments called into question the usefulness of the selection interview as a means of choosing the most appropriate person from among the field of candidates. This led to an increase in interest in the development and use of less subjective techniques which did not become really popular until Equal Opportunities legislation began to be policed effectively.

At that point many organizations which believed, quite genuinely, that their methods of selection – be it for new hires, internal promotion, redundancy or any other purpose – were fair, began to be confronted with irrefutable evidence (for example the small numbers of minority representatives who had been selected for the higher echelons) that there was some element of unfairness present in the system.

There was thus a premium on using the more objective approaches (aptitude tests; biodata; structured, relevant and well designed exercises; assessment centres) not only to increase the chances of making better selection decisions but also to have good evidence for the rationale behind those decisions.

The ability to use these more sophisticated selection techniques effectively is not acquired without effort. As a consequence it is probable that organizations now rely more and more on specialists – whether they be internal or external – to assist in making sound selection decisions.

This situation naturally sets up tensions around the process of selection. It is very unlikely that a candidate will be chosen and appointed to a position as a result of a decision made by the HR specialist. On the other hand if the decision-maker is, as is usually the case, the successful candidate's future line manager, the question will arise as to the extent to which the process has been corrupted by virtue of the fact that the decision-maker is untrained in complications of selection.

That this is not an idle speculation is emphasized by the thrust of the McPherson report into the handling by the Metropolitan Police of the investigation of the murder of the black teenager Steven Lawrence. McPherson found evidence of institutionalized racism within the Metropolitan Police: such a situation is symptomatic of the bias that is loaded into one person's judgement of another and unless objectivity is rigorously pursued it is probable that any organization will show evidence of some category of '-ism'.

16   Recruitment and the Internet

Like many other aspects of organizational life, recruitment and selection is being radically affected by the spread of information technology. The clearest impact of this is in the use of the Internet as one of the interfaces between the organization and the marketplace. The Internet is now used not only as an advertising medium but also as a speedy communication medium between organizations and their potential recruits.

Once the Internet becomes the predominant means of communication in relation to recruitment it is foreseeable that there will be a shift in the roles of the recruit and the recruiter.

Once an electronic link between the organization and a potential employee is established the speed at which communication can take place implies that the necessary delays inherent in any paper-based system as job details, application forms, references and letters are moved, via public mail systems, can be more productively managed if not entirely eliminated.

Organizational web sites and notice boards add to the advertising media open to employers and could lead to a subtle shift in the roles and responsibilities within the recruitment process. It may be that in the future there is a greater onus on the potential employee to initiate contact with an organization rather than wait to respond to specific advertisements.

17   Application of Knowledge of Selection

The application of learning about the recruitment and selection process is relevant to future managers from two aspects – that of the recruiter/selector and that of the recruit.

The selectors' contributions

For selectors there are two areas to which this learning can be applied.

Firstly it is incumbent upon the manager as selector – as opposed to the HR specialist as selector – to be aware of the contribution made by the selector to the selection process. This contribution comprises not only the active participation in the drafting and/or approval of the job description, person specification, advertisement other documentation and to the selection process, but also the subconscious, unwitting and unintentional elements that inevitably obfuscate the assessment of candidates and the actual selection decision.

There was evolutionary pressure on man, as a species, to develop the capacity to make rapid judgements based upon little evidence – 30,000 years ago man was living in a relatively hostile environment! Making use of this facility within the relatively benign world of recruitment and selection is probably counterproductive in two ways. If selection decisions are based only upon evidence that is less than fully explored they are unlikely to be the best decisions from the organization's point of view and they are less defensible when questions of fairness and equality of opportunity are raised.

Objectivity

Secondly – and partly in order to counter the problems posed by the inevitably subjective nature of the process – the manager needs to pay attention to those aspects of the process that are designed to raise the level of objectivity. The key contribution which can be made by the manager relates to the formation of the person specification – the description of the attributes of the ideal person whom the manager is seeking to recruit. This is an area to which the manager, as selector, should give quality effort. Drawing up the person specification requires careful – though not necessarily extensive – thought. The finished document should be accurate and realistic – and the reasons why particular attributes are being sought should be documented so that they can be fully understood at all stages and by all those participating in the process.

It is against a well-drawn person specification that candidates will be judged at the long- and short-listing stages and selection stages. Additionally it will guide the choice of selection techniques.

The candidates' viewpoint

As candidates there are also two areas to which this learning can be applied, which are essentially the above two areas seen from the reverse viewpoint.

In the first place it is essential to recognize the crucial importance of the person specification to the recruitment and selection process. Many modern organizations actually distribute the person specifications with the application material. Even if this is not done many of the attributes listed in the person specification should be clear from the advertisement. Armed with this information it is incumbent upon potential recruits to judge the extent to which they meet the criteria.

In these days of electronic communication it is tempting to think that nothing is lost by despatching applications for jobs for which there is little match between the candidate's assessment of him- or herself and the ideal specified by the selector. This implies that for desirable positions there will be a substantial field of candidates, which in turn implies that getting past the hurdles of long- and short-listing may be something of a lottery. Accordingly candidates should do all in their power to mould their applications to increase their chances of moving onto the short list.

This is accomplished by adopting two basic approaches.

First, it is necessary to ensure that the application addresses those aspects of the person specification that are known – showing how, and the extent to which, the candidate meets the selection criteria. Here it is necessary to bear in mind that the person specification describes the ideal post holder and that most candidates will not match all the requirements; applicants should therefore indicate how their lack of some element of the specification can be addressed.

Second, the application should set out to make it easy for the selector to find material that can be explored during the selection stage: thus if the application form permits (as most do) personal statements of fitness for the job, it is sensible to provide solid evidence – such as past experiences – of the required attributes.

The second area in respect of which candidates can apply their learning is in relation to the selection process itself. Having secured a place on the short list the candidate needs to recognize the difficulties connected with the way in which selection decisions are made and to appreciate that there may be no way in which the selector will be induced to favour him or her – the 'chemistry' between them will not be right.

This implies that candidates should approach selection with two objectives:

a)   to be the successful candidate, and

b)   to learn as much as possible from the process either to help the transition from candidate to recruit, or to enhance the chances of success in future applications.

A well-prepared candidate will help selectors to respond to the person specification by contributing, and emphasizing, evidence of the required attributes as suggested by the documentation.

Summary

Now that you have studied this chapter you should be able to:

● Participate knowledgeably in the recruitment process;

● Participate knowledgeably in the selection process;

● Critically examine key elements in the process;

● Describe the main types of workforce flexibility;

● Approach selection procedures with appropriate caution;

● Succeed as a candidate for selection.

17

TRAINING, DEVELOPMENT AND CAREER MANAGEMENT

Objectives

After studying this chapter you should be able to:

- Distinguish between 'training' and 'development';
- Outline the process of training;
- Explain the concept of the 'learning cycle';
- Explain what underlies career management;
- Develop strategies for managing a career.

1 Training and Development

The distinction between 'training' and 'development' is that training has to do with the job currently being performed, whereas development has to do with preparing for a future job or for a future range of jobs or simply broadening the contribution that the individual can make to work or life in general. That having been said, the terms are often used quite legitimately as synonyms because the theoretical basis is the same for both training and development. The choice of vehicles to impart the lessons to be learned may well be different – probably because of the more immediate payback required from training – but the choice of methods is only one aspect of a relatively extensive process (see section 3 below).

Another essential difference between training and development relates to the 'locus of control' of the activity. With training this will probably reside in the organization rather than the individual whereas the reverse is true where development is concerned (see section 11 below).

2 Training

There are two basic objectives to training:

(i) to save time, and

(ii) to ensure that the employee achieves a certain basic level of competence.

This requires some explanation.

Adults learn from a variety of sources but throughout their adult life – in contrast to their childhood – they undertake relatively little formal education. The richest source of education in respect of their jobs are those jobs themselves and the basic objective of any formal training they undertake should be to equip them to maximize the learning that they can derive from actually doing the job.

This implies that training should be focused on the job, geared to raising the trainee to the appropriate level of competence to enable him or her to perform the job – and thus begin learning from it. Put glibly, this may require the trainee to move through four stages of learning:

1. Unconscious incompetence   'I don't know that I can't do it'

2. Conscious incompetence   'I do know that I can't do it'

3. Conscious competence   'I do know that I can do it'

4. Unconscious competence   'I don't know that I can do it'

The idea that the job itself is a learning vehicle also implies that, left to his own devices, the jobholder would (if sufficiently motivated) reach the stage of conscious competence *in due course* and so a payoff from the investment in training can equate to the time saved.

There are subsidiary objectives to training such as:

(iii) ensuring company-wide consistency

(iv) ensuring appropriate levels of safety

 (v) backing-up change

(vi) reinforcing attitudes

3   Systematic Approach to Training

It is well established that, from the organizational viewpoint, training benefits from a planned approach following a process such as that outlined and the described below.

Figure 17.1: Systematic training process

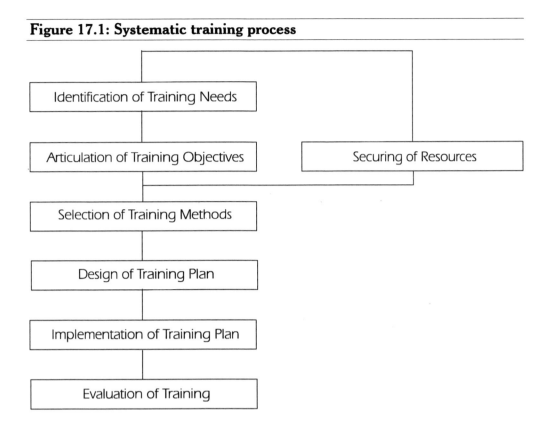

The concept of the learning organization

This is a philosophy that organizations can choose to adopt. Although it is difficult to define precisely, the concept of the learning organization is much talked about in both academic circles and in organizations. One definition of the term is provided by Pedler et al. (1991) as 'an organization that facilitates the learning of all its members and continuously transforms itself'. It is an acknowledgement that in these times of constant change, there are continuous opportunities for learning, from totally new and evolving situations to learning from past mistakes. One of the key objectives of learning organizations is to make the link to improved performance, so that learning is demonstrated through improved work outcomes.

4   Training Needs

The identification of training needs is a complicated procedure often undertaken for organizations by training consultants. There are, however, a number of pointers which indicate an actual or possible training need. Among these are:

ACTUAL	POSSIBLE
Induction	Absenteeism
Promotion	High labour turnover
New product	Customer complaints
New system	Low performance
New technology	Health and safety statistics
Legislative changes	Rising costs
Change	Grievance/discipline statistics
Planning for career move	Conflict
Strategic plan	Low morale
Manpower plan	Competitive pressure

Training objectives

The articulation of training objectives is another complicated area because in many cases the effects of training are not susceptible to direct measurement and so it is difficult to say whether the objectives are or can be achieved. Currently the trend is to ensure that the objectives are expressed in 'behavioural terms'. This means that they specify what the trainee will be able to do at the end of the training (which he or she could not do before), the standard that the trainee will have been able to achieve and the conditions under which the trainee will be able to exhibit that standard.

As an example, if an organization were to introduce a new performance management system – indicative of an actual training need – then the training objectives could be that by the end of the training all managers within the company will be able to:

● Determine targets for their subordinates in line with organizational business plans;

● Agree specific targets with subordinates;

● Assess the performance of their subordinates against the agreed targets;

● Carry out a performance review interview with their subordinates within one month of the end of the period under review; and

● Complete accurately the performance review documentation by the specified deadline.

5   Training Methods

The training methods should be selected in order to achieve the training objectives in the most cost-effective way. This is not to imply that training should not be regarded as an investment, but there is, for example, little point in incurring the cost of sending staff away on a training course when the same objective can be achieved by training that takes place in the workplace itself.

This raises a fundamental point about training for jobs. Remember that training objectives should state the conditions under which the trainee should be able to exhibit the outcome of the training. If the investment in training is to be maximized the ideal conditions are 'while performing the job itself'! This implies that the best place for the training to occur is actually on the job. Thus, for example, interview training is best accomplished by the trainer observing the trainee carrying out a real-life (as opposed to a simulated) interview and then giving appropriate feedback.

On-the-job training is expensive if it requires the services of a professional trainer – but that is not always the case.

The following methods of **on-the-job training** exist:

Sitting next to Nellie	Training manuals	Trainee logbooks
Coaching	Mentoring	Programmed learning
Job rotation	Assignments	Demonstration
Delegation	Action learning	Embedded training

To these can be added the methods of **off-the-job training**, among which are:

Training courses	Seminars	Workshops
Television programmes	Lectures	Textbooks
Simulations	Business games	Role plays
Case studies	Computer-based training	CD Roms
Web-based training		

6 Design and Implementation of the Training Plan

A good training plan will not only seek to achieve the training objectives, it will also be designed to ensure that those objectives, when achieved, will be transferred back to the workplace. This means that training is not something that can profitably be considered as divorced from the job.

An effective training plan involves a partnership between the three areas that are fundamentally concerned with the training. These can be described both in an organizational and in a personal sense. They are:

ORGANIZATIONAL	PERSONAL
Line management	The trainee's boss
The training establishment (whether internal or external)	The trainer
Those who need the training	The trainee

The most important contributor to this partnership is line management/trainee's boss – often referred to as the 'stakeholder'.

It is the stakeholder who is most interested in seeing that the right needs are identified, the right objectives set, the right training delivered and that that training is transferred to the working environment of the trainee.

Thus the training plan should be agreed with the stakeholder at organizational level, and at the personal level the stakeholder should positively contribute to the training process by briefing and debriefing the trainee.

Briefing involves discussing three things with the trainee:

(i)   Why the trainee is undertaking this training

(ii) What the training objectives are

(iii) What the trainee's personal objectives are

Debriefing involves discussing with the trainee:

(i)   What objectives were achieved

(ii) How the stakeholder can help the trainee to ensure that the learning is transferred to the workplace.

7   Evaluation

It is, of course, the stakeholder who pays directly or indirectly for the training. The stakeholder thus has a prime interest in ensuring that the training is effective. The trainer should also want to establish that the training plan has worked by setting up mechanisms that measure the extent to which

(i) the training objectives were achieved, and

(ii) the learning was transferred back to the workplace.

8   How Adults Learn

The above exposition takes an approach to training that has an organizational orientation, but it is important that the perspective of the individual is not lost. A fundamental reason for this is that people do not all learn in the same way.

An American psychologist – David Kolb – identified two key aspects of the adult learning process:

1.   each adult is a blend of four distinguishable learning styles, and

2.   a full learning experience arises only when all four of these styles are catered for.

The learning styles are:

- Concrete experience – i.e. the learner undergoes an event that is in some way novel;

- Reflective observation – i.e. the learner thinks back over an experience (whether his own or that of another which he has observed) in order to determine what can be used to change the learner's way of doing something or 'way of being in the world';

- Abstract conceptualisation – i.e. the learner moves from the particular (e.g. an experience or a training event) to the general (e.g. a job or a task within a job) by drawing generalized conclusions from what has been experienced and/or observed which can be applied to life or at work;

- Active experimentation – i.e. the learner determines what he or she will do differently in future and begins to put it into practice.

Given that we are each a blend of the four styles we can maximize the learning we derive from any learning event by ensuring that we incorporate all four styles into our experience of that event. For example, if you are to go on a training course it is usually suggested that your boss should brief you beforehand. This gives you the opportunity to plan your approach to the course and decide on what areas you are going to concentrate (active experimentation). You then experience the course (concrete experience) following which your boss should debrief you with the objective of asking you to review your experience (reflective observation) and draw conclusions as to which parts of your experiences you can incorporate into approach to life or work (abstract conceptualisation). Your debriefing should finish with an action plan highlighting how you will implement these new ideas or practices into your work (back to active experimentation).

The most potent learning event that managers experience is the job they do. Unfortunately, many managers fail to capitalize on their own experience – largely because they ignore the lessons that can be derived from a knowledge of learning styles.

If learning is structured it tends to follow a cyclical pattern:

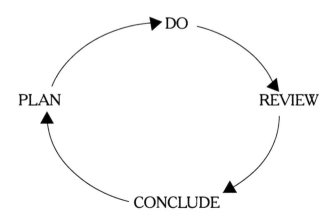

The above is only an example, and although maximized learning should follow the same cyclical pattern it need not begin with the experience – but could begin with any of the four stages – for example by:

- **reviewing** press reports of a competitor's activity;

- **theorizing** on the basis of some technological, fiscal or legal innovation or

- **planning** the introduction of a change and hence a new experience.

9   Using the Learning Cycle

So much for the theoretical input! What practical use can you make of this?

You can use the concept of the learning cycle both as a development tool – to ensure that any learning experience you undertake is as rich as possible – and as part of your approach to your forthcoming exams.

- Look ahead to each period of study – determining in advance what it is that you expect to derive from it.

- Participate as fully as possible in each learning session, having particular regard to those aspects which were highlighted during your planning.

- Make sure that you run over each session in your mind – or in discussion with colleagues – shortly after it has finished. Ideally this should be within the next 24 hours, but it need not take very long.

- As each session or topic is concluded look for the patterns between what you have learnt and what you already know about this and other subjects.

- Finally remember that managerial life goes on all around you in the workplace and elsewhere. When you have studied a topic look for practical examples of good and bad practice while at work. Think about them, and about how you would do things differently; if possible discuss them with your colleagues and bosses.

10   Changing Attitudes to Development

When training is considered from the organizational viewpoint there seems little doubt that the principle beneficiary of the training is the trainee's boss, given that training is designed to maintain or improve productivity.

The position is not the same with regard to development. The boss may have little **direct** interest in seeing employees develop – given the definition of development at the beginning of this chapter. Here the boss is likely to have to absorb the costs of development (at least in part) while, provided that the development is successful, it is the employee's next boss who will reap the benefits.

This is an aspect of the changing nature of the psychological contract between the organization and its employees. While the concept of the 'job for life' was still prevalent it was in the interests of organizations not only to train but also to develop their employees – because neither activity represented a sunk cost. Now that employees are engaged by organizations to do jobs rather than have careers, it is a predominantly altruistic act for the organization to develop employees – although the organization does get the benefit of fresh input as developed employees leave and are replaced.

As a consequence, responsibility for personal development has shifted from the organization to the employee. Since personal development is a key aspect of career management it is as well that individuals have a clear understanding of theory underlying training and development.

11 Fundamentals of Training and Development

Stated simply there are three areas in which adults can be trained – knowledge, skills and attitudes. A model for the way in which learning is achieved involves three aspects:

- Input – whereby the trainee receives something that is new – or reinforces some previous input;

- Process – whereby the trainee internalizes those elements from the input with which he or she is able – or prepared – to deal, and

- Output – whereby the trainee demonstrates what has been acquired by virtue of the training undertaken.

As an example of this model in practice, return to the training problem of the introduction of a new performance management system. The training plan, in part, could comprise:

	Input	**Process**	**Output**
Knowledge	a) Details of the new system and its supporting documents b) Interviewing theory	a) Practice at filling in the new perf. mgmt. form b) Discussion on the pitfalls of interviewing	a) Successfully completed forms b) Action plan on how to put theory into practice
Skills	a) Case study charting aspects of performance b) Video demonstrating how to feedback on performance	a) Assessment of the performance depicted in the case study b) Interviewing practice on the basis of this assessment	a) Agreed rating of the performance depicted b) Discussion around the observed interview

	Input	Process	Output
		– undertaken and observed by trainees	
Attitude	'Keynote' address by senior manager stressing the importance of the new system	Question and answer session to allay any suspicions and enthuse recipients	Action plan to cascade learning to subordinates

Notice how the above outline plan caters for all four of the learning styles.

12   Managerial Development

In his book *Management Development Strategies for Action* (1993), Professor Alan Mumford describes his conclusions from research designed to discover how directors learn but which is probably more generally applicable, particularly so as managers' careers develop.

He concluded that formal management development processes (i.e programmes of development, courses, distance learning modules, mentoring schemes etc.) were important but insufficient and often inefficiently provided. On the other hand informal processes (those that are not formally planned) were insufficient and inefficient because managers lacked the skills to maximize the learning experience (i.e. they did not apply the 'learning cycle' model).

By discussing – retrospectively – the learning events experienced by the subjects of the research, Mumford was able to get them to articulate both

a)   the content of, and

b)   the processes involved in their learning experiences.

Mumford thus identified the need for a model for management development that included both formal and informal learning experiences.

This chart is as follows:

Type 1	Informal managerial – accidental processes (basically 'learning on the job')	
	Characteristics	<ul><li>occur within managerial activity</li><li>explicit intention is task performance</li><li>no clear development objectives</li><li>unstructured in development terms</li><li>not planned in advance</li><li>owned by the managers</li></ul>
	Developmental consequences	Learning is real, direct, unconscious and insufficient
Type 2	Integrated managerial – opportunistic processes (learning opportunities that arise within a job but where the developmental aspects are identified in advance and exploited – through e.g. 'coaching' and 'action learning')	
	Characteristics	<ul><li>occur within managerial activity</li><li>explicit intention is both task performance and development</li><li>clear development objectives</li><li>structured for development by boss and subordinate</li><li>planned beforehand or reviewed subsequently as learning experiences</li><li>owned by the managers</li></ul>
	Developmental consequences	Learning is real, direct, conscious and more substantial
Type 3	Formal management development – planned processes	
	Characteristics	<ul><li>often away from normal managerial activity</li><li>explicit intention is development</li><li>clear development objectives</li><li>structured for development by developers</li><li>planned beforehand and reviewed subsequently as learning experiences</li><li>owned more by developers than managers</li></ul>
	Developmental consequences	Learning may be real (through a job) or detached (through a course), generally indirect, more likely to be conscious and relatively infrequent.

13 Career Management – Strategies

The idea that responsibility for personal learning and development has shifted from the organization to the individual fits neatly with the idea that – more so than in the past – individuals must accept responsibility for managing their own careers.

A career has been defined as 'a succession of related jobs arranged in a hierarchy of prestige, through which persons moved in an ordered (more or less predictable) sequence'. Career management involves determining (at the least) what the next job in the sequence will be.

In the context of 'career management' it is important to have some idea of what outcomes we expect from a career. The fundamental questions that need to be answered are:

'Do I want to work?' and 'Do I want to work for myself or for an organization?'

Rather like the learning cycle there can be a cyclical approach to the management of a career, (Ball B (1997)):

Figure 17.2: Cyclical management of a career

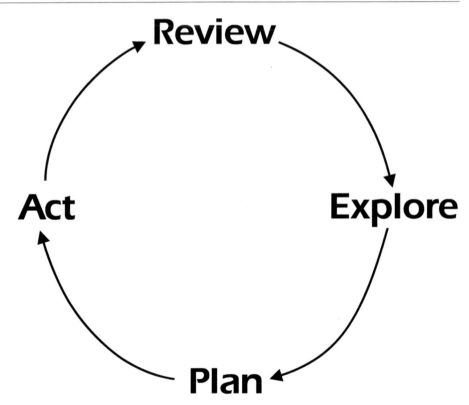

Thus having determined the answer to the fundamental questions posed above, the careerist will carry out a personal SWOT analysis as a basis for reviewing what options are open.

Knowing what you can offer to the outside world is only one part of the equation. It is also necessary to ascertain what the outside world can offer to you by exploring what is available within the world of work for an individual with your particular blend of strengths.

This is, perhaps, the key element in a career strategy because it may require a dismantling of traditional patterns of thinking about sequences of jobs. In the past it was more likely that career progression would involve moving from a job requiring one set of skills to one requiring a different set of skills but within the same industry (frequently within the same organization). Now it is more likely that the job move is to one that has a broad match of skills with the preceding job although the environment in which these skills are to be used may be radically different.

This approach reflects the emphasis on 'competencies' which has been prevalent during the past decade. Competencies are critical skills, knowledge and attitudes that a job holder must have to perform effectively and, provided that the knowledge needed falls broadly into a generalist rather than a specialist sphere (as is the case with management), there is a wide range of opportunities to transfer from one working environment to another.

A danger in this development within the field of career management is that the careerist does not know into what fields his or her competencies are transferable – hence the next stage – explore – in the career planning cycle. It is necessary for the careerist to establish and maintain an awareness of the areas to which he or she is attracted and which would find what he or she has to offer attractive. A useful source of intelligence to aid this exploration is the services of 'career management' or 'outplacement' consultants whose reputations rest on an ability to match individual competencies to job requirements.

A comparison between what is revealed by the exploration and what is shown by the individual SWOT – in terms of strengths and weaknesses – will probably lead to the identification of a gap and hence to a development need. The individual will then plan to achieve two things:

a)   supplying the development need, and when fully equipped with competencies

b)   an approach to the job market designed to satisfy the next stage of the career.

14   Career Management – Tactics

At a more tactical level the individual can best enhance the chances of achieving career goals by paying attention to the following areas:

a)   Have a clear idea of what the career is intended to achieve within the context – if possible – of an overall life plan. This enables the employee to make more informed judgements about career opportunities as they arise.

b)   Establish career goals that are realistic and flexible – and be prepared to adjust them as circumstances change.

c)   Plan career moves up to three or four jobs ahead – and have several options available for each move.

d)   Develop a 'network' – in this context a grouping of careerists with broadly similar interests who communicate informally – and networking skills.

e)   Take opportunities to raise profile both within the current organization and within the field covered by the network.

f)   Take training and development opportunities that are relevant to the overall career plan.

g)   Choose bosses carefully, opting where possible for those who can contribute to personal development.

h)   Always strive to help the boss to succeed.

Summary

Now that you have studied this chapter you should be able to:

- Describe how organizations should approach the training of their employees;
- Critically examine the structure of training and development events that you attend;
- Plan your own development activities;
- Exploit learning opportunities to their fullest extent by application of the learning cycle;
- Adopt a systematic approach to career management.

References

Pedler M Burgoyne J & Boydell T (1991) *The Learning Company: A Strategy for Sustainable Development*, McGraw Hill

Ball B (1997) *Career Management Competences: the Individual Perspective* in *Career Development International* Vol. 2, No. 2 pp 74-79)

Wilensky (1964) 'Varieties of Work Experience' in Borow H ed. *Man in a World at Work* Houghton Mifflin

18

PERFORMANCE MANAGEMENT AND REWARD SYSTEMS

Objectives

After studying this chapter you should be able to:

- describe the principles of performance management;

- describe the principles of appraisal systems;

- critically evaluate the role of performance management and appraisals in work organizations;

- explain the theoretical framework of job evaluation, work and job design;

- evaluate the impact of different types of organizational reward systems;

- discuss the significance of reward systems and their link with organizational goals.

1   Introduction

This chapter explores the issue of how organizations try to motivate employees through the use of performance management systems. An integral part of this system of performance management can be the appraisal process sometimes linked to a reward system. This chapter will also examine the appraisal process and the different types of reward systems (both extrinsic and intrinsic) used by organizations, and their effects.

2   What is Performance Management?

Performance management can be interpreted in different ways. In some organizations it means a comprehensive appraisal system, in others it refers to an attempt to redirect the whole organization towards superior performance. It does have a wider meaning than just annual programmes of appraisal and target-setting; it encompasses a cycle and range of activities within this cycle, including assessment of the performance of a job and linking this to reward systems.

It is used by organizations to try to achieve strategic goals through better motivation, monitoring, evaluation and rewards for performance. Performance management is more concerned with clarifying the organization's needs for business performance and setting up a process to ensure these are delivered.

There are a number of key activities involved in performance management:

- Determine the performance expectations – by evaluating the job and its activities;

- Support performance – by providing induction, training and development activities;

- Review and appraise performance through an appraisal system or something similar;

- Manage performance standards by feedback and rewards.

The underlying themes are therefore:

- Achievement of objectives linked to training and development;

- Providing feedback on performance, thereby identifying new needs;

- Evidence of both extrinsic and intrinsic rewards;

- Rewarding personal development and achievement.

Performance management has been introduced by many financial service organizations over the last decade as a system that ties individual pay to qualitative or quantitative objectives through profit-sharing and merit pay. The stress is on high performance throughout the organization. It aims to link individual objectives with strategic ones and provides the organization with some financial flexibility by relating some element of the reward package to performance.

The three key elements of a structured performance management system are:

- Job evaluation in order to determine performance criteria and standards and the base rate of pay;

- Setting objectives linked to the job role and the objectives of the organization;

- Appraisal to determine the performance of an individual and therefore any variable pay element that should be received;

- Establishing reward systems to help to determine fringe benefits.

It is proposed to examine appraisal systems, job evaluation and reward systems in this chapter.

3 Performance Appraisal Systems

Appraisals are normally designed in broad terms to measure an individual's contribution to the organization in as objective a way as possible, providing information for the organization on the skills and capabilities available and information for the individual on opportunities, reward and feedback on performance. Appraisals may therefore provide information on assessment of current performance, future potential and reward.

Appraisals may fulfill a number of roles:

- Information for determining rewards
- Assessment of training needs
- Assessment for career development
- Information for HR planning
- Identification of potential
- Assessment of an individual's motivation
- Information on performance improvement and management
- Information for succession planning

It could be argued that it is difficult for an effective performance appraisal system to fulfill all these different needs at once and some writers have argued that different systems should exist for different purposes. However, there is then an issue to address of how many systems it is feasible for an organization to maintain.

At the minimum an appraisal system should:

- Give feedback on an individual's performance (this obviously has some links with Porter and Lawler's model of motivation discussed in Chapter 11);
- Make salary decisions as fairly as possible;
- Give employees the opportunity to participate in decisions that affect them;
- Allow for career planning, training decisions and counselling.

However care must be taken when introducing appraisal systems. Problems can arise because of:

a) The design of the forms used (are the criteria standards that have been set fair and reflect the job content?)

b) Preparation for implementation of the systems – have both appraisers and appraisees been briefed as to the objectives and structure of the system and appraisers been trained in interviewing techniques?

c) The administration of the system – is it administered carefully to avoid subjective bias etc.?

The 360-degree appraisal (where feedback on an individual's performance is sought from all the parties with whom there is contact) is becoming more frequently used. It appears to be able to resolve some of the problems of traditional appraisal systems because it provides feedback from colleagues and subordinates as well as superiors. The key to success lies in maintaining confidentiality and ensuring an independent party is available to provide feedback.

4   The Balanced Scorecard

Another approach, which can be integrated into a performance management system, is the balanced scorecard. This is designed to assess an individual's performance in a balanced way across different areas, namely product, customer, finance and internal management processes. It is argued that in the past managers have focused on short-term financial measures such as sales growth and operational income and although financial measures are important others are equally important. The importance of these other measures should be reflected in the way individuals are assessed.

The balanced scorecard approach involves four key steps:

a)   Deciding a vision for the future;

b)   Deciding how the vision will provide competitive advantage for the shareholder, customer, internal management processes, innovation and growth;

c)   Determining from these the critical success factors for performance;

d)   Identifying the critical measures to determine how successful the individual and therefore the organization is.

5   Job Evaluation Processes

One process that helps us assess the worth of jobs is job evaluation. It is defined by Armstrong (1993) as:

The process of establishing the value of jobs in a job hierarchy.

Although it is possible to determine job values by negotiation or on the basis of broad assumptions about market rates and the internal relationship between jobs, a more analytical approach is normally adopted using a job evaluation scheme, with market rates and pay surveys. A good job evaluation scheme should remove some of the uncertainty about the fairness of rewards by using a more objective basis for deciding pay.

The aims of job evaluation are to:

●   provide a rank order of jobs for the organization. This can then be used to determine the salary level and the status of any job position;

●   ensure judgements about job values are made on objective grounds;

●   provide a continuing basis for assessing the value of jobs.

There are two major categories of job evaluation: non-quantitative and quantitative techniques.

The non-quantitative techniques involve the comparison of the whole or parts of jobs and placing them in a rank order. There are two major non-quantitative schemes, job ranking and job classification. The quantitative techniques involve allocating points or values to the various elements of jobs, which are then combined to form a whole. An example of this technique is points rating. The next section examines each of these techniques in turn.

Job ranking

This ranks jobs by comparing whole job descriptions. A paired comparison method is sometimes used, where two jobs are compared. In such cases two points are awarded to the higher-ranking post, one where each is considered to be of equal rank, and none to the lower-ranking job.

Job classification or grade description

This job evaluation scheme begins with a series of hierarchical grades. Each one is then assigned a description or classification. The description has to cover the various duties that may be involved in the post, and includes enough detail to make the classification of jobs clear. It must detail the type of work as well as the level of ability and provide key jobs for the identification of grades. Each job within the organization can then be slotted into the appropriate grade.

Points rating

This system breaks down each job into a series of factors which are then weighted in terms of points. The total number of points awarded to a job will decide the grade of the job. An example of a well-developed points rating system is the one produced by HAY/MSL. The benchmark jobs within this scheme represent a particular grade within the job evaluation system. These jobs are recognized as standard and have an agreed value assigned to them and so provide help with the position of other posts. The HAY/MSL scheme is one commonly used in the financial services sector. This scheme emphasizes know-how, accountability and problem solving as the three key components in grading jobs.

Job evaluation does involve (whichever system is used) some subjectivity, because human judgement must be used to establish an order of jobs or in assigning values to them. This in turn means that the job evaluation system must allow employees the right of appeal against a particular evaluation. It will normally be heard by a separate appeal panel which will check that the job has been evaluated correctly using information previously provided and any new evidence.

Having established what a job evaluation system involves, the next stage is to determine the base pay using a particular salary payment system.

6   Determining Base Pay

Reward systems can be broadly divided into two different types, extrinsic and intrinsic. Extrinsic reward systems provide recompense regardless of the individual's performance, whereas intrinsic reward systems reward the individual according to the individual performance that has been achieved.

There have been a number of significant changes in the nature of extrinsic reward packages over the last ten to fifteen years.

The traditional view of extrinsic rewards was characterized by:

- a belief in equity with maintenance of internal relativities;
- a tendency to focus on the pay arrangements for groups of staff rather than individuals through collective bargaining;
- a concern for clarity and order with structured, rigid pay schemes and clear rules for progression;
- a wide range of fringe benefits established to cope with the lack of differentials arising from the past incomes policies;
- an emphasis on job evaluation as a means of establishing new pay levels.

The new approach to extrinsic reward systems that has evolved over the last decade has emphasized:

- pay systems need to be market-driven, because external factors are more important than internal relationships in pay;
- individual rather than group focus, with individual contracts of employment and individually agreed levels of pay;
- flexibility with an ability to respond to organizational and business changes;
- integrated pay systems with three or four broad bands for grading rather than 10 or 12 separate hierarchical grades;
- an emphasis on getting value for money.

Some of these elements have had much more of an impact than others. Paying for performance has been widely adopted in most financial services organizations but most still use a job evaluation system to determine base rates of pay.

Base rates of pay – salary systems

Most salary systems provide the opportunity for progression through the salary scale according to experience. This opportunity for progression provides motivation for improved performance in the future as well as encouraging high achievers to remain with the firm. In order to ensure that a progressive system is as efficient as possible and can be easily controlled, it needs to:

- be divided into defined areas or zones;
- have incremental systems to indicate the rates at which individuals can progress;
- have guidelines for determining merit increments.

Incremental systems of pay can vary from rigid fixed procedures to flexible systems where management has complete discretion over the award. Within financial service organizations, the incremental system has historically been fairly tightly controlled, with a scale of increments according to promotion and experience.

There are a number of advantages and disadvantages associated with salary scale systems. It is perceived to offer several advantages, including:

● it is clear and published to all employees;

● it is predictable, so budgets can be anticipated for employer and employee;

● it offers incremental rises;

● performance bonuses can still be incorporated.

However, it is acknowledged that problems also exist with their use:

● salary is paid irrespective of results and effort;

● pay structures are rigid;

● it encourages promotion because this is the only way of really increasing income substantially;

● there can be anomalies between grades, for instance someone at the top of one lower grade may be carrying more responsibility than a newcomer who is earning more in the grade above.

7 Determining Variable Pay and Fringe Benefits

Variable pay has been introduced by many organizations over the last decade in an effort to reward individual effort and contribution. As the term suggests the amount paid varies according to an assessment of the individual's performance.

Performance-related pay

With less opportunity for promotion and fewer layers of management and staff (known as broad banding) many financial service organizations have introduced performance-related pay (PRP). In this way good performance can continue to be rewarded and recognized when no promotion opportunities exist. However, there appears to be no agreement on how effective this system of payment can be. There are two main groups of opponents:

1. Those who believe that there is something fundamentally flawed about the design of a PRP system, especially when it is used on an individual basis, and no amount of investment in its design and implementation will address this issue.

2. Those who believe that the system is basically sound, but that it is the failure to learn

from and correct the faults that has caused problems to arise.

Those belonging to the first group would argue that the assumption that money motivates employees to higher effort is flawed, and that rather than motivating the whole workgroup only a few are favoured under PRP. This is seen to lead to a lack of motivation for the majority of the workforce. It is also suggested that PRP has been developed from payment schemes relating to the manufacturing industries, and that is not appropriate for roles where limited quantitative judgements can be made.

The disadvantages of using PRP could be summarized as follows:

- it is not always easy to set targets for individuals to achieve because some are qualitative rather than quantitative measures, and this can be time consuming and costly;

- the setting, monitoring and evaluation of performance against targets is time consuming;

- it is not always easy for the employee to budget because with performance-related pay income is uncertain;

- salaries cannot be published because there is no uniform standard or scale;

- it can be very difficult to judge performance objectively, especially where the employee's performance may be measured in qualitative terms.

However others would argue that PRP offers some significant advantages, namely:

- rewards should be related to effort;

- there is not the same necessity to promote in order to increase rewards;

- the system can be integrated with corporate goals and a performance management system;

- it is easy to incorporate into an organization if it can use quantitative targets to assess performance against;

- it can be used to reward desired behaviour;

- it encourages the achievement of targets and increased productivity can fund the increased pay.

Within the financial services sector, as well as the move towards performance-related pay there has also been a move towards broad banding of salaries in line with delayering. This move towards broad banding de-emphasizes status and grading, reduces the pressure for promotion and regrading, blurs the edges around pay decisions, and makes it easier to move people laterally across the organization.

Skill-based pay

Based on the concept that individuals are valuable to the organization if they are highly skilled, some organizations consider a payment system based on skills or competencies. This system is not widely in use at the present time. Some of the problems that organizations still need to address are how to assess an individual's level of skill accurately and how to prevent individual payment for a skill not currently used in a job.

Fringe or additional benefits

Within most salary systems there is a range of fringe or additional benefits, which are available for different categories of staff, for example:

- bonus schemes, profit sharing;
- non-contributory pension schemes;
- low-interest housing and assistance with transfers;
- sick pay;
- paid holidays;
- company cars;
- medical benefits.

Some organizations are now introducing cafeteria or flexible benefits systems to allow the employee to select an individually tailored package of benefits from those on offer. With a sum of money allocated for fringe benefits they can chose which benefits they want up to the amount allowed. Their choice of benefits can change in line with their needs at any particular time. The hope is that this will benefit the employer in terms of both recruitment and retention by providing a competitive edge.

Summary

Now you have studied this chapter you should be able to:

- Discuss the role of a performance management system;
- Analyse the steps involved in designing an effective appraisal system;
- Critically evaluate the different job evaluation systems;
- Compare the various types of reward systems available and the effects of each.

References

Armstrong M (1993) *Managing Reward Systems*, Open University Press

Hackman J R & Oldham G R (1980) *Work Redesign*, Addison Wesley

Mullins L J (1996) *Management and Organizational Behaviour*, 4th ed. Pitman

19

DIVERSITY

Objectives

After studying this chapter you should be able to:

- define managing diversity;

- clarify the differences between equal opportunities and managing diversity;

- describe the role and influence of the legislation in relation to equal opportunities and managing diversity;

- explain why managing diversity is important in business;

- outline an approach for the effective implementation of diversity management in an organization.

1   Defining Managing Diversity

According to the Institute of Personnel and Development (1997), managing diversity means 'that people should be valued as individuals for reasons relating to business reasons as well as for moral and social reasons'. Therefore factors such as gender, age, background, race, disability are harnessed to meet organizational goals as effectively and efficiently as possible maximizing the talents and potential of all involved. Managing diversity recognizes that people from different background, race, age, gender etc. will have differing interpretations of the same situation and, in valuing these differences, organizations can learn and improve the way the work is done.

In recent years there has been a greater awareness of the need for organizations to manage proactively the diverse nature of their workforce. This concept of diversity complements equal opportunities, HR and quality management. It has three main purposes:

- to help employees who are perceived as different from the majority of their colleagues to succeed and develop their careers;

- to create an environment where all can work together combating prejudice, harassment, stereotyping and undignified behaviour, and to allow people to be valued as individuals;

- to help to effect cultural change.

2 What is Driving Diversity Issues?

There are a number of factors affecting managing diversity in organizations:

1. The increasing age of the workforce. By 2001 one in three will be aged over 40 and yet there is prejudice about the employment and training potential of older people.

2. The increasing number of women in the workforce. Since 1975 the number of women in employment has increased by 34% to 12.2 million in 1995, while the number of men has fallen by 0.5% to 15.6 million. Between 1994 and 2001 male employment will rise by only 3%, female by 11%, and women will make up 45% of the workforce.

3. The increase in part-time working. Between 1994 and 2001 part-time working increased by 22% and full-time decreased by 1%.

4. The acknowledgement of caring responsibilities for both children and the elderly with 2½ million men and 3 million women having caring responsibilities for elderly dependents.

5. Discrimination and harassment experienced by those entering or already in employment.

3 Equal Opportunities and Managing Diversity

Equal opportunities is broadly about achieving:

● Equal chance, providing the same chances for all

● Equal access

● Equal share, ensuring access and representation are gained at all levels, and the only lawful discrimination that is justifiable and necessary is on merit

Despite the equal opportunities legislation being in place for some time, some people are disappointed because the legislation has failed to deliver equality of opportunity for all. Managing diversity builds on the legislation and established approaches put in place by the Equal opportunities drive. Managing diversity seeks to establish a climate where people want to do more than simply achieve statistical goals. They want to aim for best practice at all times, and constantly be ahead of and go beyond the basic principles established by the legislation.

The table below summarizes the main differences between equal opportunities and managing diversity:

Table 19.1: Main differences between equal opportunities and managing diversity

Equal Opportunities	Managing Diversity
Focuses on removing discrimination	Aims to maximize employee potential
Seen as an issue for disadvantaged groups	Seen as relevant to all employees
Seen as an issue for personnel and development practitioners	Seen as an issue for all managers
Relies on positive action	Does not rely on positive action

The next section provides an overview of the relevant legislative framework relating to diversity issues.

4   Legislation and Managing Diversity

The area of employment legislation is vast and this section can therefore only highlight some of the key elements that affect the employer and employee relationship, in terms of discrimination and managing diversity.

Discrimination

Discrimination is said to occur where an employer treats one person less favourably than another in the same or similar circumstances, whether intentionally or not, in respect of the employee's sex, race, colour or marital status. There are three major acts in this area: Equal Pay Act, Sex Discrimination Act, and Race Relations Act.

Equal Pay Act (EPA) 1970 (amended by the Equal Pay Amendment Act 1983)

This states that men and women should be treated the same where they are employed to perform like work or work rated as equivalent. Employees should be paid the same and have the same rights if they are performing like work or work rated as equivalent or of the same value. The situation becomes complex when defining jobs of equal value because the Equal Opportunities Commission has argued that the evaluation is more related to the sex of the job occupant than the job itself. The Equal Pay Amendment regulations are significant because they followed a long dispute between the UK and EU. The 1983 Act widens the scope of the 1970 Act so that jobs can be compared even though evaluation is not available. This allows, for example, check-out operatives and warehousemen to be compared in terms of their value to the supermarket organization.

Sex Discrimination Acts (SDA) 1975-6 (amended by the Employment Act 1989)

There are three types of discrimination:

1. *Direct discrimination* – where the employer makes it clear applicants of one sex will not be considered for the post (this discrimination was removed by the Sex Discrimination Act 1975).

2. *Indirect discrimination* – where neutral conditions for employment or promotion mean they affect one sex more than another, e.g. height when it does not materially affect the performance of a job.

3. *Victimization* – when one employee is treated less favourably because he or she has instigated proceedings against the employer under the EPA (1970) or SDA (1975).

Race Relations Act 1976

This covers discrimination on the basis of colour, race, and nationality, ethnic or national origin. Once again discrimination can be termed direct or indirect or victimization.

5   Women and Employment

Although financial services organizations obviously abide by, and in some instances exceed, employment regulations as far as discrimination is concerned, the vast majority of managers are male (over 80%) although women form more than 60% of the workforce. From the days of their earliest employment women in banking generally occupied clerical and secretarial roles, and even as late as 1967 it was expected that the banks were providing a limited period of employment for women until family commitments took over. For male employees banking was seen as a lifelong career.

During the 1970s attitudes began to change, with women taking less time off work to bring up children and the number of single-parent families increasing. With the introduction of the Equal Pay Act in 1972, job evaluation and grading systems were also introduced. This enabled banks to introduce a career structure within clerical grades and people were paid for the work they did rather than according to age and sex. Maternity provisions, which were introduced in 1978, had little effect on increasing the number of women in senior posts, because most women with a baby wished to work part-time and the banks did not allow that. Only two-fifths of women with a baby were doing paid work in 1979. However, over the last twenty years there have been significant improvements in terms of encouraging career progression and employment of women.

Steps have been taken within the industry by appointing staff to be specifically in charge of equal opportunities, and by introducing new family friendly schemes whereby some employees with children can have a five-year career break.

6   Why Managing Diversity is Important for Business

Managing diversity aims to combat prejudice, stereotyping, harassment and undignified behaviour in the workplace. However as well as satisfying social and legal demands, the Institute of Personnel and Development (1997) claims that managing diversity should be encouraged for business reasons. Managing diversity can be a means of improving customer care and market share by reflecting customer backgrounds, needs and attitudes in the workforce. It can encourage the development of organizational ethics and values as well as enhancing HR practices. Managing diversity reflects societal changes, ensures compliance with legislation, and leads to the adoption of best practice.

7 Implementing Managing Diversity

Some organizations have tried to introduce an approach to managing diversity by establishing value systems based on trust, fair criteria for HR systems and procedures, and ensuring that all forms of harassment and bullying are dealt with. These organizations are also seeking to address the diverse needs of customers and to ensure organizational awareness of international culture. Some organizations also have in place specific policies to address the issue of equality for female employees.

One of the first things to obtain is the commitment from the top. The chief executive, board members, directors, senior managers and line managers as well as individuals all need to acknowledge that managing diversity is a mainstream issue and that it can bring a competitive advantage to the organization.

Nigel Meager and Hilary Metcalf (1988) suggest the following framework to assist in the implementation of an effective policy:

- Make a clear statement of policy/intent

- Create specific managerial responsibilities for managing diversity

- Monitoring activities

- Make the necessary changes to current practices in the areas of

  - Training

  - Recruitment and Selection

  - Promotion

  - Performance appraisal

  - Career development

  - Disciplinary/ grievance

Summary

This chapter has defined managing diversity and equal opportunities. It has summarized some of the key pieces of legislation that influence managing diversity in financial services organizations. It has also suggested an approach for a managing diversity policy in organizations and highlighted the importance of this topic for businesses today, including how organizations can use the flexible firm model for mutual advantage.

Now that you have studied this chapter, you should be able to:

- define managing diversity and explain the main factors behind the drive for managing diversity;

- appreciate the differences between equal opportunities and managing diversity;

- describe the role and influence of the legislation in relation to equal opportunities and managing diversity;

- explain why managing diversity is important in business;

- outline an approach for the effective implementation of diversity management in an organization.

References

Braddick W A G (1991) *Management for Bankers*, 2nd ed. Butterworths

Fincham R & Rhodes P S (1992) *The Individual Work and Organization*, Oxford University Press

IPD (1997) *Managing Diversity*, An IPD Position Paper

Meager N and Metcalf H (1988) *Equal Opportunities Policies: Tactical Issues in Implementation*, The Institute of Manpower Studies.

Croft Norton & Whyte (1999) *Management in the Financial Services Industry*, CIB Publishing

20

FINAL THOUGHTS...

Congratulations! You have finished working through the main areas of the management syllabus. However your work is not over. Now you have to prepare to pass the examination!

This workbook is designed to reflect the syllabus and should be regarded as essential reading. However you should not confine your reading solely to this text because *on its own* it is unlikely that it provides enough depth to enable examination candidates to pass. Like all undergraduate students you are expected to read as widely as possible and this has been emphasized within this workbook. This should include broader reading to enhance your understanding of the subject's relationship to the wider environment and more detailed reading to deepen your understanding. The Institute provides help and support on these issues.

To gain the maximum benefit from your studies and the investment you have already made:

- Keep up to date with current trends, legislation etc. Remember this workbook reflects the trends and issues at the time it was written, and students need to demonstrate an understanding of current issues and how they are developing in the financial services arena.

- Gain different perspectives on key issues and topics of debate.

- Broaden your knowledge of the general areas relating to the subject.

- Deepen your understanding of individual topics.

- Enhance your research skills and include the ability to identify and select relevant material and information.

It is essential that you make regular and extensive use of all library facilities available to you. You should read the financial press, appropriate journals and relevant in-house publications and guidelines whenever possible and you are strongly advised to explore the wealth of information that can be found on the Internet. This point is emphasized because your examination and coursework will be concerned with trends and issues prevailing at the time.

Finally, refer to the *CIB News* and CIB Examiners' reports throughout your period of study. Recommended reading lists are produced by the Institute and updated regularly and, as well as this workbook, are critical to your success. Copies are available on request from the Institute and from the website: www.cib.org.uk This reading will enhance your understanding of the concepts and theoretical underpinnings of the subject. It will enable you to consider and evaluate alternative ideas on the topics and use these as evidence in your examination **paper and assignments.**

Remember most candidates who fail do so not because they do not know the subject but because they do not write their answers in a way that allows them to obtain optimum marks. So, practice and get feedback from your tutors and use the advice given in the Introduction to this book. And finally... Good Luck!

Index

Index